THE ROAD SOUTH

THE ROAD SOUTH:
A Memoir

Shelley Stewart

WITH NATHAN HALE TURNER JR.

WARNER BOOKS

An AOL Time Warner Company

Warner Books, Inc., 1271 Avenue of the Americas, New York, NY 10020

Visit our Web site at www.twbookmark.com.

 An AOL Time Warner Company

Printed in the United States of America

First Printing: July 2002

10   9   8   7   6   5   4   3   2   1

Library of Congress Cataloging-in-Publication Data

Stewart, Shelley
    The road South : a memoir / Shelley Stewart with Nathan Hale Turner Jr.
    p. cm.
    ISBN 0-446-53027-1
    1. Stewart, Shelley, 1934– 2. Radio broadcasters—United States—
Biography. 3. African American radio broadcasters—United States—
Biography. I. Turner, Nathan Hale. II. Title.

PN1991.4.S84 A3 2002
791.44'028'092—dc21
[B]   2002016819

To my mother, Mattie C. Stewart, who would have been one hundred years old in August 2002. And to my brothers, Bubba, Sam, and David.

PROLOGUE

I KNEW MY SHELLEY THE PLAYBOY radio persona had taken on a life of its own, but I was shocked to see how the airwaves had connected me to the brain waves of white teenagers in 1960 in Birmingham, Alabama. A predicted crowd of three hundred to five hundred was instead eight hundred strong at Don's Teen Town near Jonesboro that early-summer night. A sea of energetic and buoyant white-bread youths were grooving on what the White Citizen's Council called race or jungle music.

The club operator/manager, Ray Mahoney, shaking and pale with fright, interrupted the platter-party show to tell me that my fans had been complemented with a contingency of fanatics decked out in trendy white robes. Outside were more than a dozen cars and trucks carrying eighty or ninety Ku Klux Klansmen, a group that made its national headquarters in Tuscaloosa, forty miles away. Across the road were carloads of state troopers and Jefferson County sheriff's deputies who may have been competing with the Klansmen to see who would get me first.

As a radio performer I knew how to seize my audience. Shelley the Playboy's roll call on WENN had the airwaves hopping as white kids phoned in from places like Dora and Sumiton, West End and Woodlawn, and black youths called from North Birmingham, Titusville, and Southside. Music bridged all social and cultural boundaries and was a language that everyone could appreciate whether through snapping fingers, tapping toes, or dancing the twist. Music uplifted hearts and made a mockery of the deep chasms gouged by the insidious social machinery of separation by race and class.

This same music was now apparently a threat to the white power structure. I had already been labeled "Shelley the Plowboy" by the infamous Birmingham Police Commissioner Bull Connor, who warned the white community about the evils of jungle bunny music. Somehow in 1960, the music was blasting a sour note for those who propped up the solid wall of segregation and intolerance that had hamstrung the South and the nation for decades. The fear of racial integration or, bluntly, miscegenation was a burr under the saddle of the whole gang of them. Perhaps they feared music was an opiate that would lull the white community into a knee-jerk reaction of brotherhood.

Regardless of the cave in which their attitudes had evolved, a raw expression of hate and bigotry was amassed outside the teen club personified by individuals wearing uniforms of the KKK and, perhaps, state troopers and Jefferson County sheriff's deputies.

Mahoney informed me that the KKK mob had demanded my presence outside. In no hurry to be remembered as a martyr, I respectfully declined the invitation. The host then grabbed the microphone and tossed the audience an inflammatory message. "It seems like the Klan doesn't feel like our friend Shelley the Playboy is good enough to entertain here," he said.

"Like hell he isn't!" the crowd roared back. The words had touched a nerve, and the teens went after the Kluxers like bees swarming over a honeycomb. After the melee erupted, my brother David, my friend Wallace Montgomery, and I snaked our way through the chaos toward the car. Several Klansmen danced in close in an effort to swing chains at our heads.

A few white girls then pressed themselves against us. "If you hit them, you are going to have to hit us too," they screamed. The chains went limp at the sides of the antagonists.

The teens kept the Klansmen busy fighting and gave us time to pack our gear into my '58 gray Impala convertible. On my final trip to the car I had to bang on the window to get Wallace and David's attention so they would unlock the door since they were both hugging the floorboard in an effort to hide from the mob's view.

Rocks and gravel scattered like a shotgun's buckshot as we sped off with a batch of lawmen on our heels like deer harried by a cougar. The Impala peeled rubber down the Bessemer Super-highway toward the Lipscomb home of a friend, Mary Mason. We pulled into the Mason backyard and parked, breathless as if we had been running an uphill marathon.

An hour crept by, and we realized we could not remain en-sconced at the house forever. I let the top down on the convert-ible to confuse any pursuers about the description of the car. Some old clothes, caps, and head rags in the trunk and a little dirt helped transform us into work-weary laborers. Now we were ready to leave the Mason yard and take our chances with the po-lice and/or Klan.

It wasn't long before a police roadblock near the superhighway would put our disguises to the test.

"Hey, boss, what's going on?" I piped up as we rolled to a stop at the barricade.

"Y'all know a nigger named Shelley?" said a policeman. "If you see him, tell him his ass is ours. He's been over there mess-ing with white girls. He won't see daybreak."

Fright had forced Wallace to urinate on himself like a tiny toddler.

"Okay, boss. We'll tell him. His ass is yours," I said as we pulled off.

Later that day the radio station WSGN broadcast a report that I had been slain. By the time folks realized the news was erroneous, I was safely at my apartment on Eleventh Avenue North in Fountain Heights. That evening friends and acquaintances toting shotguns guarded my residence until emotions had a chance to cool off.

———

THAT INCIDENT WAS ONE OF many memorable occurrences in more than fifty years of radio broadcasting. This career saw its genesis as a teen at WBCO in Bessemer and WEDR in Birmingham and blossomed with my stewardship of WATV, one of the nation's rare black-owned stations.

My radio life has been a roller-coaster ride zipping past new frontiers in broadcasting and cresting on a grand horizon of talk radio. The style I developed for radio started in the 1950s and has always been a blend of showmanship and communication. I have always packaged my appeal to the masses rather than the classes. A formula I used was to envision the emotional response of a man or woman dropping a coin into a jukebox, whether it was to listen to a Ray Charles tune or a Little Richard melody, and I introduced the record accordingly.

"H-e-e-e-y Lawdy Mama!" was a phrase I used often. "Timber! Let it fall!" was another utterance.

Communication is a key to understanding and progress in a competitive, fast-paced world where misinformation can cripple a community and a nation. Radio is one particular medium that can obliterate the isolation characterizing the disenfranchised. It can uplift and enhance and cultivate souls beaten down in countless ways, obvious and subtle.

I recognized this early on in my career and couched many of my broadcasts in jabs at social ills, particularly the overt racism of the '50s and '60s. Many common black folks also got a thrill hearing me talk about escaping from the boss man's workload and the absurdity of intraracial snobbery that had a foothold among the black middle or upper class. Nothing was sacred to me. The early-morning radio talk show I host now on WATV actually uses this same biting philosophy, minus the music.

My personal life has been a zigzag journey from poverty and abuse to a place in which, I am proud to say, I have gained the respect of many in the broadcast industry and outside of it. But many people who are familiar with me as Shelley the Playboy, talk-show host, or Shelley Stewart, radio and communication executive, know only tidbits about the real Shelley Stewart.

If an individual is a sum total of his or her experiences, then what I am was sculpted by the absurdity of being fed rats as a child and the cruelty and abuse from a father, stepmother, and aunts. What I am is also a reaction to life with my young brother in a horse stable beginning at age six and a half and the love and shelter given to me when I lived in the basement of a white family at a time in the 1940s when lynchings in the South were still too common and segregation was an expression of custom and practice. And what I am is a person who embraces the realization that you can't put money over people. I have never forgotten my roots, and even now I will spend time talking with and trying to assist the brown bag–carrying winos and other down-and-out inhabitants of the alleys of my native Rosedale, Alabama.

———

I WAS FORTUNATE IN THE early years of my entertainment career to have rubbed shoulders with Otis Redding, Lou Rawls, Sam and Dave, Arthur Conley, Jeannie C. Riley, and Tom T. Hall.

Back in the mid-'50s Sam Cook, B. B. King, and Bobby "Blue" Bland would stay at my house in the Titusville section when they came to Birmingham to entertain at places like the old Madison Nightspot and the Grand Terrace Ballroom. In those days Motown founder and record mogul Berry Gordy and his brother George were up-and-coming record promoters trying to publicize singer Mary Wells. Berry would sleep at my house because he couldn't afford a motel, and there were few decent public hotel accommodations for blacks in the city.

————————

BEYOND BEING A DESCRIPTION OF a whirlwind life, I hope my story will do nothing if not inspire. If I can overcome the hurdles of poverty, abuse, and racism, then so can anyone. If life throws you a lemon, turn it into lemonade; accentuate that which is positive and life affirming. A person who maintains a faith in God and focuses on noble principles and fruitful goals can accomplish much.

Too many talk shows are populated with guests who are blaming Mama and Daddy for lives swerving out of control or already crashed in a ditch of despair. The time is past for self-pity and pointing the finger of blame at the Oedipus complex. And the time is past for self-hatred from those suited in an inferiority complex.

Now is the time to follow your inner voices over the din of a world bombarded with the sounds of discouragement and pessimism. In our nation we spend foolish amounts of time trying to separate under the guise of skin color or race. But if you look at the last four letters in the designations African American, Puerto Rican American, Mexican American, or white American, you will notice the words *I can*. The individual can place this phrase into an assertive context: *I can* overcome the most formidable of barriers to achieve success, whether it is within the maze of human relations or the obstacle course of the business world. Optimism and idealism are beleaguered but not dead. Hope and understanding may often be dormant, but they are not disemboweled. The individual is essential to a wider humanity, and lives nurtured in faith and determination can prove indomitable against astronomical odds. As I always say, Life is hard by the yard, but it's a cinch by the inch.

Shelley Stewart

THE ROAD SOUTH

CHAPTER ONE

A Nest in Rosedale

LET ME SHOW YOU how I deal with something that shows me its teeth," said the tall slender man as he hopped about in his ritual dance in the yard of the shotgun house in Rosedale, Alabama.

"I'm in control! Watch the show!" he commanded as my brother Bubba and I beat sticks on tin cans in a mock drumroll. The possum snarled as the black man reached into the makeshift trap. Avoiding its sharp incisors, he grabbed the creature by the tail and escalated his chant as our homemade drums shouted a persistent beat.

"Here's Poor Sam, ladies and gentlemen, boys and girls. Watch the show!" he insisted. The man danced and strutted about for another minute, waving the animal in the air with the dexterity of a cheerleader shaking pompons.

Suddenly, he eased the possum down to the ground and pinned it there with an ax. Next, he stood on the mammal, placing his feet on either side of the tool. In a flash, he yanked the animal's tail upward, breaking its neck.

My father, Huell (Slim) Stewart, took pride in killing, whether it was wringing a chicken's neck or executing a possum. People say that back down in Russell County, Alabama, he worked as a butcher with a special talent. The story goes that as entertainment for white people he would stalk a hog around its pen, stab the swine to death with a long knife, and drink its blood. Around Rosedale he was also known for his violent nature, which saw him as a protagonist in cuttings, stabbings, and beatings that made him a feared man in the neighborhood.

An incident was described that concerned a confrontation between my father and a man named Homer over a gambling debt. The man began chasing my father around a house with a knife. Witnesses were astounded to see my father flee from a confrontation, but they noticed that he was making a wider circle each time he and his pursuer circumvented the gambling house. Apparently, Slim Stewart had spotted an ax embedded in a tree stump in a corner of the yard. Finally, on one trip around the house, my father was able to reach the ax and wait for his pursuer to appear. With one blow of the blunt side of the chopping tool, he knocked the man senseless. Until his death years later, Homer's head bore an indentation as a result of the blow.

By the time we were born, Slim Stewart was a small-time gambler, a respectable drunkard, and a thief. No, not the penny-ante rogue that you can find on many street corners. He achieved this ignominy when he stole the life of a humble woman that my three brothers and I had a chance to love for only a microsecond in the breadth of time.

I use the word *father* as a biological description rather than as an endearing one. Memories of my life with Slim and my mother, Mattie, are buried in layers of time and embalmed in sorrow, anger, and resentment. Our time together as a maladjusted nuclear family was dreadfully short, but the images haunt me six decades later. That time in the 1930s was a repository for the seeds of despair that drove me to weep every day for fifty-seven years of my life.

I NEVER KNEW EXACTLY HOW my mother and father met. I was aware that Mama was raised on a farm in Cordele in South Georgia with her parents, Willis Johnson and Emily Butts Johnson. They had four children, three of whom were girls, but their father worked them as hard as you would work men on the farm, chopping wood and carrying out other backbreaking chores. The Johnsons were an assorted mix of tall and short people, ranging from one aunt who was barely five feet tall to another measuring six feet in height. Grandfather Johnson was a hard-working man who developed a good-size farm in his community. The place slipped from his grasp after a bad crop year, and he ended up demoted to tenant-farmer status, scraping for sustenance on some other man's land.

On the paternal side, my father came from a huge family of about a dozen siblings. His father, Alonzo, was a cotton gin foreman at the Southeastern Compress warehouse in Russell County, Alabama, and his mother, Rosa Lee, was a housekeeper and cook for the families of assassinated attorney general candidate Albert Patterson and foundry engineer Frank Morton. A U.S. census schedule from the mid-nineteenth century listed my great-grandfather as spelling his name Steward, which he had apparently adapted from a plantation owner of the same name in neighboring Lee County. The current spelling of the name began with grandfather Alonzo.

Also, it has been established that a branch of the Stewart family passed into the Caucasian race. Alonzo's sister, Molly, was quite fair in complexion and ended up marrying a white man named Ben Franklin in Phenix City. After Franklin died, the family moved to Michigan and the children passed for white, although ancient U.S. laws require that a person with one-sixteenth of Negro blood be classified as black or colored.

Exactly when and where the Stewart and Johnson families intersected is unclear. In recent years I learned that my mother had once lived in Columbus, Georgia, a stone's throw across the Chattahoochee River from Phenix City in my father's home county of Russell. The proximity of the towns suggests that my parents could have met during that time. My mother lived in a boardinghouse on Tenth Avenue North in east Birmingham when she first arrived in Birmingham and began working as a maid for the Felton family. This was a low-income section dotted with pipe-making plants and a railroad car shop and inhabited by nameless, faceless, and otherwise invisible African Americans. By the time she moved over Red Mountain to Rosedale to increase her proximity to work in the well-heeled community of Mountain Brook, she and Slim Stewart were married.

My father and mother produced five offspring, born in the basement of old Hillman hospital in Birmingham. At the time, hospital cellars were designated for the care of African American patients in the segregated South. Huell Jerome (Bubba) Stewart Jr. was the oldest, born in 1932. I was next in line, debuting in 1934, and was called Shurley during my early life through some odd corruption of my actual name. Next in the pecking order were Sam, born in 1937, and David, who brought up the rear guard in 1939. Another son, Alonzo, named after my paternal grandfather, was sandwiched in birth between me and Jerome. He died of natural causes before I was born.

My mother's job was typical of what a lot of black women did in those days to make ends meet. If they weren't lucky enough or smart enough to be a teacher or perhaps a nurse, they usually sweated in someone else's kitchen or minded someone else's youngsters.

And work Mama did. She scrubbed floors and cleaned in the homes of the Feltons, and subsequently the Morgans, until beads of perspiration poured off her brow. She always took us with her out of necessity, love, or a combination of the above. Jerome, a.k.a. Bubba, and I would walk along beside her. Sam and David traveled via stroller. She would park the stroller in the backyard, where we would wile away the time while she worked, usually while humming or singing a spiritual.

"Were you there when they crucified my Lord. . . . Sometimes it causes me to tremble."

My mother sang with such earnestness and dread that Bubba and I often felt that she sensed the presence of an unforeseen misfortune that awaited us all. Most often she seemed depressed and humorless. But when she did laugh with a woman friend who visited the house, it was a deep, hearty expression that made her sons feel good. Her hugs also made us feel good.

ROSEDALE, WHERE WE SPENT sections of our early life, is a poor enclave on the crest of Red Mountain, a southern finger of the Appalachian mountain range that stretches all the way to Maine. Just over the hill from the state's hub city, Birmingham, the Shades Valley neighborhood was first settled in 1885 when black residents began buying lots and building small houses there. Its name came from a rose grower who was also a town founder. In 1911 a streetcar line was erected, which ran from Jones Valley on the other side of the mountain through the center of Rosedale. This transportation enabled the whole area to be developed, and consequently, in 1926 Rosedale and Edgewood merged to form Homewood.

The majority of the people in Rosedale were maids, yard-men, handymen, and laborers, and the town's modern-era growth was generated by the fact that it provided a handy source of labor for the surrounding white communities, like Mountain Brook, an upscale section to the east. Often, a husband and wife were employed by the same white family.

Less than a mile to the west of my house was the abandoned Valley View Red Ore mine whose dark, foreboding entrance was so frightening that I would not cross its threshold during the days when Bubba and I would wander through the area. Nearby, a disused bed of the L&N Birmingham Mineral Railroad ran along the northern flank of Red Mountain just below Vulcan Park and extended from Irondale on the eastern side of the metropolitan area to Bessemer on the west. About two miles to the south of our neighborhood was Lake Edgewood. Howard College, a Baptist school that was to evolve into Samford University, didn't locate there until the 1950s.

Rosedale straddles both sides of U.S. 31, a road that linked the state's southern and northern counties. Along the highway there were black restaurants like Fess's Place and Waterboy's Grill. The town consisted of about 150 homes, but clusters of children in each dwelling pushed the population to about five hundred people. The area near Dunn's Drugstore provided the imaginary dividing line between "Pecktown," the white section, and Rosedale, or "Niggertown," the black community. An area a few blocks north of Rosedale was informally called Three Points because it was apparently where three neighborhoods intersected. In that area was a restaurant called Chicken in the Rough. Oftentimes blacks would go to the back door of the establishment with pans, and the cooks would give them raw chicken necks, heads, and feet that they could take home and cook for a day's meal.

THERE WAS NEVER MUCH LAUGHTER in our household. Our father never took us to a park, or a movie, or a ball game, none of the mundane expressions of warmth that were a staple of *Father Knows Best* and might make small children feel loved or valued. Rapport between our parents was uncomfortably hostile. In a verbal confrontation, the dialogue of insults and curses between my parents usually ended in a dead heat since Mama could hold her own fairly well in that arena. But at five-feet-seven or five-feet-eight, standing her ground physically against my father was another matter entirely, and she endured frequent slappings and punchings.

Slim Stewart was well suited for the work he did. On my true birth date, September 24, 1934, the *Birmingham News* heralded on its front page the pending prosecution of Bruno Hauptmann, accused in the kidnap-slaying of Charles Lindbergh's baby. On the fourth page an item ran talking about rail production at the Tennessee Coal and Iron plant in the western section of Birmingham. That's where my father worked, TCI, not in steel production but in the tin mill. A strong back was an asset in the mills. And at a muscular six-foot-three, his brawn and surly disposition led him into knife fights and general mayhem, which inevitably devoured my mother as a victim.

On the day that marked the beginning of her end, Mama was preparing Sunday dinner and humming. Her favorite tune was, "Precious Lord take my hand, Lead me on, let me stand. I am tired, I am weak . . ." Maybe that was the melody soothing her tattered soul that luckless Southern day.

———————

THE DAY MY MAMA'S LIFE was extinguished began my lengthy waltz with sadness. That summer day in August 1939 began like any other but was to end with an act that seemed to serve as an omen for dispiriting relationships to come at the hands of relatives and guardians.

———————

MY DADDY SAVORED EXPRESSIONS like "mule's milk" and "cat's pajamas." And he could always enjoy his gin. To his credit, he never drank so much that he could not go to the tin mill and put in a day's work. But I was afraid of my father's furies, which were in part molded and shaped by the nimble hands of a world riddled with humiliation, degradation, and social castration, and which had cast people of color onto the scrap heap of second- and third-class citizenship.

We would never see much of Daddy. He would turn up on the weekends as if by appointment. His appointed mission, it seemed, was to fuss, and fight, and harangue Mama. The conflict that sunny Sunday was rooted in issues that always seemed to lurk in the background—gambling and money. On this day, he had left Miss Martha's shot house around the corner and come to our home at 2604 Eighteenth Place with the devil in his pocket and little else. Bubba and I saw him ambling down the sidewalk and ran to the house to tip off Mama.

"Give me some money," he snapped upon entering the kitchen.

"The little money I've got I need to use to buy food for the children and pay for our insurance policy," Mama said. Enraged, my father began to strike her. She stumbled. He grabbed her, but she broke away and sprinted down the hall with him on her heels like a leopard in pursuit of an antelope.

Daddy clutched the ax that had rested by the stove in the kitchen. "Don't hit Mama," Bubba and I yelled from the hallway. David and Sam were asleep in the front room, oblivious to the unfolding horror.

"Lord, don't hurt me or my children," she pleaded as she cowered in the rear bedroom near the window. Daddy swung the ax, striking her in the chest with the flat side of the weapon. Mama tumbled out the window into the arms of a waiting pecan tree. Caught in its leafy tentacles, she hung upside down. Daddy rushed outside, pushed her leg loose from the branches, and Mama plummeted to the ground like a ship's anchor.

"Oh, Mattie, I'm sorry," he moaned.

The ambulance from Strong Funeral Home came and took her to Hillman Hospital in Birmingham. Women in the neighborhood brought us plates of food and looked in on us. My mother's sister, Emily Williams, who lived on our street, also would drop by and briefly check on us. We did not see our father, and if he visited home, it was most likely late at night when we were asleep.

Mr. Davenport was a man who sold coal and wood in the community. He also rang the bell in the Bethel African Methodist Episcopal (A.M.E.) Church tower. This was our main communication in the black community, our tribal drums. If the bell rang quickly, this meant someone was ill, and those available would come to render assistance. The men would tend to men, and women would care for women. If the bell rang slowly, it meant an individual was deceased.

One morning, as my brothers and I sat on the porch, the bell began a cautious peel.

"Somebody's dead," said Bubba.

Mrs. Pryor and Mrs. Malone, neighborhood residents, walked past our home and down to the church. Others soon swarmed to the site to determine for whom the bell tolled.

After a few minutes had passed, the crowd moved as one body toward our perch on the steps. Individuals within the throng picked up each of us boys and held us.

"Boys, everything is gonna be all right now," someone said. "Your mother is dead, but God knows best."

Bubba and I began to weep, but the two younger boys, Sam and David, were, of course, not cognizant of what had occurred.

"Daddy killed Mama," Bubba said.

"He sure did," I answered.

"Did you hear what they said?" a man asked others in the party.

Two Homewood policemen, Officer Smith and Chief Scott, came to the house to inquire about the death a few days later. Bubba and I told them about the surreal confrontation that had quickly escalated into a fateful incident. Daddy predictably informed them that Mama had jumped out of the window during a spat and landed in the tree. Apparently nobody bothered to check her injuries to see if they were consistent with our pronouncement about an ax murder.

In those days, a black person's life wasn't worth much more than a jar of sand to the white power structure, and Mama's life was granted about the same value. Also, as young juveniles, our words didn't muster the same credibility as an adult's. Her Jefferson County death certificate bears a telling reference in that the individual reporting her demise was listed as "self." The case was closed, and the law never inquired about the circumstances of Mattie Stewart's demise again.

We had my mother's funeral at Bethel A.M.E., and we buried her at Grace Hill Cemetery. My father, brothers, and I rode to the services with my mother's sister, Mamie Pickens, and her husband, Henry, in their black Model A Ford, which used a hand crank to start its engine.

As we rode southward over Red Mountain back into Rosedale, the grown-ups began conversing about our future without Mattie C.

"What are you going to do with these boys?" Aunt Mamie asked.

"I don't know," Daddy said. "Why don't you take them?"

The grown-ups disappeared inside our home, and we boys stayed on the porch. After a few minutes, the adults came out with a few bags that contained our modest wardrobes. We children climbed into Mamie and Henry's Ford and sped off with them to our new home in Collegeville, about seven miles from Rosedale.

Apparently our father was as affected by his severance from us as a man parting company with personal property. Of course, Bubba and I weren't overwhelmed by this more pronounced breach from an already distant guardian.

We had seen Mamie and Henry perhaps once before our mother's death. After all, they resided on the other side of Birmingham. The journey on the streetcar would have been formidable: Climb on the Number 39 Edgewood and ride downtown, then change over to Number 22 Boyles/Tarrant City for a trip to Vanderbilt and Coosa Streets, and finally walk at least two miles to their house. The fact that Mamie and Henry rarely drove to our home could be laid at the feet of sisters pursuing separate and distinct lives, or the more obvious impediment—Slim Stewart.

Uncle Henry had a laborer's job at the Louisville & Nashville railroad car shop. Their home was comfortable but modest in the gritty low-income neighborhood that saw many of its residents working as laborers at U.S. Pipe and Sloss, two companies within the metropolitan area's steel and iron fabric. We boys slept on pallets, and the food was plentiful since the couple raised hogs and chickens. Bubba and I spent time trying to potty train Sam, but David, of course, was still in diapers.

We stayed with the Pickenses from shortly after Mama died in August 1939 until right before Christmas of that year.

That's when Aunt Mamie and Uncle Henry apparently saw the light in a revelation from hell. "I'll be damned if I'll take on the responsibility of raising somebody else's children," said Mamie, a tall, big-bosomed woman. "I'm taking you back to your daddy. I'll be damned if I'm cleaning some baby's shit."

We soon discovered that new people lived in the death house on Eighteenth Place. Slim Stewart had moved over to Central Avenue near the streetcar line in Rosedale with a woman named Marie. Aunt Mamie and Henry dropped us off in a field right next to their house on Twenty-seventh Court.

Henry took our bags and set them out of the car, and Mamie ordered us to follow. "Your daddy lives over there. I don't give a damn if you go root a hog or die poor," she said, the words trailing off as they sped away.

———————

IF A RAT IS BATTERED AND FRIED *and cooked to a golden brown and your stomach aches because it only contains gastric acid, when you do eat, the meal tastes like the finest Manhattan restaurant cuisine.*

Marie Thompson protested with vigor when she discovered that we had been deposited that December day of 1939 like dirty laundry outside the household she shared with Daddy, her sister Louise, and her young niece Nettie. She proclaimed that we were not welcome in the small, two-bedroom home that sported a tiny dining area and a back porch.

We were allowed to remain on the premises at our father's insistence. But the catch was that we would have to stay on the dreary rear porch. So, there we were, four young children, ages seven, five, two, and a few months old, doomed to consort with Mother Nature's offspring: rain, snow, hot and cold air.

Blankets were thrown on the floor, and a kerosene heater was placed in the middle of the porch. The next day a mattress showed up. Lattice was put up to reinforce a cardboard wall erected to deflect wind and rain. A blanket was hung to give the adults privacy when they used the toilet. All four of us slept on the mattress, which always wore the fragrance of urine since we routinely peed in the bed. David, of course, would soil the homemade cloth diapers Bubba and I manufactured for him. This situation lasted all winter.

Sometimes, Bubba and I would go down near U.S. 31 and perch outside of Damon Lee and Sons' coal yard. We would wait for Lee's teenage grandson Afton Jr. to show up at the business and would throw rocks at him. The youth would retaliate by throwing chunks of coal at us. However, he did not know that this was a ruse; we took the coal home, placed it in a bucket, and lit a fire on the back porch to keep warm.

———————

SPRING 1940 BROUGHT NATURE'S WARMTH, rejuvenation, and the promise of new beginnings to most people. For us it meant that the soggy mattress, damp with urine and caked with grime, began to swell with maggots and bedbugs. We made tasty meals for the insects, which munched on us constantly since we never bathed.

Our caloric intake consisted mainly of one meal each evening, handed out the door to us on the porch, mostly leftovers from the Jefferson County Tuberculosis Sanitarium where

Marie worked. Our utensils were pans rather than dinner plates; an old sewer pipe pulled double duty as our table. We lived days crafted with cookie-cutter sameness. Each morning with the radiance of dawn we hurled ourselves toward a mission to stamp out our personal version of world hunger. Bubba and I had blossomed quickly into skilled scavengers, and our savanna was a couple of blocks down the street in Pecktown, the white section. We were looking after our two younger brothers since we basically had been abandoned by our father and Marie. Our stepmother's motto was: "I don't have a child to die and I don't have a child to cry," which meant she did not feel any obligation to treat us as anything more than creatures of contempt. So, for diapers we cut up potato sacks and used the cloth quite creatively.

In the mistiness of morning, we became the hunter-gatherers for our tribe on the back porch. Sometimes Bubba and I found a cane pole and string and followed adults in the neighborhood down to Lake Edgewood on fishing expeditions for catfish. We would bring our catch to the backyard and begin preparing them for a meal. This was done by cutting off their heads and gutting them with a clothes hanger and tossing the fish in a pan over a small fire. When we killed birds around the neighborhood with an old BB gun, we followed the same procedure. But it took a whole mess of birds, which were often sparrows, to make a meal.

More often, we would visit stores like Piggly Wiggly, Hill's Grocery, Dunn's Drugs, and Shaia's General Store, the backbone of the white business district. Our trips were not designed to shop for goods but were for scavenging purposes. On most mornings Hill's and Piggly Wiggly would set out perishable goods that were deemed not fit for customer consumption. Molded bread and apples and oranges on the brink of rotting became the staples of our diet. If we were lucky, the dairy-truck driver would hand us a bottle of milk or the bread man would toss us a loaf of cinnamon rolls.

Competition for our morsels came from a source we had not expected. For fun, Bubba and I would find old paint cans and use a broom straw or blade of grass to paint ants in the field next to our house. Each morning we would place bets on whether a red or white ant would emerge from the mound first. Once we followed the colorful ants down the alley and discovered they were dining at the same "restaurants" at the back of Hill's and Piggly Wiggly that we patronized. And, like the ants, we hoarded our food. Our stash would be shared with Sam and David and squirreled away from the grown-ups in the house, especially Miss Marie.

A source of nourishment for baby David was Mr. Benson's cow, which grazed down the street from our house. Bubba and I would often sneak over and milk the bovine, squirting the precious fluid into a ragged baby bottle. At the end of the day, Benson, I'm certain, had to take stock that the beast was at least a quart or so shy of what a healthy creature should have been mustering. In later years I was to reveal our Robin Hood roles to Benson, to his amusement.

The only time we got food prepared in the house was on weekends. Daddy had a chicken coop in the backyard, and we would smell Miss Marie cooking the staple of Southern black folks' diets—fried chicken. Daddy also had large rat traps in the yard by the chicken house, the jaws of which represented instantaneous death for pesky vermin. But we never actually saw what he caught since we were warned to stay away from that section of the property.

On Sundays the grown-ups would fix us a treat of what we assumed was fried chicken. One particular weekend we noticed Officer Smith parked outside the house. After we were served our dinner, Smith came forward and confiscated the food and placed it in a brown bag. Later that week he returned with Nurse Avery from the Jefferson County Health Department. He proclaimed that we were eating rats and warned Slim and Marie that they would be locked up if the situation was repeated. We never got meat with our Sunday dinners again.

A neighbor, Ennis Daniels, who was also a drinking companion of my father, had blown the whistle. He had noticed Daddy skinning and cleaning the rats, putting them in a boiler, and carrying them inside. His conscience had prodded him to call the authorities.

"Boy, if Mama was here, this wouldn't be happening," Bubba lamented. "Why don't he kill Marie like he killed Mama?" we both wondered.

THOSE DAYS WERE FULL OF TEARS AND PAIN that gnawed at your gut. The source of this angst was the loss of a mother's embrace and the burden of childhood chased away by cruelty and circumstance and replaced with weighty responsibilities more appropriate for a thirty-year-old. Life on a back porch is a claustrophobic existence. When you top that off with barren crumbs of emotional warmth, you've got the recipe for despair and bottomless gloom. The need to care for Sam and David created a situation in which Bubba and I never strayed far from home. For leisure we tracked our ants down the alley or created homemade knives and spears and tossed them at makeshift targets, a skill at which we became quite adept.

Bubba and I came and went as we pleased. We were our own parents and guardians encased in children's bodies and starkly aware that our lives depended on our instincts for survival in a world coated in unrelenting misery. The days flowed like currents of the Alabama River on its journey to the Gulf of Mexico; in some places swift, but in many others languishing or plodding along with mind-numbing tedium.

Daddy enrolled me in a surrogate school at Union Baptist Church. Two fires in 1939 had transformed Rosedale School into a heap of wood and brick. Youngsters in turn had to be sent to Union for the first four grades, Friendship Baptist for the second four, and Bethel A.M.E. for the high school years.

Meanwhile, each day represented a land mine in the quest for survival and mere emotional fulfillment. On occasional Sundays, though, Bubba and I would go down to Friendship Baptist and plant ourselves on the outside of the brick building and listen to the songs and the preaching. You could always hear lively proselytizing and "shouting" in the black church, a tradition that could probably be traced to the brisk worship of Southern slaves. I thought all churches were like that, but later I learned that white congregations expressed their faith in calmer seas of music and ritual.

A song reverberated through the walls of the church and caressed our ears: *Our mother, she is gone, she is gone. Our mother, she is gone, she is gone. And she won't be back no more . . .*

The congregation and choir moaned these words in traditional black gospel earnestness. Bubba and I wailed in sadness and grief awakened from slumber, another reminder of our virtual orphanlike status and lives void of love as a result of Mama's destruction.

The fight for survival was also coupled with striving to stay on the good side of the temperamental Slim and Marie. If you compared Slim and Marie's relationship with the one my father had with our mother, Mattie C., there would be at least one obvious departure in similarity. Slim and Marie had a good time together mainly because of a common denominator—gin. My mother did not drink, nor did any of her siblings. Slim and Marie didn't necessarily love each other. They *enjoyed* each other's company, and liquor was their permissive chaperon.

Marie was a peculiar woman anointed with unfaltering, self-perpetuating spite. We couldn't please her even when it came down to what name we were to call her.

"Hey, Miss Marie," Bubba and I would greet her when she returned from work at the tuberculosis sanitarium.

"Why don't you try calling me Mama?" she corrected us.

The next day, buoyed by her instructions, we decided to use Marie's recommended greeting. "Hey, Mama!" we yelled.

"I ain't your damn mama," she retorted. We just couldn't win with her.

But life walking on tiptoe was inevitably doomed. In about the middle of 1940, Marie greeted my father at the door of the house proclaiming that she was missing twenty-five dollars in gold pieces and accused us of stealing them from her room, a place we had never been. She had obviously misplaced them or was lying in an effort to cause grief to me and Bubba. Our protests of innocence ricocheted off deaf ears, and Daddy immediately sided with Marie. He grabbed a two-by-four piece of lumber and began viciously to beat Bubba and me. We wept and dodged and ducked, but those maneuvers didn't help us escape this basketball-player-size man with long legs and even more imposing arms.

We wound up as casualties in a domestic battle zone. The injuries: Bubba had a cut eye and my arm was broken in two places. Daddy put me on the streetcar and took me to Hillman Hospital. He reverted to the same acting talent he had used when Mama was taken to the medical facility after he had knocked her out of the window with the ax.

"He fell. I told that boy to stop running," said Daddy.

"No, he beat me," I exclaimed.

"He's lying. Maybe we can pray for him to stop his lying," he said.

The doctors gobbled up the malarkey and, to my amazement, closed their eyes and joined him in a pious moment of prayer. A cast was placed on my arm and remained there for two weeks until my father cut it off after my limb was healed. It was not long after this beating that I discovered Bubba was gone—a runaway at seven. My father and Marie revealed not even a modicum of concern or worry about the matter.

"Bubba's probably gone off and got himself killed," Daddy said nonchalantly.

The beating was an even clearer omen that life with Slim and Marie would never be mistaken for an idyllic scene depicted in a Norman Rockwell painting.

"Shelter" at Aunt Emily's House

Aunt Emily was next in line of birth behind my mother, Mattie. She resided across the street from our former home on Eighteenth Place in her own fashionable shotgun house. A few weeks after Bubba's departure, I decided to leave Slim and Marie's place in search of a more humane and saner existence. We had seen Emily intermittently during our young lives and knew nothing of her personality. Most of the time she and my mother would talk back and forth across the street from respective perches on their front porches. Since she was the sister of my angelic mother, I figured that I would be well received.

Emily welcomed me into her peculiar-smelling home and said it would be fine for me to stay with her and that she would not tolerate any inkling of my father's well-known violent temperament.

"I'm not taking any of Huell's shit," said Emily, a brown-skinned, husky woman whose face was decorated with moles, a trademark of my mother's side of the family.

A maid by day, she had extricated herself from rural Georgia but had brought its ambiance with her. My aunt relied on a kerosene lamp rather than electricity, and she chopped her own wood too.

"I can do anything a man can do. My daddy taught me how," she said.

Emily placed a cot for me in the front room where her bed was. That cot alone was a quantum leap up from the mattress on the back porch at Slim and Marie's place.

A chicken house sat in her side yard, and she taught me to feed the birds, wring their necks, cut wood for the stove, wash dishes, and do other chores. I abruptly stumbled onto the source of the house's stench. In the kitchen at the rear of the habitat was a brooder in which Emily kept chickens. She had thrown dirt on the floor, and a menagerie of fowls had unrestricted roaming rights in the room. The door between the middle room and the kitchen was kept closed in a futile attempt to keep out the odor.

Emily, I discovered, was one who apparently believed in voodoo. She would mix up unusual concoctions that smelled of sulfur. A dry form would be placed under my bed and other places in the house. A liquid version of the potion would be sprinkled under the front and back steps of the quarters. Sometimes my aunt would order me to pee into a jar, and then she would disappear into the next room carrying my bodily fluids like a scientist attempting to unravel a medical mystery. What she did with the urine, however, was anyone's guess.

Overall, despite the peculiarities, I had concluded that it

wasn't a bad living arrangement. But I soon discovered that Emily possessed her own Pandora's box of unmentionables. Marie and Slim were cold, indifferent, and mean. Emily unveiled a wicked style that my young mind found almost incomprehensible.

The sadism started in the middle of the night about a week after I had moved into Emily's house. After I had finished up a tedious dishwashing chore and gone to bed, Emily jarred me out of a deep sleep. "Wake up now!" she commanded, beating me with a frayed cord.

"What is it, Aunt Emily?" I asked, suddenly wide-awake.

Through bleary eyes I then saw that she had taken the dishes I had washed earlier and placed them in the middle of the floor.

"I want you to wash these dishes again," she said amid hard, furious blows. Emily never said whether the dishes were not clean enough. Just "wash them again." And I was not to use the wood already in the stove to heat up water with which to do the job. I had to go out and chop some more logs.

After the stove was heated, I washed the dishes and went back to bed. Later on that night, the process began again.

"Damn it to hell. The white folks are my boss, but I'm your boss and you are going to do what I say," she yelled.

Every week there was a hard blow, a slap, or a swift kick. Her motives, I surmised, were meanness, madness, and maliciousness. However, Emily had her own rationale. "I'll cower you down, boy, so the white folks won't have to do it," she often uttered during the disciplinary sessions.

One beating in particular is ingrained in my head. Curiosity had gotten the best of me, and I asked about her name. The fact that her last name was Williams rather than Johnson puzzled me since I did not see any suggestion of a husband. My mistake. Emily burst into a fit of rage as the inquiry parted my lips.

"Boy, you don't ask grown folks their business," she sputtered in commentary to an assault.

Emily and I had little to do in the house but sit in the front room and stare at the fireplace. When she tired of spitting tobacco into the flames, and she was sure that I was within striking distance, she would eject the brown gunk into my face and dare me to wipe my face clean.

The realization that I had traded Slim and Marie's mess for a parallel world of equal or worse quality hit me like two Louisville & Nashville freight trains colliding at fifty miles per hour over the Tennessee-Tombigbee River.

I saw my father at a distance. Often I would catch glimpses of him socializing down at Fess's Place on U.S. 31. One day our paths crossed down in Pecktown, the white section. I attempted to flee, but he quickly caught up with me and left me with a heartfelt expression of contempt.

"I'm glad you're gone. You stay up there with that damn bitch, and you don't come back to see Sam and David," he snarled.

———————

I WAS A PRISONER AT EMILY'S. Once I came home from Union Baptist School, I could not go outside the yard. But I was so petrified by her warning that, more often than not, I would simply stay inside the house.

When Emily asked a neighbor named Miss Odell if I had crossed the threshold of the property, the woman, through either confusion or malice, said yes. Emily made a valiant effort to outdo herself because of Miss Odell's comments. Needless to say, I was severely punished. She tied my hands at the wrists with rope and, employing screws used for hanging heavy plants, created a pulley. All my clothes were stripped off, and I was hoisted up toward the ceiling, the end of the rope tied to the bed. She then started whipping me with the cord until I felt blood trickling over old bruises. Grains of salt were rubbed onto the welts. I was left hanging there all night where I urinated and defecated on myself and the floor. Emily, unperturbed, sat there in a chair just about the whole night and watched me until sleep overpowered her.

After Emily had awakened, she grunted an explanation. "I'm doing this so the white folks won't have to do it," she bristled. "I'm breaking you in like my daddy taught me to break a mule. I'm breaking you down, boy."

Emily then freed me from the contraption but kept me cloistered in an attempt to hide the signs of torture from the outside world. She got word to my teacher, Mamie Foster, that I had the mumps and kept me at home for a few days. I never told Mrs. Foster or anyone else about Emily's actions.

Mrs. Foster had shown me some of the rare moments of kindness I had experienced in my short tenure on earth. She happened to live in the neighborhood and would pass the house and see me sitting on the steps in my narrow world of confinement. Also, she had been among the throng who came down to our porch to comfort us after the Bethel A.M.E. bell tolled my mother's death. One day she dropped by and presented me with two pairs of short pants, two shirts, and a pair of shoes, all brand-new. The first new duds for a boy whose wardrobe consisted of tattered hand-me-downs. The teacher took me down to Wiley's Barbershop for a haircut after getting my aunt's permission. She really seemed to care and was an oasis of warmth in a desert of emotional indifference and cruelty.

"Something's different about you, and you are going to be somebody," she would tell me. "You can be whatever you want to be. You are going to be all right."

Mrs. Foster's encouragement was crucial to me. Her compassion and interest did much to uplift my young soul. But at home, Emily's cruel nature had constructed a madhouse of horror with more surprises in waiting. Tipping the scale at 180 pounds, it was not unusual for Emily to pick me up over her head like a sack of potatoes and body slam me in wrestler fashion. She would then take her foot and stomp down on my abdomen. For years the place was sore to the touch. When I was an adult, a physician noticed an old bruise and thought I had been in a bad wreck. I traced the injury to Emily's dancing on my torso.

Emily also seemed to obtain sadistic gratification from killing animals. She bragged about how she would cut a "son-of-a-bitch hog's throat" and took pleasure in watching chickens flutter and convulse after she had wrung their necks. On one occasion we were in the backyard "pipping" chickens. The birds would eat seeds and consequently suffer calluses on their tongues. Then they couldn't eat and would get sick. Pipping consisted of holding the fowl's beak open and puncturing the hard places on its tongue with a needle.

Rhode Island Reds and other breeds scampered about the chicken yard, about thirty or forty birds. "Bring me that one," said Emily, motioning broadly with her right hand at the dozens of chickens strutting about the place.

"Which one?" I asked, confused.

"I said, damn it to hell, that one!" Emily growled, waving her hand abstractly and walking toward me at the same time.

"But . . ." I started. Suddenly a terrific blow to the left side of my head left everything dark. I don't know how long I was unconscious, but my eyes opened to see Emily standing above me, hands on hips. She clutched a four-quart metal broiler pan, her weapon of choice.

"Damn it. When I say bring me that chicken, you come to me and say 'Aunt Emily, I'm bringing you *that* one.'" I still wear a knot on my head as a memento from that day and, in a poetic sense, a reminder of my whole life with Emily, a woman educated only in the ways of the devil.

I was to discover years later that I was not the only person Emily had apparently bedeviled. Emily's brother, Charles Johnson, all but blamed her for their mother's death. It seems that, as a teenager, Emily was a wayward child who disappeared from home for several hours. Their mother apparently searched for her in foul, rainy weather and was rewarded with pneumonia, which killed her after a few weeks.

––––––––––

MY ACTIVITIES AT EMILY'S HOUSE were a kaleidoscope of boring undertakings. I would get up and do my chores, go to school, and come back home and stay inside. Most of the time I would do homework and entertain myself reading schoolbooks.

I foolishly thought I had witnessed all the harshness Emily had in store for me. One morning she went over Red Mountain into Five Points South and noticed a man named Houston selling vegetables and fruits at a stand on Twentieth Street near Fourteenth or Fifteenth Avenue South. Later that night she awakened me from sleep for what I assumed was another hair-raising dishwashing session.

Emily had taken off all her clothes, and a middle-aged black man with a medium build was there, also nude.

"Take out your pecker and rub it on Mr. Houston's pecker," she said. "Rub it on there so yours will be big like his one day." All the time she was pulling my shorts off and laughing, and so was Mr. Houston. Simultaneously crying, scared, mad, and confused, I rubbed my penis against his.

This was another layer on the cake for me. It pushed me even further into a realm of disdain for Emily. After about the third time she and Houston sexually abused me, Emily started telling neighbors I was a big liar principally because she assumed I had spilled the beans on what had been happening to me behind the closed doors of her house. Just like my father, Slim, had done when he broke my arm in two places, Emily covered her butt with fraudulent declarations regarding my own honesty.

The nights and days all blended together in a mosaic of surprise beatings or stompings or slappings with no provocation. All of this was done by a guardian who was supposed to shield a child from the seaminess of life. And it was executed by the sister of a woman whom I regarded as a sweet, divine creature molded in the image of God—my mother, Mattie C.

Mr. Houston and my aunt kept company for a few weeks, and the ritual they had cooked up for me took place almost every time he came over. Eventually, the vegetable man faded out of the picture, taking his vileness with him, but I was still left with the ogre that was Emily.

While other children, plain and privileged, were nurtured, I was being destroyed, not outright, but slowly and purposefully and with malice aforethought. I knew no other world, and there was no one to rescue me or offer a hint of a brighter tomorrow. I could foresee no relief from this existence in my shortsighted vision.

Oftentimes I wondered what better world sat beyond the confines of Emily's yard. On occasion I would scoot from my perch on the front steps, meander to the fence, and look up and down the street as I contemplated an escape from the life of torment. Each time fear would inflate my spirit with anxiety about the unknown. If I walked away from the house on Eighteenth Place, perhaps I would be shifting my lifestyle from bad to worse. I would be a child alone against a huge, impersonal world that might swallow me up like an African lion devouring a juvenile water buffalo. Each time, fear forced me to return to my so-called refuge.

Finally, one day about ten months after I had first moved in with my aunt, courage from an unknown source seemed to radiate through my tiny body. The time to act had presented itself. I walked to the fence, opened the gate, and strolled from Emily's house of abuse with no intent of falling under her clutches again so long as I drew a natural breath. I was only six and a half years old.

CHAPTER TWO

Horse Stable and Papa Clyde

IT WAS THE SUMMER OF 1941, and in Dixie the summer roared like a lion. The humidity made the steel mills and iron ore mines that much hotter. The chance to go barefoot and shirtless was a paramount concern for most youngsters. A kid might run under a yard sprinkler or take a dip in a swimming hole. Most blacks didn't have the benefit of nice swimming pools in those days, and a creek or quarry was the only relief from the oppressive heat. Tulips had given way to azaleas and roses, which stamped a bold signature on the landscape.

My hefty mission was to put distance between me and Emily's hatefulness. I walked down to U.S. 31 and maneuvered over Red Mountain toward downtown Birmingham. I stopped at a corner on the other side of the mountain where I noticed a lot of blacks were standing. It was right outside the Birmingham Electric Company. This, I learned, was where many Negroes caught the bus to go back over the mountain to white neighborhoods in Mountain Brook and Homewood where they worked as maids, yardmen, and a host of other menial jobs.

I stood there with nothing but the clothes on my small back, lost in the wilderness of black humanity. My whimpering was ignored, so I used a rickety bus as my North Star to freedom. I followed the vehicle's trail of exhaust fumes as it moved haltingly through the city's Southside, passengers embarking and disembarking, the bus accelerating and then stopping, stopping and accelerating. It traveled just slow enough for me to keep it in sight.

An inner voice prodded me as I approached Eighth Avenue South. I was "directed" to make a right turn. Another few blocks and I was compelled to make another turn. I hadn't eaten all day, but I continued to walk.

You can't sit here long, the inner voice whispered whenever I sat on a curb to gather myself. The messages abbreviated my interludes, and I trudged on with no obvious sense of direction. After a few hours I ended up in a little community with cobblestone streets dotted with quaint stores. A sign read "Crestline Village," a neighborhood in the well-to-do city of Mountain Brook.

I was nearly dying of hunger, so I naturally made a beeline to the alley behind a grocery store to forage like I had done in the trash bins behind shops in the white business district of Homewood. A garbage can sat like a lonely banquet table. Partially rotten apples were recovered as I rummaged through the container. A banana, bread, and other morsels left me stuffed.

Sleep and shelter were my next concerns. After supper my wandering brought me to Euclid Avenue. Nice homes greeted me as the sun began to lower its gaze. On one piece of property, a white fence surrounded a large two-story wood-frame house. Farther back on the land was a barn, which I approached. As I got closer, I noticed a light emanating from a little room in the building. Fear welled up inside, but the inner voice commanded me not to turn back. Just as I was about to run, a slight young boy stepped out of the door into the half-light.

My eyes widened with joy and amazement as the unknown

figure became familiar: It was my older brother, Bubba, whom I had not seen in months. "How did you find me, Shurley?" he said.

"I don't know," I said, just as puzzled.

Bubba asked me about our two younger brothers, Sam and David. I told him I had not seen them except at a distance, and that had been weeks earlier. He apologized for leaving me behind.

I related the miserable experience I had endured at Aunt Emily's house, and he assumed blame for what had befallen me. He explained what I already knew, that he couldn't take any more of the oppressive life with Daddy and Marie. Now I had parted company with that duo as well as Aunt Emily. Our dealings with family members was leaving a discouraging trail of disappointment and suffering in its wake.

Bubba was now about nine. I was almost seven. But we both knew our battered bodies and emaciated souls had aged us light-years beyond childhood. The barn, I learned, served as stables for the Stringfellow family, but they boarded and groomed the horses of others. Bubba lived in the building and earned his keep and meals taking care of Tennessee walking horses there. Another boy living in the stables named Peewee was also bewildered at my appearance out of nowhere. A native of Bessemer, Peewee was about ten years old, walked with a slight shuffle, cared little for his personal hygiene, and was senior in tenure among the stable boys.

Bubba and I covered more ground in our retrieval of old times, depressing as they were. He gave me his cot to sleep on, and he curled up on the floor of the compartment that I learned was the tack room. The stable was divided into six stalls on one side and five on the other, plus the tack area. That section housed bridles, curry combs, soap, and other grooming items, and served as the groomsmen's living quarters.

We turned the kerosene light off at about 8 P.M. so the horses wouldn't be disturbed. That night I slept more peacefully than I had in months. Four-legged beasts may have been my neighbors, but at least the inner voice had directed me to an aspect of my life I thought I would never experience again—Bubba.

DAYLIGHT PEERED INTO OUR SANCTUARY too quickly, and we faced it with the hesitance of youths who would rather stay nestled in easy slumber. Bubba and Peewee began the day grooming some of the walking horses, and I just observed. Breakfast was to be provided by the horse trainer's wife, Mrs. Wilma. But first I was to meet the trainer himself.

"Damn, I go to bed last night and there're two niggers, and here I come this morning and it's three niggers," said a thirty-something white man wearing an old hat pulled down over his ears.

Bubba introduced me to Zollie Derryberry, the horse trainer for the stables. "This is my brother Shurley," he said.

"Jerome, you told me you didn't have no kinfolk," said Derryberry, a brown-haired man with a medium build who liked to chew tobacco. "How many more of you coming?" he prodded. "How long you gonna stay here, boy?"

I shrugged off these questions.

Derryberry lived in a modest, well-kept house on the southeast corner of the Stringfellow acreage with his wife, Wilma, and their three sons. He never objected to me staying in the stables, and since I could not handle the big horses, it was agreed that I would perform lighter chores such as piling up horse manure for use as fertilizer and helping his wife keep their dwelling spic-and-span.

The Derryberrys were decent folks but, like most other whites you ran into in those days, believed in segregation. As long as you "knew your place," everyone got along just fine. That's how it had been in the South for three hundred years; master and slave had evolved into boss and domestic servant. But the common denominator was servitude, and most blacks played their roles flawlessly, from the maids and yardmen who walked from their homes in Rosedale to work at white residences, to me, a stable boy. We all accepted the paternalistic social system in a spirit of accommodation with an eye on survival.

Mrs. Wilma, a matronly, friendly woman, gave us our food. She struck me as the only white woman in Alabama who didn't want to have a black maid or cook; she'd rather do it herself. All of the cooking, except for the food that came from the big house inhabited by the Stringfellows, was dished out by her and was actually quite delicious.

I arrived at the stables with nothing but the clothes on my back, but Mrs. Wilma outfitted me with her children's discards. Zollie Jr., the eldest of their three sons, was two years my senior. He and his brothers, Harold and Larry, did little work around the stable. Mrs. Wilma presented me with shoes the boys had outgrown but, sadly, my feet were smothered in them too. A knife or a pair of scissors enable me to cut off the ends of the footwear so my toes could poke through. Scraps of leather from the stable were used to pad the shoes to ensure maximum durability.

One of the sons had a difficult time reading, and I would read with him, to Mrs. Wilma's astonishment.

"Hey, this boy can read. Where you learned to read?" she asked.

When wealthy whites visited the stables and the Derryberrys made mention of my literary skills, my head grew exponentially and my chest swelled with unbridled pleasure. Magazines and books would be placed in front of me, and I would leap into action. Page after page. Word after word. A lot of magazines came to the Derryberrys in the mail. *Life. Saturday Evening Post.* Bunches of them. Whenever the family would discard them in the trash, I rescued them for entertainment and nuggets of knowledge. At night I would read to Bubba and Peewee, all the while building one heck of a library.

Mrs. Mamie Foster had taught and guided me masterfully in the first grade at Union Baptist and helped lay the foundation for my affection for the printed word. I was secretly proud that I was a capable reader in a sea of Negro illiteracy.

Reading and chores around the stable and Derryberry house consumed the summer days. That fall saw me ready to go back to school. The closest Negro school was in Irondale, a good five miles away.

I told Mr. Derryberry my intentions. "How you gonna go to school and work, boy?" he said. Bubba declared that he would cover for me and do my work, piling the manure and whatever else.

"Let him go to school if he can get there," Mrs. Wilma persuasively argued.

The first morning of school I arose with nervous enthusiasm for a new adventure and started out at about 7 A.M. on the trek to Irondale Elementary. The school bell rang at 9 A.M., and I made it with a few minutes to spare. The facility was a simple old wooden building harboring urchins in grades one through eight—nothing to brag about in those days of "separate but equal" education. By the time I returned to the stable in the afternoon, Bubba had completed my chores. There was nothing much left to do but homework, talk, sing, read, pitch horse-shoes, and share dreams and thoughts of a brighter future or simply hit the hay.

Bubba, I discovered, exhibited masterful skill with the horses, many of which, of course, weighed hundreds of pounds. Mr. Derryberry had earned a reputation as a great trainer, but to see what a nine-year-old boy could do with the beasts was quite impressive. Several days a week we would help catch the huge, spirited animals. Derryberry would lead them over to the fence on which Bubba stood. From his perch, he would then step into the saddle. The horse would rear up on its hind legs and violently buck its body in an effort to toss off the human cargo that was holding tightly onto the reins. But after about thirty minutes, the meanest equines would become as mellow as lambs. In addition to breaking horses, my brother could make the animals trot, canter, stretch, and kneel. I almost believed that he could prompt the creatures to rear up and do a tango if the spirit moved him.

Weekends seemed to crawl by, but we still had to earn our way and that meant grooming and walking the horses for the owners who came by more frequently on Saturdays and Sundays. As stable boys we were apparently invisible to patrons, who would talk with abandon employing racial slurs. The expressions of bigotry were revealing but hardly fazed us as we continued to perform our tasks with the horses.

A glorious break in the daily tedium came in the form of the horse shows that were usually held in various cities in the state. A trip to Pulaski, Tennessee, for a show was my first view of the world outside Alabama. It provided an adventuresome opportunity to sleep in cots in the trailer with the horses, dodging their long tails as they swished back and forth, scattering pesky flies. Bubba could not only tame horses, but he was equally proficient as a rider in the shows, and I was his manager. A lofty title. My chief duty was to spit-polish the black boots he wore so he would look presentable among the other horsemen, most of whom were young black men or boys. Bubba took first- and second-place trophies on one excursion. The mementos of achievement were among the few things he and I had to cherish.

––––––––––––

DURING THE TIME AT THE STABLES Bubba and I would contemplate the fate of our younger siblings, Sam and David. We assumed that if they were with Slim and Marie, trouble was riding on their shoulders. We hatched a plan to go back and rescue them from that back porch. But, realistically, we knew they were too young to work at the stable, and the notion was discarded as unfeasible. However, many nights Bubba and I would join hands and pray for their well-being.

Lurking in the shadows of our minds was the fear that Slim Stewart or perhaps Aunt Emily would come after us to inflict bodily harm, or send an emissary in their stead. We decided to learn self-defense strategies. These took the form of throwing ice picks at targets constructed out of just about anything. Our training sessions were relentless and took place after chores and schooling had been completed in the evenings or on weekends. A bull's-eye would be drawn on a fence or board with paint or crayons to help enhance our skills during the sessions. Sometimes we would roughly sketch the image of a man, complete with head, heart, torso, and limbs. The ideal picks had smooth handles and were aerodynamically suitable to slice through the air with ease. We would throw overhanded, underhanded, and at odd angles in an effort to hit a target. Sometimes we pulled the target with a rope to create the effect of firing on the run. Peewee would practice his own marksmanship with us, but we had no idea whom he was training to assault or defend himself against.

Another form of leisure was using BB guns to scare off birds that bothered the horses. This provided an avenue for sharpening our survival skills since we would practice shooting at targets around the stables like cans, twigs, and such. We even mounted matches on a post and shot at them from several yards away. Our skills developed to the extent that we could light a match when we hit it with a pellet.

The Stringfellow property was our whole world in many ways. But sometimes I would leave the acreage and wander through nearby Crestline Village near the shops and daydream and pine for something beyond stable life. On one occasion, as an eight-year-old, I came face-to-face with the dark side of my personality, which all humans probably possess in a Dr. Jekyll vs. Mr. Hyde dualism. A middle-aged Negro worker came out of one of the shops. I wasn't often prone to begging, but I asked him if he could spare some change so I could buy some candy. If the Derryberrys or Stringfellows were not around the stables, Bubba, Peewee, and I had to fend for ourselves. No sooner had I made the request than the man kicked at me like I was a mangy dog stealing scraps from a picnic lunch table. Although the man missed, I didn't. Again and again I pummeled his head with a stick until I had drawn blood and he stumbled away. I had been beaten by Aunt Emily and my father, but I knew I would never allow myself to be mistreated again.

———————

OUR ROUTINE IN THE STABLES PERSISTED: grooming and exercising the horses, piling up the manure for use as fertilizer, pitching horseshoes, singing, and talking about the grand dreams that stable boys were inevitably prone to conjure. The Derryberrys and visitors to the stables continued to ambush me with quizzes about what I was reading or the performance of the stock market. This was kindling that stoked a burning desire to be known as more than just another ignoramuslike colored person in the tradition of the archetypical Stepin Fetchit. Reading was my crowning glory.

Life with Papa Clyde

Clyde Smith was always dressed elegantly, and his shoes shone like a Marine's belt buckle when he visited the stables to ride his horses or fetch them for an equestrian show. His Packard convertible boasted a rich rumbling sound, and when he turned onto Euclid Avenue approaching Stringfellow Stables, he would race the engine as if to herald his arrival. Diamond jewelry on his hands and wrists sparkled like the eyes of a lover, and he never starved for wads of cash. Mr. Clyde struck up a pivotal conversation with me one day in the latter half of 1943.

"Hey, Shurley, come here and read. How you doing in school?" he queried. "You still going to school? . . . How long you going to stay in this barn?"

I told him that I figured to keep trudging to Irondale School and live at the stables as long as humanly possible. Mr. Clyde was in some ways a mysterious man. Although he loved to tell jokes, they were invariably as dull as dishwater. He conveyed an "I'm in charge" attitude built on the inner confidence of a self-made individual who juggled work as a developer, restaurateur, and small-time gambler or "policy-maker," which was like directing a miniature lottery. Some said he made and peddled moonshine or whiskey.

"By the way, old Percy that works for me says folks talk

about the boy at school that's so smart," he said. "That's you. I didn't tell him I knew it was you. I tell you what. I'll let you go to school, but I'm not going to take you away from the Stringfellows. If you go to the highway and walk away, I'll let you stay at my place. It would be better than this stable, and I'll let you go to school."

The proposition sent ambiguous impulses through me. Mr. Clyde's habitat had to be more comfortable than a place where the washroom was the horses' grooming tub and bushes were our commode. The Stringfellows and Derryberrys had provided a haven, but I was, in effect, a stable hand conducting odd jobs around the horses and Derryberry house in exchange for boarding and some meals. Clyde Smith was apparently offering me the roof of a house over my head without a compulsion to work off a debt. And he said his house would be closer to school, a logistical fact that would make it easier to feed my passion for learning. But, despite the lures of the Smith proposal, separation from Bubba was a fly in the buttermilk. We had been reunited in a miraculous fashion, and now I would be separated from him again. I took the offer to my brother in hopes that he would help me make a decision.

"Mr. Clyde, he a good man," said Bubba. "What you gonna do, Shurley?"

"I don't know. I guess I'll stay here, Bubba. I won't see you," I said.

"You'll see me," he replied.

Mr. Clyde, a middle-aged man with reddish hair parted down the center, consented to bring me to the stables whenever he went riding his horses so I could see Bubba. That was a key element of persuasion in the decision to make the transition from a world of minimum sustenance into a hopefully more beneficial lifestyle.

I trekked across the pasture and kept looking back at Bubba, watching his small frame become less discernible with each step taken. A few minutes scooted past before my ears caught the sound of Mr. Clyde's powerful Packard approaching.

"Get in," he said as he maneuvered the vehicle up to me on the dirt road. As we hurtled down U.S. 78, I marveled at the sleekness and performance of the first convertible in which I had ever ridden.

Soon we encountered a huge rock house on a hill about 250 feet from U.S. 78. Smith had dynamited the rock from the surrounding terrain and used the minerals to build the structure, which had a rear parking area that could accommodate about a dozen cars.

"What you doing with Shurley?" asked Mr. Clyde's wife, Bessie.

"He's going to stay downstairs in the basement," he replied matter-of-factly.

Mama Bessie was a stately, sophisticated red-haired woman, a Southern belle in the best sense of the word. She was also a chain smoker. Her laugh sounded like a man's and seemed to roll from deep within her belly. She voiced no opposition to Mr. Clyde's plan.

Mary Sue, Clyde's stepdaughter, was a polio victim with gnarled arms. She was in her early twenties and walked with the aid of crutches.

"Mr. Clyde told us you love to read. You and I going to be all right," she said, adding that books were her great pleasure.

The basement of the house was to be my quarters, and a cot was placed there for me. A toilet and washbasin, furnace, coal bin, and pool table were also a part of the place I would call home. The coal dust on the floor was a minor irritation for a child who had slept in the stable. Finally, here was a decent room that surpassed a horse stable's tack room, crapping in the bushes, and receiving meals at the back doors of the Derryberry and Stringfellow houses.

The back door was the most commonly used entrance for the rock house, which contained three lovely bedrooms. Smith and his wife, Bessie, occupied a bedroom in the rear, while Mary Sue stayed in the front bedroom. Sandwiched between the front and rear living quarters were a guest bedroom, a dining room, a library, an immaculate living room, and other nooks and crannies for a total of twelve rooms. A tourist court motel, the Rock Castle, was next door to the house and was made with the same rocks. The Smiths also owned the Pines, another nearby motel.

Country and western music placed on the radios at the house, and the lyrics seemed odd: "I had to take a tater and wait" or "Old Uncle Bill went to the hill drinking mountain dew." This is how the lyrics came across to my ears, but I presume that they were more substantive to the ears of the Smiths or others who really enjoyed melodies of that type.

Mr. Clyde, I deduced, took a shine to me apparently because I wanted to learn. I discovered that he had been observing me for a while before he asked me about moving to his home. He surmised that I was intelligent and hungry for knowledge. The trip from the stables to Irondale School was at least five miles and took me two hours, but from the Smith house it was a breezy thirty-minute walk.

The word on the street was that Mr. Clyde was what was called a policy or lottery operator. He was known in the Negro sections of Irondale, Southtown projects, downtown Birmingham, East Birmingham, and other communities. He also apparently had a stake in several little shops and restaurants in the black community.

Clyde Smith admitted that he was well fixed for money but

did not seem to feel that such materialism was the apex of human existence. He lived on simple but earnest philosophies that he espoused often, such as the likelihood of catching more flies with syrup than with vinegar and the belief in the masses of people rather than the classes. Although he could have blended in with big shots in the community, he seemed to be more comfortable around Negroes and lower- to middle-income whites. While blacks called him Mr. Smith or Mr. Clyde, whites just called him Clyde.

Mr. Clyde took me down to the black section of Irondale known as the Bends. We went into a store, and he bought me some pants, shirts, and low-cut shoes to supplement my threadbare wardrobe. Next he escorted me to get my unkempt hair trimmed. All of the black people knew Smith and greeted him warmly in a monotonous chorus.

"How you doing, Mr. Clyde?" came the salutation.

Tears still flowed that first night under Mr. Clyde's roof like they had every night since Mama was killed. The warmth of the Smiths was uplifting to me, a nine-year-old boy, but of course, their humaneness couldn't completely salve the emotional wounds plastered with the scar tissue of time.

The journey through the woods to Irondale School meant I ran the risk of tearing my clothes, so sometimes I took the longer three-mile route down U.S. 78. On an average day I would arise, eat breakfast, and head through the woods to school. Some days Mama Smith or Papa Clyde would drive me down the highway and let me out at the Golden Rule restaurant. I would then walk the few blocks to the school from there. If someone had seen whites dropping me off at the institution, it might have caused problems for me and the Smiths, who were aware that they had to use a degree of caution and not openly invite scrutiny or needless conflict.

At school, children teased me about my body odor and banana-colored teeth.

"I bet you ain't had any stuff," girls taunted.

They were right, of course, but prepubescent innocence made me indifferent to that barb. Aces in the hole for me were my good grades and learning skills.

"Well, at least I can read," I would respond.

"Yeah, well we could read too if we tried," they retorted.

Isolation from the community was a hallmark of my tenure at the Smith house since I could not raise suspicion by having a classmate drop by and play. Aside from when I was at school, I was away from the black world. Clyde's immediate family, of course, knew I lived there, and so did Big Percy Kelley, a black handyman who did work for the Smiths. He always wore overalls and stylishly kept one suspender hanging off his broad shoulders. He and Papa Clyde always seemed to enjoy each other's company and had a magnificent time seeing who could tell the biggest lie in the form of jokes, which were often vulgar and crude, the kind usually told only between men. Many days Big Percy would drive up in his old raggedy pickup truck to work on some project at the rock house and greet Papa Clyde with the usual salutation.

"I've got one for you to hear this time, Mr. Clyde," he would say. He would then relate some gag, and both men would invariably burst into laughter. Clyde would often fall on his knees in mirth or press a palm against the house as if attempting to keep it from sliding off its sturdy foundation; Percy, not to be outdone, might end up guffawing to the point of falling down on the ground onto his back, feet up in the air.

"Mr. Clyde," Percy would say. "You ought to be ashamed of yourself."

Their interaction was the only time I had seen a black man

and a white man share the same whiskey bottle. Clyde would tell his joke and pass Big Percy the liquor. In their own way, the two men were close friends and did not truly seem to be just boss and handyman. Symbolically, their bond reflected the tortured, timeless relationship between blacks and whites in the South: from one perspective separate and apart, but from another sharing a common, intimate culture dictated by the shames and glories of a collective history.

Every day two black guys named Darnell and Caleb would come by the Smith house. Apparently they were the legmen in Clyde Smith's policy business. They expressed concern that I was staying with a white family. Clyde would never tell them anything about my background and dismissed them and other nosy transgressors with terse words: "That's my boy; you stay out of his business."

Usually, when the two legmen showed up, I made myself scarce. The gambling was a side of his life that Clyde did not share with me. He was the money man. If it worked like other such enterprises, people would select or be assigned a series of numbers, and Clyde's function would be to bet that they would not win, so to speak. I have no idea how much money he raked in, and I think my ignorance on the topic was not accidental but by design. If Papa Clyde was actually peddling and making moonshine, as some alleged, I never saw it. This type of activity was wedged in the adult world, and as a child, I had no burning interest in such schemes. What was within my purview was the business side of the man, the hard-driving, negotiating, wheeling and dealing Southern gentleman in all his mesmerizing charm.

While I still loved to read magazines and books, Clyde Smith told me to always develop common sense as a companion to academic learning. During the week he was busy designing and constructing homes in developments in Irondale and in Bluff

Park, south of Birmingham. On the weekends he would let me accompany him to learn old-fashioned nuggets of truth and urged me to keep my eyes and ears open to absorb the information presented to me.

At the subdivisions, I took the opportunity to watch carpenters and plumbers work and ask tons of questions. No one ever chased me off, probably because they knew I was with Mr. Clyde, and they dared not reveal the usual irritation adults displayed with pesky children. Carpenters would sometimes produce a section of lumber and allow me to experiment with what was called a carpenter's square or some other tool. If Papa Clyde noticed that something was not put together properly at one of the sites, he would order the men to tear a structure down and make them tell him what was wrong with it. More often than not he would end up having the upper hand. He liked to say, "I'll let you do things my way."

MY RESPONSIBILITIES AT THE HOUSE were never backbreaking. Taking trash out of the kitchen, raking leaves, and picking up refuse in a rear parking area were some of my duties. The Rock Castle Court motel was a few yards from the house and contained about twenty rooms or cabins that boasted bed, shower, and commode. All brands of whiskey were available, and cabins 1, 2, 3, and 4 had garages attached. My job was to carry ice and towels to the rooms. The truth was that the motel catered to a transient business, which meant that most of the people using the facilities were often on a sexual rendezvous. The staff and I would recognize different cars as belonging to regular patrons and knew that certain men preferred cabins with garages to conceal their cars and ensure privacy. Often the customers were married to other people. We would see white men drive in with their maids or black girlfriends. But we knew that no Negro man would dare be seen bringing a white female to the establishment, although, knowing Papa Clyde, he may not have cared if they had.

Smith fulfilled a fatherly role in my life much more so than my biological dad, Slim Stewart, had ever thought of doing. We would often go riding together in his car, an odd coupling and a stark sight in 1940s Alabama, or for that matter, the whole dog-gone race-obsessed United States: this young Negro boy of nine years and a middle-aged white man who were always together when the law of the state made many interracial interactions illegal. And where the law left off, centuries of Southern mores took over to maintain the wide valley between the races.

Many people saw us together and, eager to explain our oddity, assumed I was the son of their maid. Since segregation was strictly enforced in the world outside the rock house, we had to focus on logistics.

"I know what you like to eat, the same thing I do," said Papa Clyde as we visited Jeb's Seafood, a popular restaurant across from the train station in downtown Birmingham that did not cater to Negroes. He sauntered into the building, purchased the food, and returned to the car where I waited.

I understood that Papa Clyde had gotten into confrontations with whites who had made derisive comments about our relationship. People wondered if we were related by blood.

"Clyde, I see you got your boy with you," said a man on one outing. "No way you'd be taking care of that boy if he wasn't yours."

I was well fed at the Smith house and ate whatever they consumed. Clothing was adequate, but I was not showered with toys. Even when I asked about the possibility of receiving a bicycle, Smith had a practical answer.

"Where you going to ride it?" he said. "We're too close to the highway. You'd just get your damn self killed." That was also the rationale for why I never got a basketball. It would likely roll down the hill to U.S. 78; I'd follow and be smashed by a car speeding toward Atlanta.

The crux of the covenant with Papa Clyde was that I would be closer to school and have better living quarters. Material possessions were never mentioned as a part of the bargain. The Smiths' whole attitude seemed to emanate from regard for another human being who, after all, was still a young child. My excitement over learning never abated, and the Smiths were, in effect, like private tutors. Mama Bessie could often be seen taking a sip of liquor and summoning me to bring my workbooks in for review. She would coax me not to be satisfied with mediocre work and always go beyond school requirements. I should read four chapters if I was assigned only one chapter, for instance. Often Clyde would say, "Boy, when you get out of high school, I guess I will have to send your ass to college."

Clyde was cognizant of the fact that I was longing for an intangible element missing from my short life and seemed aware that I needed to expunge bothersome details from my system. When I assured him that I did not want to leave the Smith family, he urged me to talk things out. Often we would just end up singing a song together, or he would do something comedic to make me chuckle. After a while I became more comfortable with telling him about the death of my mother and the abuse from relatives. It was not until after I had lived with the family for almost a year that I discovered that Papa Clyde had gone to Rosedale and double-checked some of the allegations about Slim, Marie, and Emily with people in Rosedale. Detective work of that type would have been relatively simple for a man with intimate knowledge of black neighborhoods because of his small-time gambling endeavor. This explained why, during our wide-ranging trips through the metropolitan area, he apparently avoided driving near the Rosedale relatives' houses. The closest we got was about a mile away when we stopped at the Twenty-third Street Grill on Birmingham's south side, an establishment Clyde apparently owned. However, I never told him about Aunt Mamie in Collegeville, and sometimes we drove within eyesight of her house.

———————

ALTHOUGH CLYDE WAS A STERN MAN, he never lifted his hand to me. Some days when I got on his wrong side, he would often bellow an empty threat, which I never took seriously. Even when he and Mama Bessie had words, nothing much became of the matter. Either of them might put the fuss to rest with the harmless magic words, "Go to hell."

Clyde never used the words *Negro, colored,* or the popular racial slurs. Actually, the way he handled my whole situation was the darnedest phenomenon. Our trips to the black community, the at-home school sessions, and the opportunities to watch him conduct business seemed to have been crafted by a skilled psychologist. He undoubtedly wanted to make sure I had a foundation rooted in a solid, sensible perspective, even though I was essentially encased in a white world.

I went back to see Bubba at the stables once not long after I began living with the Smiths. But the winter of 1945 was the last time I saw him because Papa Clyde sold his horses and erased any official reason for him to go there. I later learned that Bubba had gathered his meager belongings and disappeared into the Alabama landscape. I wept again for the loss.

Reading periodicals and doing homework were my chief pastimes at the Smith house. The New Testament became a project for me, and I read the book twice forward and once backward. On Sundays I would go over to the Bends in east Irondale and perch on the outside of a church and listen to the Negro pastors winning over their congregations with emotional, gut-wrenching sermons. I sat in the tree outside the church because I had been turned around at the door once by an usher because I did not have the proper attire.

"O-o-oh Lord! In the sweet bye and bye . . ." they would declare.

A mirror in my basement room allowed me to learn to preach by mimicking the spine-tingling delivery and exaggerated gestures of the ministers. I felt like some of the songs were aimed directly at me.

"Sometimes I feel like a motherless child . . . A long way from home . . . Sometimes I wish I had never been born." That song irritated me because these people sometimes felt motherless when I was without a mother 100 percent of the time. The impact of the song was so penetrating that I would even dream the tune, and it seemed to vibrate through my head during waking hours as a personal theme of orphanhood.

My performances in front of the mirror involved working myself to a fever pitch while delivering spellbinding speeches during which I would begin to laugh or cry, caught up in my own eloquence. This was an escape from a nagging loneliness; in many ways the person in the mirror was my Negro companion in the white world in which I lived. In my mind I could visualize thousands of people in an audience behind me engrossed with my messages. I would pray during these sermons with my eyes open. The idea came to me during one of these sessions that my mother's death was a crucifixion. When my father knocked her out of the window of our house on Eighteenth Place in Rosedale, she landed in the tree in almost spread-eagle position reminiscent of Jesus on the cross. The blood that I saw on her ankle as a result of her body impacting the tree was like Christ's blood after he was pierced in the side by soldiers. Jesus, according to the Bible, died so that humanity might live. My mother had died so that her children might live in that she was killed after she refused to give our father the money she had saved for our food and insurance policy. I also thought about my own near-crucifixion when Aunt Emily used a pulley to hang me from the ceiling, whipped me with an ironing cord, and rubbed salt into my wounds. Although it seemed like the vocations of preaching or acting would have been natural progressions after these performances, I never seriously considered those undertakings.

MUCH OF MY TIME WAS SPENT in the company of Mary Sue and Mama Bessie since Papa Clyde was roving between enterprises during the day when I was at school. When Clyde and Bessie would go off for the evenings, I would stay in the guest room to keep close watch over Mary Sue. She was not the kind of person you would leave alone because of the severity of her condition. Sometimes I would lie across the foot of her bed while we read magazines and books together. The young woman's close relationship with me rewarded her with insight into the black experience.

"Shurley, I think I know now what it is that the colored have to go through," she said. Mary Sue explained that from observing me she realized that because of limited opportunities for Negroes, many did not have a chance to show their full potential. She said that if I were given a chance, I would demonstrate that I was as smart or smarter than many whites.

Mama Bessie, for her part, counseled me on racial identity.

Thicker lips and a broader nose signaled obvious physical differences between the Smiths and me. Bessie would always tell me I was a nice-looking boy and to be proud of my looks, although I was already. Despite being ridiculed for my appearance at school, I never considered myself to be ugly.

Soon no room was off-limits to me. The Smiths' relatives and friends were cordial, but I kept a distance when they were around. An attitude prevailed that I was "that boy." Gradually, I began eating in the breakfast room more often, sometimes at the same time the family was having a meal. On one occasion, Doc, the blacksmith from Stringfellow Stables, stopped by on a social visit and saw me eating at the family table.

"I hope you break those damn dishes," said Doc, a tall redheaded man.

"What are you talking about?" said Papa Clyde.

"You let a nigger boy sit down in your house, that nigger sitting there at your table," he said, pointing and glaring at me.

Before the blacksmith could spew any more venom, Papa Clyde decked him with a knuckle sandwich to the chin, sending him sailing over a chair.

"What's wrong?" Doc said in befuddlement. "All I said was you let that nigger"—Papa Clyde interrupted with another blow. He made it clear that the blacksmith was never to use that term again in describing me, although Doc defended the expression as a harmless word he always used toward Negroes. Papa Clyde would hear none of it. This was his house and he set the rules under its roof. He admonished me never to accept being called that slur.

Doc was a younger man and larger than Papa Clyde, but he did not try to defend himself, a fact I attributed more to Clyde Smith's status in the community pecking order than Doc's self-restraint. The pair drank themselves into a stupor after the incident as if nothing had happened. But Doc never crossed the threshold of the Smith house again.

I was not totally surprised at Papa Clyde coming to my defense. Both Clyde and Mama Bessie always displayed a strong, independent nature. I saw this characteristic again after Mary Sue voiced concern about my future with the family.

"He's little now, but what will people say when he gets older?" she said.

"Not a damn thing!" Mama Bessie retorted.

Papa Clyde was not a churchgoing man, but he would often state that the world was full of laws, but the axioms stated in the Ten Commandments represented the ideal truths that people needed to chase after and live by.

———

PAPA CLYDE AND I ACTED OUT our father–son relationship with exuberance and earnestness. One excursion was to check on some property he owned in Thorsby, thirty miles south of Birmingham in Chilton County. We drove down U.S. 31 to the town, the site of his sugarcane farm. The spread was worked by nine or ten blacks plus a white foreman. I was so intrigued with the cane operation that I arranged to be left there for a few days so I could see how things worked.

The houses were small and dreary, like slave quarters. Each contained a bed and lantern. I stayed in the Smith house, which was used as the overseer's domain, and slept on a cot after the foreman noted my grimy clothes and steered me away from the bed. The next morning we began harvesting the cane. My job was to grab the staff and stack it after another worker cut it with a sickle. Breads of perspiration glistened on mahogany skin as we cut, grabbed, and stacked over and over, singing, chanting, and telling jokes that made time accelerate like a hounded fox.

The mystique of residing in the Smith house with the over-seer prompted one of the men to broach an inquiry. "We know you stay with the white folks, but we don't know how you do it," said a man. "Do your daddy work for Mr. Clyde?"

I nodded in affirmation, figuring this would be the least complicated way to answer the intrusion without going into a convoluted life story and history. The fellows had more or less accepted me as one of the crew. I really knew I was in the fold when five of the guys, all in their late teens or early twenties, in-vited me to the picture show that afternoon over in Jemison. The dusty ride there was a bonding escapade as we sang and joked all the way to the movie house, where we sat up in the balcony or the Negro section. After the show I elected to stay in the work-ers' quarters with the rest of the guys.

I soon grew restless and felt overly familiar with the farm and its workings and wondered when Papa Clyde was coming back for me. To my relief, he drove down to Thorsby on the third day and spirited me back to less taxing circumstances. There was a world outside the Smiths' house, but the farm represented a mere fraction of it. It was great to pal around with other Negro males, but the strenuous, hot work made the minor chores I did around the motel and the Smith house even more appealing.

CHAPTER THREE

Mamie Returns

THE SOUTHERN LANDSCAPE CHANGED like the chameleon it was, taking grand hints from fickle Mother Nature. Seasons driven by a cosmic scheme displayed themselves and then receded from view like luggage on an airport conveyor belt waiting to be claimed. I had become more comfortable and secure with my surrogate white family after almost three years with them. I was still making good grades at Irondale School, taking taunts from classmates, and weeping at night.

One Saturday in the fall of '47, Papa Clyde and I were outside in the yard talking when he alerted me to an approaching visitor. "Who is that colored woman coming up the driveway?" he said as I turned to look toward the end of the yard. "She's a big one."

I looked. Colored woman. Determined stride. Big sunbonnet. Finally, my memory was rattled enough to notch a name on this imposing form.

It was Aunt Mamie. I hadn't seen her since the day after Christmas in 1939, the day she dumped my three brothers and me out in the field in Rosedale, washing her hands of us. *What unmitigated gumption,* I thought, *for her to show up now.* My first impulse was to flee, and my adrenaline urged me to do so. As soon as she was about ten feet away from us, I turned and looked for an escape route.

"You better not run," Aunt Mamie commanded.

This was a woman who always dressed beyond her years, and today was no different. Big hat. Old scarf. It was Mamie, thrust forth like an image from a discarded negative ushered to crisp reality in a photography darkroom.

"Hold it, Shurley," said Papa Clyde, grabbing me by the arm. "Who is this?"

"That's my auntie," I said. "What do you want, Aunt Mamie?"

Mamie had her speech rehearsed. "That's my sister's boy, and he has no business living here with you white folks," she said. "He's underage, and I came to get him."

"I'm not going with you," I said.

The adults began to argue, but Papa Clyde realized that he didn't need to have the police poking around in his business. They knew about his gambling enterprise, but they conveniently looked the other way. Clyde was aware that Mamie could make trouble even for him, a white man. He wanted me to stay with him, but his hands were tied.

"I love you, Shurley, but that's your aunt, and the law is on her side," he said.

Tears welled up as I entertained thoughts about running away back to the stables or anywhere rather than Mamie's house. I hesitantly packed my clothes for departure from the rock house.

"Can Shurley come back and get the rest of his stuff?" Papa Clyde asked.

"I'll think about it," Mamie answered.

I hugged Papa Clyde and bid him farewell. Mama Bessie and Miss Mary Sue were alerted to my pending departure, and copious tears flowed all around, except from Aunt Mamie, of course. This family had represented the true meaning of the word *shelter*. That was what I had been seeking when I moved in with Aunt Emily back in 1940. But her haven turned out to be a torture chamber. The Smiths were my family in a deeper sense than my father, stepmother, and Aunt Emily, and, I suspected, Mamie would not be much better than the rest of the kinfolks. I told the Smiths that I would be seeing them later and walked away from their rock house that was built on a foundation of warmth and kindness.

IN EVERY EXPERIENCE THERE IS A LESSON to be gleaned like the flecks of gold a prospector finds sifting through sand in the Yukon territory. A precious nugget of wisdom was collected from Papa Clyde and his family: Love has no color. Only the demons of narrow vision and cultivated fear make humanity want to classify who should be accepted and appreciated. Once when I wandered away from the Smith home and walked over to the business section of Irondale, I found that I had gotten a little hungry. I asked a Negro man for few cents with which to buy something to eat. The man kicked at me and cursed me. A white man saw what had happened and went into the colored entrance of a restaurant. Minutes later he returned with a hamburger, potatoes, a pie, and soft drink for me. The vignette is not told to glorify or condemn a particular race. But this was another lesson that a person's skin color is only an expression of nature and does not make him good or bad. It is the heart and character that reside underneath superficial appearance that truly matter. Race and color are often political, empty designations, but love and kindness are essential to the progress of one race only—that which is fully human.

In a wider view, it was remarkable to me that it took whites to show me the kindness and acceptance I never got from my blood kin. The Smith family's oasis of warmth in a desert of hatred that blanketed World War II–era Alabama gave me an extra dimension of fortitude and understanding. I knew that all whites are not the same, and neither are all blacks. The individual must be sized up on his or her own merits, for better or worse.

———————

MAMIE'S CAR WAS NOWHERE TO BE SEEN. She held my arm in a viselike grip as we took the Number 17 streetcar back toward her house in Collegeville. After one streetcar change in downtown Birmingham, we arrived at her place, 3411 Thirty-third Avenue North in the old black working-class neighborhood. This was my first time in years in a community filled with black folks. The small frame house had two bedrooms and was well kept and clean; linoleum floors shone brightly. Even though it was in the city limits, the structure had no bathtub or indoor toilet, only an outhouse. Chickens and goats rambled around the yard.

Uncle Henry Pickens looked about the same as when I last saw him: a tall, pleasant, henpecked man who always walked around with a big matchstick hanging out of his mouth. He was still working as a laborer in the Louisville & Nashville railroad's wheel shop and priding himself on how he could pick up a fifty-pound hog without breaking a sweat.

Mamie shed light on the cloak-and-dagger exercise that had led to our awkward reunion after a separation of almost a decade. Her neighbor, Eugenia Merriweather, was an acquaintance of Mrs. Maxey, my Irondale School teacher, and their conversation touched on a smart boy at the school. Mrs. Merriweather heard the name Shurley and began to piece the situation together and told my aunt. Mamie and Henry, I learned, had watched me at the school and plotted the right time to confront Clyde Smith. It dawned on me that my "rescue" from the Smiths was not really a noble undertaking in the name of blood and kin. For Mamie, I was to be a pawn with which she could elevate her social status. Mamie didn't work, and Henry had his modest railroad job. A child pulling down good grades would be a feather in their cap, nothing more, nothing less.

A beautiful bedroom with polished chestnut furniture was situated at the front of her house. I thought this would be where I would lay my head at night, a step up from the stable and even the basement at Papa Clyde's. Mamie had other plans. I was summoned to the living room, where I found she had pushed the table against the wall and set up a cot. My life was undergoing a metamorphosis for better or worse, and I suspected it was the latter.

Mamie laid down the rules of the house, and, at an intimidating three hundred pounds and six feet tall, she was certainly woman enough to enforce them. At 3 A.M. she woke me and told me to bring in coal for the stove so water could be heated for the washtub. After dinner each night I was to prepare the stove for the following morning, she said. Since it was considered bad luck to carry ashes out of the house after dark, I was to put the grayish, powdery residue behind the stove until morning.

Each morning, dusting the floors and furniture was to be followed by slopping the hogs and feeding the chickens and goats. Her daddy, Willis Johnson, had taught her about hogs and chickens, she reasoned, and it would be good for me to know how to do this too.

"Henry needs somebody to help him around here," said Aunt Mamie, her eyes looking past me toward the ceiling (she never could look you straight in the eyes, perhaps out of contempt). "Let's see just how damn smart you really are," she said.

Clyde Smith had never hung work over my head as a prerequisite for food and shelter, but Emily did, and now Mamie was making the same demand. But I knew these chores would make me feel less like a charity case. All the same, I had traded freedom at the Smiths for jailbird status at Mamie and Henry's house. Now it was even more paradoxical how a sweet, loving creature like my mother, Mattie C., could have been a product of the same household as Mamie and Emily.

The house in Collegeville placed me back in the circle of blood relations again. But with this new status I never feared that I would run into my father or Aunt Emily. Rosedale was at least seven or eight miles to the south and over Red Mountain, a distance not traveled on a whim in those days. More important, there was never much interaction between my father or Emily and the Pickenses. Emily and Mamie, however, communicated weekly through the medium of penny postcards that bore salutations and brief messages, since neither owned a telephone.

I began Hudson Elementary on Huntsville Road that year in the eighth grade. Mamie outfitted me with four pairs of shirts and pants and some long johns. My hygiene still wasn't the best, and I endured Hudson classmates' taunts about yellow teeth and nappy hair and long johns that showed underneath my clothes in the warm Alabama autumn. Principal T. J. Settles sent for me after he noticed discrepancies in my records retrieved from Irondale Elementary. Vague responses exasperated him enough that he eased up from his inquisition, complimented me on my grades, and dismissed me. I had artfully dodged any mention of the white family I stayed with for more than three years, knowing that revelation would open a snake pit of questions.

At home kid stuff was as foreign to me as the Himalayan mountain range. No skates, toys, and bicycles. Once when I did stop to play on the way home from school, Mamie interrupted the activity with a hickory stick. A wooden fence was constructed around the house, and of course I was forbidden to cross it unless it was for school or a prescribed event, like going to the store. I would sit on the porch and watch the children play ball in the vacant lot across the street. Any stray ball that bounced onto the property might as well have been outside the Milky Way galaxy; Mamie would not give it back to them, and she wouldn't let me do so either. A virtual graveyard of kids' balls was situated under the house. Mamie earned a well-deserved reputation of cantankerousness in the eyes of neighborhood youngsters.

———————

HOG KILLING WAS IN THE FALL OF THE YEAR, and I arrived in Collegeville just in time for the excitement. While most of the swine were fed slop, the three-hundred-pound hogs destined for death received care suitable for royalty. An elevated platform called the fattening floor was constructed so that the animals did not have to wallow in the mud. They were fed only the best corn and other food products since it was believed that the creatures represented whatever they had been consuming. This practice supposedly ensured that the hogs' meat was of the best quality. It was my job to cool the animals down with buckets of water as part of the pampering ritual.

To Mamie and Henry, hog killing was serious business. They would talk about oddities like how full the moon was and even check the almanac about weather temperature. When the animals were in prime condition for slaughtering, Henry sharpened

his knives and monitored the swine with an unabashedly lasciv-
ious eye. "You sure are getting fat," he would say to the animals.

The ritual consisted of digging a slanted hole or trough in
the ground and then covering it with two pieces of lumber.
Henry jumped up and down on the boards to test their re-
silience. He had also constructed a pulley using a block and
tackle. Two barrels were also nearby.

Mamie felt that my years with the white family had robbed
me of survival skills, and my ignorance about hog butchering apparently confirmed her suspicions. Although I had helped Emily
wring chickens' necks and gut them, this was new to me.

Reading was my forte, and I had learned carpentry skills
with the Smiths, but my aunt still was not impressed. To her, I
was really living in slavery with the Smith family despite the
warm and special place I felt I held in their lives. "Clyde Smith
didn't teach you a damn thing," Mamie said. "Those white folks
have ruined you."

One morning we went out into the yard for the big event. I
had put on the uniform that I wore every day after school and
on weekends—overalls and brogan shoes. Mamie and Henry
wore denim overalls and knee-high rubber boots.

All of the pigs had been fed the previous evening except for
the hog anointed for butchering. This simple omission was a
central key to its fate.

Henry removed the boards covering the trough and tossed in
portions of corn. Mamie handed me an ax. It would be my job
to strike the hog in the head and stun him as he consumed his
last meal, like a prisoner on Alabama's death row. Henry, standing to the side with glistening knives, would take over after that.

Their instructions made my head spin, and I froze in panic
as tears streamed down my face. All I could see was Slim Stewart chasing my mother down the hall in our Rosedale home and

hitting her in the chest with the dull side of an ax. This slaughter now seemed to have been craftily designed not only as an act of cruelty for the swine but for me too.

"Boy," said Henry, laughing, "you're crying like a little ol' girl."

"You ain't worth a damn. . . . What's wrong with you?" said Mamie, as I continue to weep and tremble. My aunt jerked the ax from my hand and glared at me disgustingly as she swung the weapon in a manner that would have made Paul Bunyan proud. The dumb beast fell to its knees, and Henry held up his end of the execution scenario by plunging a knife into its heart. As blood spewed from the wound, I visualized the blood on my mother's ankle that appeared after my father knocked her out of the window and she was caught in the embrace of the pecan tree in Rosedale.

I continued to cry as we wrestled one end of the hog into a barrel of hot water; after a few minutes we pulled the animal out of the container and maneuvered the other end into the barrel. Next we draped it over a sawhorse and scraped hair off its body with knives. After that it was hoisted up into the air with a block and tackle.

"Okay, let's start the operation," said Henry. The L&N railroad laborer apparently missed his calling as a surgeon or, even better, a New York butcher. He deftly began carving up the animal. An incision down the center of its chest allowed access to the intestines that would be used as chitterlings or "chitlins." A virtual smorgasbord of delights would now be available for consumption such as liver, ham hocks, pig ears, pig feet, pig tail, and so on, ad nauseam. But while the swine would provide our sustenance, I still considered the animal's demise as the "murder in Collegeville."

HENRY STARTED TAKING ME TO GAINES CHAPEL A.M.E. in East Birmingham. Church was a culture shock, and all I had was regular everyday clothes and no suit. Or I might visit Gaines or Bethel Baptist or Douglasville C.M.E. and listen to the preaching and singing. On Mother's Day at Bethel everyone wore corsages; a white flower meant your mother was dead, and red stood for life. Memories of my own mother's death came streaming forth into my consciousness like water through an unplugged dike.

Reverend T. M. Lasser's Sunday school class at Bethel was also a joy, and I usually would stay at church all day as a refreshing change of pace from home—that is, until Mamie got wise to my secondary motives and restricted me to worship-service-only attendance.

Depression coiled around me like a boa constrictor. So much of my schoolwork was information I had already absorbed at Irondale Elementary. I wanted to study more than I did, but lights were flicked off at eight since Mamie didn't fancy education despite the pride she ostensibly felt having me under her roof as egghead-in-residence. Neither Henry nor Mamie put much stock in conversation. And there was no radio. It was a quiet house that rivaled the most solemn library. Mamie accused me of stealing any book seen in the house other than my textbooks. Magazines and newspapers were scorned too.

"What's a colored boy gonna do with an education?" they often said in moments of candor.

ABOUT TWO MONTHS AFTER ARRIVING AT MAMIE'S, I was allowed to visit Papa Clyde and used the opportunity to see if he could arrange for me to come back, but he refused. "I don't want the pressure," he said apologetically.

School, with its books and low-key competitiveness, was a delicious diversion from home life, despite the occasional taunts; it was a game, and I played it with considerable dexterity. At home I cried in the stench of the outhouse over my depressing life. After dinner each night I would leap into a sequence of chores. I tried to immerse myself in the work as a pressure valve for my pent-up frustration and anger at my treatment in the house and to suppress an inescapable residual sadness that had walked with me since my mother's murder.

I reasoned that if I could pull my own weight through benefit of a job, Mamie would stop riding me so hard and give me more freedom. The opportunity to put this theory to the test popped up when I went with my aunt and uncle to buy groceries at Yeilding's on Second Avenue North, one of Birmingham's first department stores.

Milton Yeilding asked me how I was doing in school. Before I could sputter an intelligent response to the old man's question, Mamie piped up. "He's doing fine. We make sure he's doing well," she gloated.

These two relatives were a case study in paradox. On the one hand, they basked in the light of my studiousness and intelligence, and on the other, behind closed doors, they downgraded education as a one-way ticket to nowhere for Negroes.

A cashier stroking the keys on a bulky register began to fall behind, and customers formed a conga line down the aisle. I leaped forward and began bagging groceries and, in the process, caught Mr. Yeilding's attention. He coached me on the craft of loading eggs and bread into the bags. "You make a good sacker," he said. "Henry," he told my uncle, "I might want to hire this boy."

Since this was a white man, Mamie and Henry would have to agree to the situation. The next day after school I caught the streetcar downtown and worked from about 4:15 until about 6 P.M. I drew a ten-dollar paycheck at the end of the week, which Mamie quickly confiscated. Despite the contribution to the household money pot, my Cinderella-like workload did not diminish at home, and true personal freedom remained elusive.

———————

SEGREGATION WAS A MENACE and an evil that had to be tasted on a daily basis. It was always a part of the landscape, just like the residue of defiance toward the North that many Southerners still harbored as they held to the unfathomable motto "The South will rise again." My first real confrontation with the omnipresent, stifling Jim Crow schematic occurred after I started working at Yeilding's and climbed aboard the Number 22 Boyles/Tarrant City streetcar on my way from Collegeville to downtown. After I entered the vehicle, I noticed that the Negroes were packed like sardines in the aisle toward the rear, while two or three whites sat in the front of the streetcar. Not one of the blacks attempted to sit down, although there were a bunch of empty seats all around. A board was situated about four rows from the rear of the vehicle separating the so-called black seats from the white seats. The drivers usually would place the device toward the rear so whites entering the vehicle could have first choice at the seats.

No one dared touch the board since it was against the law for anyone other than the driver to move it. Often a black man would rise and let a Negro woman have his seat in the crowded rear section of the streetcar.

After a few minutes of riding, I decided to make a plea to the driver to move the board toward the front so the Negroes could occupy some of the empty seats on the dozen or so rows the whites were not occupying. For some reason, I took the initiative that the adults had not taken. Perhaps I viewed the segregation as another form of abuse reminiscent of what I had experienced with my father, stepmother, and Aunt Emily. My relatives' harmful acts were directed toward individuals, me and my brothers. The social custom of mandated separation of the races had Negroes in general as a collective target, but the practice was damaging, emotionally and mentally more than physically.

"Sir," I said. "Would you please move the board up?"

The request was met with the driver's silence, although I knew I had spoken loudly and clearly enough for him to have heard me. A second appeal was again answered with stony quietude as the driver continued to look forward, although he could review the whole compartment from the rearview mirror in front of him. At that point I grabbed the board and moved it toward the front of the streetcar and sat down behind it. The driver saw my action and was livid with anger.

"Boy," he said, "move that board back where it was and get up out of that seat."

"No," I replied in a firm, clear voice.

"Did you hear what I said?" he said.

An uncomfortable tension started to build that radiated among the blacks, the couple of whites, and the angry driver. The women appeared apprehensive as I am sure they were wondering what made me challenge the system and destroy what would have been a mundane ride to replace it with a sense of peril. The second hand of time seemed to slow-dance with anxiety in the moment of shared drama. Soon the driver would stop the streetcar and call the police, I thought. Of course, violence was never far from the surface when blacks dealt with a power structure that had traditionally treated them as second-class cit-izens in every facet of daily life. There was always a possibility that the driver would stop the vehicle, assault me, and physically eject me from the seat. All of a sudden, a couple of black men extricated themselves from the crowd in the rear of the streetcar and sat down, which was tantamount to the cavalry riding to my rescue.

"Y'all, come on up and sit down," a man said. "Ladies, sit down."

One by one others took seats too, figuring, perhaps, that our collective boldness would rule the day. The driver, apparently dumfounded, glared at us through the mirror without trying to gain the upper hand in this confrontation that pitted the tradi-tionally subservient against the old, established order. Perhaps he thought we were crazy, but he did not push the issue any further. Of course, his hesitation may have been inspired by a Negro man I saw unfolding a pocketknife as he took a seat. The driver may have seen this also, but, for whatever the reason, the black folks won out on that particular streetcar ride.

———————

THE ONLY BLACK FOUR-YEAR HIGH SCHOOL in the city of Birm-ingham was A. H. Parker Industrial in the Smithfield section. Although some went to Samuel Ullman High on the city's south side for the first two years, Parker was the only city institution that allowed for an uninterrupted tenure. With hundreds of stu-dents enrolled, it was ranked by some as the largest such school in the country.

As the fall of '48 approached, I asked store owner Milton Yeilding to help me get a birth certificate for enrollment. He took me to the vital statistics office, and I regurgitated all the facts about my birth and family to the clerk, who took down the information like a stenographer. She sauntered away with the information but came back a few minutes later, confused. "Your name is Shelley, not Shurley," she said. "And your birthday is September 24th and not September 4th."

It was as if I was an amnesiac who was told his true identity for the first time. Things I thought were absolutes had been refuted in an instant in the stacks of musty, dingy official records of the state. But the name Shurley clung like a leech even after I made the revelation to Aunt Mamie and Uncle Henry.

While most children dreaded school, to me it was a grand adventure, another stepping-stone on the way to a career in law. I don't know why I had set my sights on the legal arena, but nothing else ranked in the same ballpark, not a job as an airline pilot or a teacher or a preacher. Law. A law career was the apex of professional, white-collar life, in my view. Perhaps, in an odd way, I thought it would allow me to pursue the justice that had escaped when my father's blow with the ax ended my mother's life and yet he continued to walk around Rosedale as unfettered as the wind. Burying my nose in books, I thought, would be a surefire ticket to a college scholarship and ultimately legal wheeling and dealing as a lawyer.

The first day of high school saw me hungry with anticipation. Even though I had saved money from working at Yeilding's, Mamie told me to walk the eight miles to the Parker High annex rather than ride the bus. I woke up at 3 A.M. to do chores and left for school by 6 with a path plotted through the Evergreen Bottoms and Acipco neighborhoods. The sturdy bed of the Louisville & Nashville railroad tracks would be used as a trail a third of the way. I was the pied piper of Collegeville. Children who had money to ride the bus decided to walk with me instead. Perhaps they traded transportation for the long stroll in order to save the seven cents fare, or they viewed the journey as an unexpected social event. But an entourage of two or three grew to about twenty or thirty by the time we got to Parker, ahead of the 9 A.M. bell.

Teasing and taunts awaited me at Parker just like at Irondale Elementary and Hudson over my hygiene, hair, and teeth. I did figure out a way to avoid wisecracks about the long johns by changing out of these at school and putting them in a locker.

Daggers ripped my heart if I got a B in any of my classes. So I found a way to get around the lights-out mandate that threatened my ambitious career plans. The route to school took me past Dolores Shines's house, and some afternoons I would stop and study a few minutes with her (and make a feeble attempt at romance). Another tactic was to study in the stockroom at Yeilding's on lunch breaks.

Gradually my popularity grew, but most girls considered me nerdish. However, the principal's daughter, Alma Vivian Johnson, now wife of Secretary of State Colin Powell, took a liking to me, perhaps because she was charmed by the image of a young man studying during lunch and recess. We pored over our books together quite often at recess, and soon a girlfriend of hers, Yvonne Echols, joined us. I had gained the attention of two of the prettiest girls in school, and everybody thought Alma and I were dating based on the fib to that effect I had spread among my classmates. Principal Johnson found out about our friendship, summoned me into his office, and warned me to keep my distance. But Alma, to her credit, brushed her father's objections aside and cemented our friendship with her kindness.

Students rapping about tough times seemed like silly crybabies to me. I knew my personal hardships would dwarf any dumb-ass anguish they claimed to endure. I still cried myself through every day like I had done since my mother's death. Loneliness was a faithful companion. I wept for my brothers and from sorrow too weighty for a teenager to bear. But bear it I did and dreamed of a providential life yet unborn.

A philosophy crystallized and took form. I would be different from every cruel and ugly thing people had revealed themselves to be. The objective for me was to be sober, not drunk, peaceful rather than violent, wealthy over poor, and educated as opposed to ignorant.

Something beyond a life reeking of horse manure had to be in store for me. I kept up my studies and made myself into the best, most colorful grocery sacker at Yeilding's. Tips started to come my way. I learned that if you worked hard and were kind, assertive, and helpful, monetary rewards materialized. Mr. Milton started bragging about me like Papa Clyde had done.

IN THE SUMMER BEFORE TENTH GRADE I again persuaded Aunt Mamie to let me ride the bus for a visit with Papa Clyde.

"My boy has come back," he cried when I got to the rock house in Irondale. "Have you run away, Shurley?" Clyde wept after I told him about life at Mamie's, and he collected his brothers and friends over to the house to see me.

"You had better be getting back to that prison," he said after a couple of hours. He drove me home to Collegeville so we could spend a little more time together and bid me adieu with a gift of a hundred dollars in small bills that Mamie wouldn't notice and impound.

WHILE I HAD ABSORBED MUCH BOOK SENSE, as Papa Clyde had suggested, I also made a point to be aware of the everyday world in which I was situated. There were happenings beyond the mundane and predictable occurrences of Parker High School and life with Mamie and Henry in the blue-collar world of Collegeville.

On Seventeenth Street in the Negro business district was a focal point of extracurricular learning called Ratkiller's Shoeshine Parlor. Ratkiller was a man named Charlie Barnett. You could sit in the business and soak up all sorts of street knowledge that would not be found within the pages of the secondhand textbooks the Alabama Board of Education issued to the Negro schools.

Pimps and prostitutes made Ratkiller's a regular stop in their corridor of activity. You would hear discussions of "copping" a woman, which was essentially purchasing her services as a prostitute. Women were the sport, so to speak. Some of them had been my classmates at Parker who had taken unfortunate detours off the road to more legitimate vocations. They had been indoctrinated about the art of prostitution and the importance of loyalty to their own sponsoring pimp. The pimps often used a "lead whore" to lure some recruits into the realm of prostitution. These women would convince attractive girls of the lucrativeness of the trade. The goal was to turn as many as ten tricks a day and rake in as much as five hundred dollars from the customers. When the pimps noticed me observing them, they would encourage me. "Hey, youngblood, listen up," they would say. "You might make a good pimp some day."

Within the confines of the shoeshine parlor I learned about card trick scams and how to pad dice so they would turn up the lucky seven on demand. I even learned about till tapping and how to open a cash drawer without the bell sounding. Drugs were floating around with names like Black Beauties and Red Pearls. I could see that I was at a juncture, pulled between two roads. One road headed toward law school, while another led toward hustling, taking advantage of weaknesses in the mental abilities and moral judgments of others.

Besides the moral void of the latter lifestyle, there was also a rather substantial risk factor. I had read about Al Capone and the gangsterism fueled by prohibition in Chicago. Capone had been imprisoned on a tax evasion charge, and his henchmen had been killed or hauled off to the penitentiary as a reward for their attempts to subvert the system. Even the conversations of the men in the parlor gave me reason to doubt the wisdom of their ventures. Many of them were older hustlers who had been in the business from ten to thirty years. Most of these guys were the recipients of fortunes washed away through bad luck, faulty thinking, or the greed that comes from taking one chance too many. For certain, I was not interested in the drugs that were prominent in underworld lifestyles. I had read about the consequences of using them, and I often saw the human wreckage from the havoc they reaped. The price of walking on the shadowy side of the law seemed hardly worth the ill-gotten gains in my opinion.

The Mask of Radio

In my sophomore year at Parker I chose to ignore the sordid appeal of the world as represented by the Ratkiller's Shoeshine Parlor crowd and poured energy into extracurricular activities as tools of distraction. An upcoming variety show was a huge event and a chance to be in the spotlight. I billed myself as a comedian despite a life barren of much laughter. Mr. Milton allowed me to go into work late at Yeilding's Grocery so I could participate in rehearsals. My performance in the variety show was well received by the audience, and this success inspired me to want to sculpt my diction and voice so they would be pleasant to the ear and command attention.

Word filtered through the community that a new black-oriented radio station, WBCO, owned by white businessman Jess Lanier, was trying to find its legs in Bessemer, a hard-boiled blue-collar suburb southwest of Birmingham. I was determined to get on the show. This would be another opportunity for me to suppress the angst that I felt every day over my early childhood.

The WBCO station manager said he was impressed with my audition but stated that I needed a sponsor. Schiff's Family Shoe Store was opening up on Third Avenue North in Birmingham. I told Mr. Langford, the store manager, that for a twenty-dollar weekly sponsor's fee I could get on the radio and trumpet the store's name to sell shoes. He agreed and threw in a job as a stock boy to seal the deal.

The radio personality I presented was an amalgamation of theatrics, sack-boy dazzle, talent show comedy, and even preaching. I was a gifted ad-libber who never followed a script for commercials. The formula was simple: Spin discs, toss out banter for the anonymous radio audience, and sell Schiff's shoes.

"I was talking to the garbage man the other day," I would say on the air. "He said he hates to pick up some folks' garbage cans cause they are so heavy they will break his back. But, hey, the big shots on the hill . . . he said he can pick up their garbage cans with one finger because there's nothing in them."

The message was a backhanded swipe at the black middle-class folks who lived in a neighborhood just northwest of downtown Birmingham. The neighborhood was to gain the nickname of Dynamite Hill since it suffered so many unsolved racial bombings in the '50s and '60s. In addition to symbolizing the superficial materialism that was a symptom of the so-called upper classes, the empty garbage cans suggested that many of these people may have been hanging onto their nice homes by the skin of their teeth, perhaps forgoing meals to meet the mortgage payments. This became the model for my broadcast persona—blunt talk combined with favoritism toward the masses rather than the classes or elite.

Every broadcast consisted of my messages or commentaries interlaced with tunes from such recording artists as Charles Brown, Luverne Baker, Faye Adams, Ruth Brown, Louie Jordan, Johnny Otis, Little Esther, Howling Wolf, and Muddy Waters. The rhythm and blues records ran for about two minutes and twenty seconds. Usually I could get about three records into a fifteen-minute broadcast. The shows eventually evolved into thirty-minute excursions. Sandwiched between music and chat were the pitches for Schiff's shoe store.

Radio was simultaneously exhilarating and liberating. It was a chance to sublimate the inwardly melancholic Shelley that walked around Parker High every day. Spinning records and chatting permitted me to suppress my troubles just as I had when I preached before imaginary audiences in Papa Clyde's basement. Adults and teenagers began to recognize me from the performances and often complimented me on the shows. But recognition took a backseat to the sense of connecting to people and being valued that I secretly craved. I was providing listeners with a sense of enjoyment, and as a collateral benefit, the airwaves presented an opportunity for a guy with low self-esteem to thumb his nose at all the taunters at school. None of them could come close to accomplishing what I did on the radio.

Aunt Mamie and Uncle Henry predictably assumed I had fallen in league with the devil. Henry was going to rescue me with a job at the L&N railroad.

"You're going to hell," Mamie warned. "You need a real job."

To complement my learning experience, I also went to WEDR on Fourth Avenue North between Fourteenth and Fifteenth Streets above the Forniss Printing Company. The owner, E. D. Reynolds, and manager, John Thompson, occasionally allowed me to spin records and gab without pay. Mamie and Henry were less talkative for several days, but they gradually realized that I would not disassociate myself from the world of radio.

———————

THE FALL OF 1950 brought the annual hog-slaughtering ritual around again. This event promised to be no less traumatic than the previous seasons that saw Mamie and Henry trying to persuade me to bash a creature on the head with an ax. Of course, every time, I would end up cringing and whimpering as I thought about Mattie C.'s fate. Two hogs that I had named Slim I and Slim II were to be killed that season. I had spent the year projecting the animosity that I felt for my father onto the animals and had grown to dislike them intensely. This attitude would make their death sentences easier to carry out, I reasoned.

Uncle Henry slammed Slim I in the head with an ax after it wandered over to eat food placed in the trough; he then dispatched the swine with a knife thrust into its heart. Since I had become a marksman with the BB guns at Stringfellow Stables, I asked Mamie and Henry if I could use their .22 caliber rifle to do what I never could with an ax in order to dispatch Slim II into hog heaven.

"Do what, boy?" said Mamie.

"Use your rifle," I said.

"Why, nobody has ever done nothing like that before," said Mamie, as if I would be breaking some sacred rule that would cause all of her ancestors from Georgia to West Africa to roll over in their serene graves.

"Hey, let the boy be a failure," said Henry. "I'll finish the hog off."

Henry retrieved his rifle from the house, and Mamie scurried behind the outhouse, ordering me to hold my fire until she was safely out of harm's way. My uncle then poured the food into the trough, and Slim II ambled over to partake in the feast. As I took aim at the hog, I could see the face of Slim Stewart superimposed over the animal in my mind's eye. Standing a few feet away from Slim II, I shot the swine between the eyes, killing it instantly.

A DESIRE TO BECOME INVOLVED IN DRAMA was implanted in my mind perhaps in the days when I stood before the mirror in Papa Clyde's basement and pretended to deliver sermons. Although I never considered acting or preaching as true callings in life, drama was a way to immerse myself in an activity and erase an inner loneliness. But pursuit of dramatic training at Parker was not as easy for me as joining the choir or participating in the talent shows. Back in the '40s and '50s, before the racial pride movement had gained a foothold in communities, Negroes were regrettably more concerned about the pigmentation of their fellow black Americans. This preoccupation with colorism was an expression of the pecking order passed down from slavery days, when light-skinned blacks were allowed to work in the Big House and darker-hued folks sweated out in the cotton fields. At Parker Industrial, as was most likely the case at many other Negro schools, there was an unofficial code regarding color. Light-skinned blacks sometimes referred to those with darker skin tones as "smokies." The dark kids were often unofficially restricted to activities such as the choir and sports such as football and basketball. Dark girls were often passed over in the process of choosing majorettes. Also, they were encouraged to pursue trades such as sewing rather than courses that were preparatory for professions such as teaching, law, or medicine.

Students who knew that I planned to join the Parker Playmakers, the school drama club, warned me that I would run into a stone wall. Sure enough, I discovered that for dramatic arts teacher Bobby Jones, a light-skinned black man, it was apparently still Alabama in the 1850s instead of the 1950s. Without explicitly stating that I was too dark for the club's production of *Seventh Heaven,* Jones said that he needed a responsible prop person for the troupe and that there was no place for me in the club as a thespian. Perhaps he thought that darker Negroes would taint the portrayal of a true heaven, but I was determined to crash those pearly gates despite Jones's opposition.

I was astounded that a race that wrestled with second-class schools and other symptoms of discrimination would be making such distinctions within its own ranks. But I always felt that if I was correct on a position, I would stand firm on the matter. Besides, a phrase came to me that Clyde's stepdaughter, Mary Sue, had used: human rights. She sometimes would complain that she felt she was deprived of her own rights because many public buildings did not accommodate people with handicaps such as the polio with which she was afflicted.

A dark-skinned teacher named Mr. Emmett, whom I respected, asked me what I was going to do, and I informed him that Mr. Jones was going to give me an audition before the dust settled around the issue. I took my case to Principal Johnson and subsequently Carol W. Hayes, superintendent of Negro schools, whose office was located in the Parker Annex Building. Since both men coached me to abandon my campaign, I ignored their discouraging words and continued up the chain of command to lodge a protest with L. Frazier Banks, superintendent of the entire school system. As I ambled down the hall in the board of education building, I encountered Banks and told him about my predicament. Banks listened patiently to my plea for human rights and then recorded my name and my teacher's name.

Principal Johnson was upset that I had gone over his head, but apparently he yielded to the pressure from Superintendent Banks and from his daughter Alma, who was a member of the drama club. Jones ignored me when I returned to the club and asked for a part in the play again. A few days later, I went back and discovered that *Seventh Heaven* had been switched for another production, *You Can't Take It with You.* I was saddled with the stereotypical dark-skinned role of a janitor and walked on and off the set, never malingering.

EVERYTHING BEGAN TO PILE UP ON ME. By eleventh grade I was working alternate afternoons at Yeilding's, Schiff's, and WBCO in Bessemer and then still had to do chores at home—slopping the hogs, feeding the chickens, and cleaning the house. There was an emotional conflict in my soul, a tug-of-war, as the outgoing personality I had created pulled against the real Shelley, thoughtful, introspective, and brooding.

One night in the late spring of 1951 I had decided to use the outhouse rather than the slop jar to relieve myself. The privy was in the backyard about fifty feet from the main house. I entered with a secondary purpose, which was to meditate on the course my life was taking. Suddenly, a voice ruptured the midnight silence.

"Shelley," the voice said. I looked toward the back of the house thinking it was Aunt Mamie but saw no one.

"Son," the voice came again. The door of the outhouse was ajar, and through the slit my gaze settled on a form several yards away near an empty lot adjacent to Mamie and Henry's property. A streetlight hung above the spot on Thirty-fourth Street and shone with purpose.

I couldn't fathom what I was perceiving in the dark embrace of the nighttime scenery. After blinking and rubbing my eyes, the form began taking on a familiar essence. There she stood like a sentry in an old gray coat, small furry hat, and familiar glasses.

"Don't be afraid of me," said Mattie C., my mother.

I had seen my father kill her more than a decade earlier. I saw her lying dead in a casket at the funeral, and now she was back talking to me in the middle of an Alabama night. My bowels locked up on me as she pressed on with her monologue.

"Don't be afraid, Shelley. I've been with you all along. You're special to me, and you've followed my directions. I'll come to you from time to time. You are my chosen son, and I'll give you directions. Obey me. Yes, things have been hard for you. I put you and Jerome together. That's my proof. Listen to me and follow my directions and don't fear. I see that you are upset, but I'll come back. Find my boys; I'll show you where they are. Know that I am with you and in you."

Mother vanished as quickly as she had materialized, and I broke the hinges off the door as I galloped toward the house screaming.

"I can't believe it! I can't believe it," I shouted, waking Aunt Mamie and Uncle Henry.

"What's wrong with you, boy?" Uncle Henry grumpily asked.

"I just saw Mama outside while I was in the outhouse," I explained breathlessly. Needless to say, I wasn't believed, and my outburst was laid at the feet of an overactive imagination. But I knew that I had somehow experienced a projection from an unseen dimension of the spiritual kingdom that briefly intersected with the finite, material world in Collegeville. Sleep eluded me that night as I pondered the ramifications of the encounter.

My mother's order was to find my brothers. Certainly, I had lost track of Bubba again, but I had always felt Sam and David were still in Rosedale with Slim and Marie. The vision became even more enigmatic. Were they still in the little village on the south side of Red Mountain? It was at least seven miles from Collegeville, but a fear of some manner of confrontation with Slim and my stepmother, Marie, was the chief reason I had not attempted to return to the neighborhood to visit my younger siblings. The vision had given me much to ponder.

The shelter at Aunt Mamie's and even at Papa Clyde's rock house in Irondale could not fill the emptiness I felt in my spirit as a consequence of earlier abuse and witnessing my mother's killing. Chores, school, and work at Yeilding's, Schiff's, WBCO, and, informally, WEDR presented me with a nonstop lifestyle, but my long-range plans were still motivated by high-minded aspirations. I had disregarded the appeal of the lifestyles at Ratkiller's Shoeshine Parlor and Uncle Henry's suggestion that I become a mechanic and forget law school. I steadfastly looked to black trailblazers like singer Marian Anderson, athlete Jesse Owens, and scientist George Washington Carver for inspiration in my life. One day, I presumed, people would say the name of Shelley Stewart and preface it with the adjective *great*. After all, I knew that I could speak better than President Harry Truman, whom I had heard on the radio. An eloquent speaking voice would serve me well in the career of law, and I would chase those dreams until I caught up with them and converted them into a tangible reality.

GANGS HAVE ALWAYS THROWN their weight around. In the 1950s the Gilley thugs were bad boys shrouded in menace with a brand of violence that included bullying, harassment, and beatings. Jealousy over a female's attentions, or an unintentional bump in a crowd, were deemed justifications for assault. Their brand of justice was to be avoided at all costs. Luck ran out for me in my ability to tiptoe out of the way of the hoodlums when I climbed down off the school bus "special" one morning during my senior year at Parker in the fall of 1951.

"It's your time to pay now," one of the punks growled in my direction. "It's time for you to pay your back dues. I'm gonna kick your ass, but I'll let you go this time."

This fellow was one hooligan who took pride in keeping a promise. The Gilleys meant business, and all the students were acutely aware of that fact. Some children even stole money from their parents so that they would have enough cash with which to respond to an extortion demand.

The school session darted past that day as I consumed myself with the crisis that had ensnared me. The spectacle of having my ass kicked troubled me during work at Yeilding's that afternoon. Aunt Emily and my father had pummeled me enough for two lifetimes, and now, here was a ruffian itching to use my head as a football. I had drawn a line in the dust and vowed never again to passively accept getting knocked around like a rag doll.

Mamie and Henry kept a .32 caliber automatic pistol under their bedroom mattress, and I knew that a 12 gauge shotgun was on hand for deer hunting. On the dreaded morning, I hid the pistol in my book satchel and headed out the door to school.

As I walked toward the bus stop, I inserted a clip in the gun and shoved the weapon into the back of my pants and let my coat further conceal the firearm. The idea of an Old West shootout raced through my head as our rickety yellow school bus sped toward Parker Industrial School. As we approached the building, I could see four members of the Gilley gang planted on the Eighth Avenue bus stop. At least a couple of dozen children were my traveling companions, but I ventured that the ad hoc welcoming committee was prepared to roll out the red carpet for me specifically.

"Got our money?" the punk asked in his encore performance for me as I disembarked from the bus.

"I've got five dollars," I said, as they followed me to the side of a little store near the school.

"Nigger, you had better have brought it. We were gonna whip your ass," a boy said.

"No, I don't believe you are going to whip my ass," I replied boldly.

"Get his ass," growled one of them.

I yanked the pistol out of my pants waistband from under my coat and started firing toward the boys' feet. Three shots were squeezed off in rapid succession. More bullets weren't expended for fear that I would actually hit one of the guys or an innocent bystander.

"This nigger's crazy," they bellowed, scattering like a frightened flock of sparrows. In the commotion I ran around a corner and tossed the gun under a house.

Authorities inquired about the incident, but no one broke the code of silence and fingered me, the gunslinger. Apparently I was a hero to many of the students since I had stood up to the Gilley menace in big-time fashion. Accolades poured in throughout the day. The praise came during classes and after the bell rang when students changed classes. After school I recovered the gun from underneath the neighborhood house and headed home, plotting how to replace the spent cartridges and return the gun to its resting place underneath the mattress before it was missed.

The gratification that had enveloped me that day as school hero would not last till sundown. Standing up to the Gilley gang had set in motion an unimaginable series of events.

Aunt Mamie and Uncle Henry met me at the door when I returned home. Mamie had discovered the pistol missing and directed me to the back porch. Attempts to explain were brushed off like dandruff chased from a groom's black tuxedo. She seemed to relish taking the smart boy down a peg or two.

"You're just like your damn daddy, no good," she said. "You're not going to live to see twenty-one." Each word lanced my heart like a porcupine quill. "You're just a liar and probably cheating in school. Take those damn clothes off," Mamie stormed on. She ordered Uncle Henry to hold the shotgun on me while she aimed the pistol. Henry reluctantly complied as my aunt grabbed an ironing cord and broke a broom handle across her masculine knee.

"I'm going to whip his brains out," she said.

Aunt Emily and Slim Stewart's actions gravitated into my mind along with my sacred vow not to let a painful history repeat itself.

"I'm not going to take a whipping, Aunt Mamie," I said calmly. My refusal to allow my temper to become unleashed only made her eyes bug out more and chased her own rage up to another barometric level.

"You gonna fight me?" she shrieked.

"I'm not going to take a whipping," I repeated.

"You get the hell out of here," she said. "You'll never get a chance to get back in this damn house again."

I nodded in affirmation that I was leaving, although Uncle Henry coached me to accept the beating and stay. Aunt Mamie checked my belongings and confiscated a few items. The world outside the humble North Birmingham abode was not hospitable, but it was no more intimidating than it was when I walked away from Aunt Emily's home in Rosedale at age six and a half. I strode out the door onto Thirty-third Street sapped of emotional energy, but the old faithful inner voice rose to the occasion again like a seasoned guide for the all-black Buffalo Soldiers of the nineteenth-century American West.

Rosedale lay on the other side of Red Mountain, and the Number 39 Edgewood streetcar would be my chariot to that next destination in the drama of life.

CHAPTER FOUR

Rosedale on the Rebound

TOIL. SWEAT. ROW HOUSES. Rosedale never seemed to change. The village on the crest of Red Mountain, of course, still lay under the watchful gaze of the statue of Vulcan the iron man, a mythical figure that acquired a role as guardian of Jones and Shades valleys. The geological floor of Jones Valley, site of Birmingham, was 660 million years old. In more "recent" years the uncharted wilderness was a no-man's-land on which tribes of Indians did not hunt the plentiful bear, rabbits, and deer; it was sacred ground.

The mountain presented itself to industrial men as a rich source of red hematite iron ore, which blanketed beds of shaley, impure limestone. But the ore was the treasure. It became a staple of the local blast furnaces that had saddled Birmingham proper with its nickname, the Pittsburgh of the South. During the 1880s and 1890s, iron makers discovered that Red Mountain ore made excellent foundry iron when it was "sweetened" with brown ore. Also, a special process could produce a valuable steel product.

In the shadow of the iron man and in the shadiness of Shades Valley, the maids and yardmen, general handymen and laborers who inhabited Rosedale sauntered to and from their

jobs drenched in humility like worker ants patrolling a munici-
pal mound. The town seemed seduced by a nonchalant and
trusting frame of mind that served the prosaic lifestyle well. This
was, after all, the South, where life moved at its own pace in a
way that emphasized parochialism. The modest people and
buildings seemed sheltered from the industrial progress characterizing Birmingham, which churned out iron and steel under
the auspices of Stockham, U.S. Pipe, and the Tennessee Coal
and Iron Company.

The streetcar that spirited me away from the blue-collar
neighborhood of Collegeville deposited me into the community
that I had walked away from a decade earlier in an escape from
Aunt Emily's cruelty and abuse. Now her tiny brown shotgun
home at 2611 Eighteenth Place sat like all the other row houses
that had been cranked out with an almost insane precision. They
were called "shotgun" because, if a person were so inclined, he
could shoot a gun through the front door and the pellets would
travel through the abode and straight out the back door.

They say time heals all wounds, but my emotional injuries at
Emily's hands had not yet been mended by total forgiveness and
forgetfulness. The hurt and humiliation were still fresh in my
mind, but the need for sanctuary and a chance to clear my head
outweighed any ambivalent feelings lurking in the crevices of my
heart.

As I approached Emily's house, a bowlegged young man
bounced out of the house next door. "Man, you and Romey
back at the same time," said the boy, whom I recognized as Boot,
a neighbor, about my age. Christened J. B. Wimbush, he lived
with his aunt and uncle. His assertion about Romey, a.k.a.
Jerome, or Bubba, was like an uppercut from Joe Louis. I had
not laid eyes on my older brother since I had visited him at
Stringfellow Stables years earlier.

"He been here about a week. He been in the army," said Boot.

The prospect of seeing Bubba both excited and perplexed me. We had slept on the same filthy, chinch bug–filled mattress on the back porch of the Rosedale home of my father and step-mother, Marie, unknowingly savored the same fried rats, and gone to bed in the Mountain Brook barn inhaling horse muck. Before I could collect my thoughts, Boot yelled what amounted to an introduction.

"Yonder he comes now," he said.

My gaze riveted onto a lanky figure wearing a green military uniform walking across the way near the roadside grill and a vacant lot. As the man got closer, the abstract features gelled into the familiar face of a man with whom I shared a common, tortured heritage.

A warm embrace sealed our chance reunion. Was it just an accident that I would be exiled from Mamie and Henry's home on that day and end up on Emily's porch at the same time as Bubba? Chance was the flip side on the coin of fate.

Bubba announced that he was about to embark for the hot spot of Korea after returning to Fort Riley, Kansas, at the end of his U.S. Army furlough. He revealed that he had been living with various families in Rosedale for the past few years, trying his hand at odd jobs. Recently, he had joined the U.S. Army's 87th Infantry, and during his leave he had divided time between the home of pal Junior Cunningham and Aunt Emily's house. He was at Emily's to retrieve his duffel bag.

The fact that families would open their homes to him was a testament to the fact that Rosedale was like one big connected village where neighbors ranked as kinfolk. People were not afraid to sleep on their porches or even leave their homes unlocked. It was not unheard of for one woman to walk into another woman's home and, upon finding the dwelling empty, go in and turn down a fire on the stove or make some other adjustment at the house and saunter away.

Bubba looked like a nineteen-year-old string bean in the lizard-green uniform. He wore his adult height well, which was at least six feet tall. I informed him that I had once gone back to the stables to look for him only to find Peewee, the other stable boy. As if to wrestle my exuberance into submission, Bubba then stated that he would be returning to Fort Riley the next morning.

As his words settled on the afternoon air, out of the corner of my eye I noticed a stocky, short woman ambling across Eighteenth Place. As she got a few feet from the house, our eyes locked. It was Emily, weathered by the winds of time and consummate spite, returning from her job as a maid in the home of white folks in an over-the-mountain suburb. In seconds, recognition engulfed her too. I was the little boy she had body slammed and hoisted up to the ceiling in her shotgun house reeking with the aroma of chicken shit a decade ago. Now I was over six feet tall, skinny, but nevertheless, not one to be manhandled easily even by this hefty woman.

Emily was as nervous as a cornered possum. Perhaps she thought I would strike out at her like a south Alabama rattlesnake. She measured her distance from me as cautiously as she weighed her words.

"What y'all going to do now?" she said. The question seemed to test the wind for the possibility of violence, but we cheated her of any meaningful answer. Bubba got his duffel bag from the living room, and we walked down to Waterboy's Grill on the east side of U.S. Highway 31, the main thoroughfare that snaked lengthwise across the state and linked Birmingham with

Huntsville to the north and the state capital of Montgomery and counties like Baldwin and Escambia to the south.

The grill wore several aliases. A gin joint, it was also called the Waterboy's, Miller's Inn, or Homewood Grill. Waterboy's did a brisk business despite the presence of private residences called shot houses, where liquor was served illegally, which were scattered throughout the neighborhood. It had been owned by Miller Lee, son of Damon, a business and real-estate owner who was the wealthiest black man in Homewood. Lee had packed up for California, and the business had been bought by a cement laborer with a strong rural accent named Waterboy, a.k.a. Brady. His wife, Lula Mae, was the chef whose specialities were delectable hamburgers and french fries.

No one bothered to check identification. No one cared. Bubba was nineteen and I was seventeen. We plumped down in a couple of chairs, and I sipped my first beer as the aroma of whiskey and cooking grease hung thick in the air. Bubba shoved a pack of Chesterfield cigarettes across the table. This was my first nicotine-laced taste of displeasure. I coughed and wheezed but finally settled down to some easy puffs and adult posturing.

"I heard you on the radio, but I didn't know it was you," said Bubba, referring to my broadcasts on WBCO and WEDR. My name on the radio was Shelley, not Shurley.

Bubba was amazed that I had been ejected out of the cauldron of our early hellish life in relatively good emotional shape. He was proud that I had been going to Parker and nailing down superior grades, and that I had aspirations for the legal arena. He explained that he had received some schooling in Rosedale and had gotten as high as the seventh grade. The Colored Family School Census record of 1945–1946 would show that in that grade his best subjects in the first semester were physical education, library, literature, and spelling, for which he received B averages. His average increased from C to B the next semester in science and social science, but he went down a letter grade in literature and spelling. Apparently my tutoring him at Stringfellow Stables had paid off.

The records also showed that at thirteen years of age he was six feet tall, 132 pounds, and had "a bad eye, uncontrolled blink." This defective eye, I deduced, had to be the result of our father beating him. Odd jobs and boarding with area families had helped him to survive, as did the fact that he was muscular and quick to use his fists and, less frequently, knives.

A neighborhood man, Bob Burton, would later recall that during that period a fellow named Cheeks had blindsided Bubba at a Rosedale shot house one day. A few days later Cheeks was walking along U.S. 31 when he noticed Bubba walking parallel to him on the opposite side of the street and glaring at him. Cheeks walked faster and noticed that Bubba had accelerated his own pace. The guy then broke into a gallop and raced into the Homewood City Jail and locked himself in a cell to shield himself from my brother's wrath.

I also was reminded of an element we had in common, other than heritage—a desire to kill our father, Slim, for what he had done to our mother. During the time at Stringfellow Stables I had taken a .22 caliber rifle out of the stable and made my way back to Rosedale to act as my father's judge, jury, and executioner. I remember staking out Waterboy's Grill, but he never showed up. Bubba lacked the heart to do what his head had suggested that he do, and who knows, maybe I couldn't have killed Slim either. Bubba had seen Slim in Rosedale and asked him about the location of our brothers, Sam and David, but received vague answers and shrugs in response to his questioning.

Bubba promised to send me money from his military pay, and we willed our so-called earthly assets to each other. We made our way out of the gin joint, and Bubba went to spend his last night in Rosedale with Junior Cunningham and his family. I visited a neighborhood boy named Clack Bullard, and his mother, Sister Bullard, allowed me to stay with them until I could plot my next action.

The next morning Bubba awakened me with a rap on the bedroom window of the Bullards' small frame house, and we wished each other well. A brotherly hug through the open window followed, and in an instant he was sucked into a world of dog tags and the Cold War. I stayed at Clack's about two weeks. Sister Bullard did not charge me anything even though she was a maid and the Bullards were not Rockefellers. Sister Bullard recommended that I do the incomprehensible—rent living space in the home of my nemesis, Aunt Emily.

Aunt Emily's face was a mask of coolness poorly camouflaging her apprehension. "What do you want?" she asked, fidgeting on the other side of the screen door. The wood and wire mesh barrier between us was fragile. An enraged man could have yanked it off its hinges or ripped it open with a pocketknife like a lumberjack cutting through Oregon timber. I suddenly noticed that Emily's eyes kept darting down to my side at a wooden stick I had absentmindedly picked up on the way to her house.

"I just need a place to stay, Aunt Emily," I said, half annoyed. The beatings of yesteryear were fresh in my mind, but I was not going to harm Emily. She wasn't really worth the time and trouble. I had big plans for law school and beyond, and I certainly wasn't going to blow them with an assault charge. The objective was finding a place to stay, and I knew Clack and his family were only a watering hole, nothing permanent.

We nailed down a deal. I would pay twenty-four dollars a month with the help of my salary from Schiff's shoe store to cover the house's gas, electricity, and water bills, although I learned later that Emily's monthly utility bills amounted to only eighteen dollars. Upon agreement, I walked into the little house for the first time in a decade. Only now it seemed claustrophobic.

"Don't touch anything. If I find you stole something, I'll have you killed," she said. "I'll tell the white folks that I work for. The Lonnegans love me. They don't care nothing about killing you. A black man's life ain't worth nothing."

This time I slept in the middle room instead of the rear. The brooder and chickens and dirt on the floor in the kitchen were gone, and so was the outlandish stench that once washed over the house. Chickens were still promenading around the side yard though.

The first night in the house I felt like a sheep sleeping in a wolf's lair. I feared that Emily, for old time's sake, would pound my head with a skillet and hog-tie me to the bed. Or maybe she would thrust a kitchen knife into my belly as if I were one of the Rhode Island Red chickens waltzing across the property. Emily apparently harbored similar fears since she seemed to be wide-awake too. A Rosedale standoff. I played possum most of the night, but gradually fatigue overruled fear and I was lulled into a series of catnaps.

About two weeks after I arrived back in Rosedale, I saw the man who had caused so much angst in my life—Slim Stewart. He stood next to a bench outside the pool hall near Fess's Place. I was standing on the east side of U.S. 31 when I spotted him on the opposite side of the road. This was the first time I had laid eyes on him since I had left Rosedale in 1941, more than a decade earlier. He wore the look of a man who had reached his middle years without the wisdom that is supposed to come with age. I didn't feel hatred for my father but a sense of bewilderment. What manner of man could have taken the life of a woman with whom he had created children and hardly shown any remorse? Or beaten his sons and allowed them to live on the back porch of a house and fed them rats?

After a few minutes he seemed to recognize that I was the son back from the shadows of his memory. I am sure word had wafted around the neighborhood grapevine of my return to the community, and he probably was not shocked at seeing me staring at him. His response was merely to stare back. The standoff continued for several minutes before I drifted off down the street.

The whereabouts of my two younger brothers was, of course, a nagging question. Information from Rosedale School teachers, students, and neighborhood pals indicated that Sam and David had vanished about two years after I had left Rosedale when they were roughly five and three years old, respectively. I decided to ask my father about the boys. Hopefully I would succeed where Bubba had failed in solving the mystery regarding their fate. One day I approached him warily at his perch outside the pool hall and made the inquiry.

"What the hell are you asking me for?" he growled.

The dialogue between us was brief and consisted mostly of my father cursing me for interrupting his afternoon with such an inconsequential question.

"Got any money?" he asked, after I turned and began walking away.

———

ROSEDALE SCHOOL HAD A HUMBLE population when I enrolled there in October 1951. Parker Industrial High, a school with five hundred seniors, was collegiate-size in comparison to Rosedale, where the graduating class topped out at about twenty-five souls. The curriculum at the Rosedale School was not exactly what you would find in the classes at Andover Academy in Massachusetts or some other fancy prep school, but not many Alabama educational facilities could claim that distinction either. Books, science labs, and other resources at most Negro schools were meager to start with under the separate-but-equal doctrine handed down by the U.S. Supreme Court in the *Plessy vs. Ferguson,* and the hand-me-down policy of the Alabama education system. I had already studied physics in the eleventh grade at Parker. The contents of many of the books that we used at Rosedale were moot as far as I was concerned. Studying hard, to me, was about as useful as Albert Einstein obtaining a degree from junior college, and it represented another source of irritation and frustration since I still clutched dreams of becoming a legal gladiator.

The principal of the school was B. M. Montgomery, also known as Fess, short for professor. The cafe Fess's Place, off U.S. 31, was his establishment. Montgomery also used his business sense to take advantage of the fact that the school did not house a cafeteria. Consequently, he bought a house a few yards from the school and sold candy, potato chips, sodas, and other snack foods out of the basement.

My teachers were Jeanette T. Jackson, Carlotta Harris, Bonnie Mae Perine, and Odessa Powell. Mrs. Harris seemed to like me especially and said that I resembled her husband, Paul, who was also tall and rather dark-pigmented. She and Principal Montgomery became confidantes for me in that I shared many aspects of my troubled past with them.

In class I was always waving my hand in the air like a traffic cop to lob a question or answer one. My grades classified me as an A and B student with a partiality for history. Mrs. Jackson, an influential instructor, served as my senior adviser and seemed annoyed that I exhibited a seemingly effortless grasp of her class.

As a young man who was not rabid about sports and showed a strong interest in learning, I was an enigma to her and others at the school. The fact that I was carrying emotional baggage but still succeeding in academics also caused them to scratch their heads.

Odessa Powell was another matter altogether. She was just a year out of teacher's college and an attractive specimen of a woman. We shared the same mentor, Mamie Foster, who had told her about my time in the horse stable and rough-and-tumble early days. She seemed quite empathic.

I had dropped the word among some teachers that college textbooks were more my speed. Mrs. Powell was one who took the request to heart and did not dismiss it as a gag. She lived near Miles College, a small private Methodist-owned school in the suburb of Fairfield, and borrowed books from the school for me to use.

Since I still ranked low on hygienic issues and was a magnet for some teasing, good grades were something none of the pea-brained antagonists could snatch away. But like any teenage male I wanted the attention and admiration of some of the cute, shapely girls. Being tall, gangly, and odorous was less than an asset in this area. If I could have traded places with Melvin Cook, my sex problem would have evaporated like a rainbow over a Mobile Bay beach. Melvin was Mr. Hotshot. A relatively small guy, he played a great game of football and was consequently up to his elbows with foxy females. He invariably greeted me with one stock question in the school halls, lunchroom, or gymnasium: "Hey Shelley, you getting any yet?"

"Not yet," I would reply, grinning to veil annoyance and shame. The "any," of course, referred to sexual relations.

The most effective way for me to squash the teasing, I figured, was to impress a girl. The Rosedale girls were suckers for the sports jocks—basketball, football, it didn't matter. The players were like combatants of ancient Rome battling in a modern arena of green grass, bleachers, and scuffed hardwood gymnasium floors.

Rosedale's sports teams seemed to need all the firepower obtainable. Coach William "Night Train" Coger had a limited pool from which he could draw players, so I volunteered my services. The desperate coach could not even turn his back on a 120-pound shoelace. I had never held a ball of any kind and never played sports. Aunt Mamie's restrictions had served to help blunt the development of my athletic prowess.

At practice, Coach Coger told me to run out on the field, veer left, count to ten, turn around, and catch the ball. I followed his instructions to the letter, but as I galloped downfield, the back of my helmet and the ball collided, to the amusement of the hyenas watching the spectacle. Before I could humiliate the team any further, I became the record keeper and benchwarmer.

When we played Dunbar High, my engine was idling fast. I wanted to prove myself worthy and walk away with some female admirer's eyes riveted on me. "Coach, is it time for me to go in yet?" I asked every few minutes.

"Boy, sit your ass down!" he barked in return each time until soon we had achieved an almost perfect stimulus and response rhythm like Pavlov's dog.

The first quarter passed, followed by the second. Finally, someone got hurt, and Coger reluctantly commanded me onto the field. "Get out there, Stewart!" the coach snapped. "I want you to go out for a pass and let the quarterback throw the ball at you." The key words were *throw* and *at*. Oh coach of little faith.

I ran out on the field toting images of my body pulverized and tossed around like a flimsy house smashed by some of the tornadoes that roared through Jefferson County most years between April and November. Dread and fright gripped me and rode my measly shoulders.

The huddle fell together like a human puzzle. *Single wing, thirty-three to the right.* This meant the ball was going to the right, and ideally I was supposed to cradle it like a baby in a mad gallop across the goal line. The powwow disbanded, and the pigskin was shoved between the legs of the center. I took off in a blind run down the field, turned and caught the ball, and fled toward the goalposts. Screams signaled that I was about to put a score on the board for the other team. I changed course, and a hard tackle knocked me out of bounds. My effort to stay on the sidelines out of harm's way had failed.

"Get your ass back on the field," the coach yelled. Everyone knew my skills as a running back were derived from unadulterated fear.

On the bus leaving Dunbar, Melvin Cook blasted me with both barrels. He needled me about the fact that I had *yet* to have sex and the fact that I kept pestering the coach with the question of whether it was time to play *yet*. Cook saddled me with the nickname of Yet. Cheerleaders, majorettes, and players hooted.

But the sheepskin was my objective rather than fancy juggling with a pigskin. I had good grades, and that was something Melvin and the other nincompoops couldn't pry from me. Shelley Stewart had his eyes on a grand prize of a scholarship and law school and a world light-years away from Rosedale.

CHAPTER FIVE

Not So Easy Money

HEY, BOY."

"Hey, preacher."

"Hey, Uncle."

The salutations rolled off the tongues of the shoe salesmen at Schiff's shoe store on Third Avenue North in downtown Birmingham, and reverberated through nasal passages to construct the high-pitched twang prevalent south of the Mason-Dixon line. The accents were as much a signature of the South as the tune "Dixie," magnolia trees, and weather that made you sweat like a visitor to a Turkish sauna.

Black women were given no courtesy titles either. The only recognition came in the form of names like Girl or Granny, Auntie or Mary. These were common greetings at the store whose clientele was mostly low-income Negroes and whites. In the 1951 climate of widespread bigotry and intolerance, a sense of dignity and self-worth was a fleeting and precious commodity for Alabama's black citizenry.

I had been a stock boy at Schiff's since the tenth grade at Parker, and the store was my sponsor on my show at WBCO. After I left Rosedale School, I would empty crates and stock shelves with boxes based on the serial number and size of the shoe.

White clerks would steer Negro customers toward the rear of the sales floor and away from the Caucasian customers. After a black patron had bought shoes and departed, the salesman's true colors would leap out in kaleidoscopic fashion.

"Man did you smell the funk coming from that woman when she sat down?"

"That nigger's feet stank. He ought to wash them."

Mr. Langford, the manager at Schiff's, took a shine to the jovial, outgoing personality I had patched together while working at Yeilding's. He decided to give me a shot at being an unofficial shoe salesman.

"Good afternoon, ma'am . . . Good afternoon, sir," I said as I directed the Negroes to our section of the floor room. Mr. and Mrs. and Miss were courtesy titles I always used when addressing the black customers. More often than not I would sell a pair of shoes to the customer, although I had to summon a white salesman for the actual transaction. A steady stream of loyal clientele frequented the store I suspect in large part because of the respect and courtesy I showered on them.

———————

THE NEED TO MAKE MONEY was a premier concern since my pay at Schiff's was less than chump change and I was giving a good deal of my weekly salary to Aunt Emily. Rosedale had always been poor, and any and every type of hustle, from the legal to the nefarious, might be considered for survival. The jobs that blacks could qualify for were more often as porters and chauffeurs and other menial, if not invisible, service positions. Consequently, when the mere suggestion of a money-making enterprise arose at Fess's Place on the west side of U.S. 31, the listeners were more than a captive audience.

The turf outside Fess's Place was the gathering place for the young crowd, fellows like Bill Readus, Alfred Millender, and Clack Bullard. Milk crates and old bread boxes were our chairs, and all of us had Ph.D.s in shooting the bull. Tales tall and low, gossip firsthand and fresh off the grapevine, floated from lips like wisps of billowing smoke from a Camel cigarette. We socialized and bonded, cursed a little, and laughed a lot. The territory was our humble equivalent of the country clubs located over the mountain and in downtown Birmingham frequented by white male fat-cat scions of the local Dixie society who had made their money in the industrial boon that Birmingham had been blessed with since its founding in the 1870s at the junction of railroads in the Elyton community.

"Man, I know where y'all could make plenty of money," the man said, his voice rising. "Y'all don't know how to make no money."

Dan was older than the rest of us—in his late twenties. Most of the other guys were four or five years my senior. His boast about knowing how to attract money was just the kind of intrigue that silenced our symphony of rubbish and refined it into a serious discussion of merit.

"Ya'll don't know how to make no damn money," Dan continued. "I make plenty of money working at the Jack-O-Lantern."

The fellows teased the man about parking cars for whites at the restaurant, an upscale nightclub and lounge in the white section of Homewood.

"I make fifty or sixty dollars every night. Them white folks love me. I make plenty of money and get drunk too because they leave lots of whiskey in their cars," he said.

After a brief introduction, I asked about the possibility of getting on at the restaurant to make doubly sure I didn't become a charity case at Emily's and to give me the peace of mind only greenbacks could secure.

"They need bus boys at the club," he said. "I'll put in a word with Mr. Leo and Mr. Abe. They love me. I'm their boy. They'll do anything for me."

That evening I went with Dan down to the Jack-O-Lantern restaurant with my appetite for personal income whetted. The place, of course, was lily white from the clientele to the bus boys' vests. I was introduced to the owners, Mr. Leo and Mr. Abe, and Dan told them I had experience busing tables, which I didn't.

"This is one nigger that loves to work," Dan said. "He's all right." It was strange to hear a Negro use the word in front of whites, although it was nothing for blacks to use it among themselves jokingly, as an expression of brotherhood and sisterhood, or as a linguistic shock device tossed out to bring home a point.

"If Dan says you are a good nigger, you are a good nigger," said Mr. Leo. Everyone laughed at this insult except me. I was bewildered. The last time someone referred to me using this slur was Doc the blacksmith. Papa Clyde had answered that remark with a blow that sent Doc tumbling to meet the floor.

After the two white men went inside, Dan attempted to explain what had happened as if to deflate a balloon that was about to explode.

"You've got to learn to work white people," Dan began. "Learn how to play 'em. You can't let them know you are smart. You can't let them know what you know. Make them think you ain't got no money. Every night I go borrow some money, no matter how much money I make each night. Make 'em think I'm broke. That's the game."

Dan assured me that if I followed his instructions, I would go far in the world. But I still burned on the inside over the racial aspersion tossed around in front of the whites and by the whites. The valet rattled on in a mission to soothe my anger and initiate me into a world of subservience and accommodation.

"I'll call you nigger and the whites will too. But don't let the word get to you. Just because they call you one don't make you one," he said. "*You* know what you are."

The episode with Dan was confusing and emotionally aggravating. I went into the club and was given a white jacket. My pay would be two dollars a night to bus tables, and the waiters were to shave off slices of their tips for me. It was a new experience for me in a place with bright tablecloths and hurricane lanterns on each table. There was even a master of ceremonies for the dinner show, and the featured acts were a comedian and a singer who sang "Stardust."

Bus boys balanced huge trays loaded down with soiled dishes. The trays seemed to float effortlessly across the room like magic carpets as they disappeared into the mayhem of the kitchen. The guys' techniques were dazzling, but I figured my own juggling skills were a match for any veteran tray manipulator's dexterity.

I overloaded the flat receptacle with dishes from my station table—glasses, plates, saucers piled upward toward the ceiling. The charade unraveled and I was unmasked as a rookie when my grip loosened on the top-heavy tray, and remnants of the patrons' entrees, beverages, and desserts spilled to the carpet. As I frantically attempted to pick up the mess and bring chaos to order, waiters came over and informed me that I would probably be banished before I had even gotten my bus boy uniform wrinkled. To deflate the tension, I began apologizing to the customers for the inconvenience. I took a few steps toward a table to offer mea culpas and received a startling awakening.

"Nigger, look what you've done to her dress," the male patron said, at once rising from his seat and bristling at me. "I ought to make you lick the stain out."

As the club owners ran over to berate me and calm the customer down, Dan's words seeped forward: Play the game. The menial job was essential to me, and I didn't want to lose it because an outcropping of boiling indignation forced me to knock the hell out of the white man. Play the game just like all the maids and butlers and yardmen and Negro teachers and doctors and lawyers who adjusted to the humiliation of back doors and filthy balconies. Play the game like all the dignified blacks who accepted being called boy or girl even if they were fifty years old. Play the damn game and accept the belittlement that squeezed my soul until I was ready to curse the way Job never did.

I began loading less on my trays and subsequently took twice as long to clear my stations. At 2 A.M. I clocked out and took inventory of my earnings for the evening. I received a quarter from each waiter, which amounted to an impressive total of one dollar in tips plus my base pay of two dollars a night.

The humiliation of my first night ate at my insides, and subsequently I initiated a strategy to make sure nothing resembling the fiasco happened again. The place opened for the cleaning crew at 3 P.M. so I dropped in a couple of hours before my shift was to start. I went through several dry practice runs of trays stacked tall with empty but clean dishes.

That evening I bused tables and heaved trays with the skill of a Ringling Brothers Circus juggler. I traipsed through the swinging doors separating the dining room from the kitchen. "Hot stuff," I yelled as I entered the room filled with patrons. "The baby's coming through," I warned anyone on the other side of the door when I sped back to the kitchen.

People were amazed at the transformation from one evening to the next. I was rewarded with five dollars in tips and was on my way to fat city. I would be able to pay Emily for room and board even though most nights I slept on the porch. When she headed for work mornings at her maid's job, she assumed that I was intoxicated when she saw me lying there, although I hardly ever imbibed more than root beer.

"Just like your daddy. Not worth a dime," I would hear her say as I feigned sleep.

I chased after the presidency of the student body in a contest that featured Clyde Jackson, popular captain of the football team and no relation to Mrs. Jackson, the teacher. But Clyde was Mrs. Jackson's choice for the position. I was the ragged-ass kid from the far side of the tracks. This was not the image a lot of the teachers envisioned when they thought of the twelfth grade class president.

I won the post, to the deep chagrin and consternation of Mrs. Jackson. It was unbelievable that the students had voted for me. I found out from some girls that I had been elected because I was smarter than Clyde, the big jock. The girls told me that I was still ugly and stank, but they wanted good representation and felt my being on WEDR and WBCO saddled me with good diction and communication assets.

After the school election Dan, the valet, told the Jack-O-Lantern owners, Mr. Abe and Mr. Leo, about my accomplishment at Rosedale. The two were shocked that I was in school and even more so that I was in activities like student government. One night they asked me to serve at a private party in a room upstairs above the lounge. I was dumfounded.

"Be a waiter?" I asked.

"I didn't say you could be a waiter, boy," Mr. Leo admonished.

"You said server. That's a waiter, isn't it?" I replied.

"I see you been hanging around that damn Dan too much," he joked.

Leo grudgingly agreed to pay me twenty-five dollars as a waiter at the party. His instructions were to take the orders down on a pad and get them correct. Don Greathouse, who was a little older than me and a Miles College student, worked the party of sixty people with me. We displayed showmanship by holding our trays aloft and announcing the courses: martini, appetizer, entree, dessert.

For good measure I was heavy on the compliments. "Beautiful dress, ma'am." "What a great tie, sir." The patrons lapped it up and were complimentary about our performances. We capped off the night with several five-dollar tips.

The next day one of the waiters did not show up for work, and Mr. Leo asked me if I could handle his station of deuces, or doubles. I quickly accepted the offer, which turned out to be a rite of passage for me.

Mr. Leo escorted a middle-aged couple to my station. After they were seated, the gentleman quickly ambushed me. "Hey, slim nigger, you nigger," he blurted. I wasn't really sure he was addressing me but was aware of other waiters snickering. Their apparently private joke eluded me as the man pressed on with his insults. "Nigger, they told me you was waiting on me. Come on and take my order," he said, now standing.

Veins in my neck fattened as I clenched my fists in impotent rage. One more derisive comment, I decided, and I would snatch a steak knife from a table and carve him like a pork roast. Despite my torment, or because of it, the other waiters seemed to double over in mirth. But I knew that I could not let my composure deteriorate at such a critical juncture in my fledgling career.

"May I take you order, sir?" I asked in response to Mr. Wallace's venom. I took the man's liquor request and went over to the bar where the waiters let me in on the gag. This man was a notorious patron of the restaurant. They informed me that he always addressed the Negroes in the establishment with a diatribe and never a name, always complained about service, and never tipped. Tommy, the bartender, said I would be bringing the order back because no matter which way a concoction was crafted, Mr. Wallace would find fault.

I returned to the Wallace table with the order and braced myself for another round of vituperation.

"What is this shit?" Wallace asked, punctuating the question with the same derogatory description of me he had used twenty times in the five minutes during which our lives had intersected. Apologetic, I told him I had not prepared the drinks, an admission that only served to enrage him even further. "You tell that boy Tommy to put some damn liquor in this drink. Fix my lady's drink right too," he ordered.

I took the drinks back to Tommy, but instead of pouring from the bottle, he did something I could not quite believe. The bartender reached under the counter and poured the contents of an odd, solitary glass into the patrons' containers. Baffled, I remembered Dan's words: "You got to play white folks."

The special container was reserved for VIP patrons, and Wallace fit the description to the letter. The glass was a veritable witches brew of disgusting ingredients. Cooks and waiters had blown their noses and spit and urinated in the liquid, which was reserved for those that waiters and bus boys could not openly retaliate against. Since venting anger toward a white man in the South meant swift retribution, the Negroes had found that the potion was a catharsis in defusing long-standing rage birthed in the cultural womb of general humiliation and degradation that blacks faced incessantly every day.

I felt intense antagonism toward Wallace, but I had to muzzle myself against raising my voice in protest. The man rained slurs on me as his female companion laughed at my debasement. His put-downs were a crude show that he had staged for their mutual entertainment and sadistic enjoyment. I returned the glasses to the table and went into an act that would have made Machiavelli proud.

"Sir, I went back and told Tommy he don't mess with you," I lied. "I jumped on him, Mr. Wallace. I told him you are my man. Taste it now."

The customer was pleased with the drink and ordered a sizzling steak platter. Back in the kitchen, Chef Cornelius took the cuts of meat out of the refrigerator and threw them in the garbage can. A cook blew his nose on them. Everyone spat on them as they sizzled on the grill, including me, even though I was not proud of it.

In serving the entree, I placed towels over each customer's lap, cheered their attire, carved the steaks for them, and elicited their glowing critiques on the scrumptiousness of the beef. A healthy ten-dollar tip was my reward for service with a shit-eating smile. It was a lesson always to be respectful to folks who serve you.

CHAPTER SIX

From Mourning to Reunion

THE BELL AT BETHEL A.M.E. CHURCH still rang with the spirit of African tribal drums, but now I hated the sound of those bells and any others for that matter. Ever since that day in 1939 when Mr. Davenport initiated the dreary, slow toll that announced the death of my mother, I cringed at the sound. The inner pain that saw me weeping in my private moments remained a constant companion. But, by traditional measurements, I was starting to make a small impact on the world around me in December 1951. The Rosedale senior class had elected me president, and I was working at the Jack-O-Lantern where, on a good week that included work at a private party, I might clear $120 in tips. Usually, though, my wages averaged ten or twenty dollars a week. I also had my job at Schiff's shoe store where the pay was about nine dollars a week. Whenever I was at Schiff's, I would go over to the radio station and play records at WEDR for the teen show for free. Two afternoons a week I would take the streetcar for the long ride to Bessemer to play a gig on WBCO.

I was confident of my ability to survive in the world. My spirit had been forged in the furnace of a roughshod life foreign to most teens my age, black or white. Also, I had become a world traveler based on the knowledge I had sopped up from books. That information had encased me in a sense of security against the constant assault on my self-esteem that sprang from being poor and a virtual orphan. The news that jolted my consciousness one chilly day that December would send me spinning around the edge of a whirlpool of anxiety. It was news that I had secretly feared and that lurked in the unconscious realm of my mind where the real and the imaginary embrace.

A knock on the door summoned me away from the book I was reading. Two men dressed in army uniforms stood outside the screen door, their faces stern and sincere.

"We would like to see Emily Williams and any other relative of Huell Jerome Stewart Jr.," said one of the men, whom I discerned to be a military chaplain.

"I'm his brother," I said, summoning Aunt Emily into the room.

The men were armed with a document but extemporaneously began to recite the message: Huell Stewart Jr. had been declared missing in action on November 6, only three days after he had arrived in Korea.

This was a scary and confusing moment for me as I tried to understand the word *missing*. Did that mean he was just lost in the Korean countryside? Or, at best, and nonsensical, did he get drunk at a wild party on a furlough and forget to return to his unit? What the heck did it mean? Emily did not seem fazed by the unsettling words. The four of us bowed our heads for a brief prayer, and then the soldiers disappeared into the darkness.

After a sleepless evening, I headed down to Waterboy's Grill to interrogate the older men. Their response to my query was an answer that burned with bluntness. A military notification like the one Emily and I had gotten was usually followed by the revelation that the soldier or sailor was KIA or killed in action.

The fact that the news about Bubba came as the Christmas holiday season approached only seemed to make me feel drearier in the midst of gaiety. A sadness settled over me that rivaled the glumness I felt on all of my motherless Mother's Days. Bubba might be dead, and my two younger siblings, Sam and David, had vanished as if they had been kidnapped and spirited back to West Africa. My thoughts ranged from confusion to anger. If Bubba had actually been killed, perhaps, I thought, he could rise from the dead like Christ did. My anger stemmed from the fact that Bubba had gone to fight against Communist aggression in Korea and possibly lost his life in the process. But in his own country he could not be buried in Birmingham's all-white Elmwood Cemetery and would be barred from Homewood High School because of his skin color. All I could do was bide my time and wait for further information.

Fireworks and shotgun blasts punctuated the night in a celebratory introduction to January 1, 1952. The new year ushered in bold aspirations and fresh strategies for most. I had been praying that Bubba would turn up alive in Korea, but apparently this was not in God's plan. Word came on January 5 that Huell Stewart Jr. was dead, and so was my hope. My next door neighbor Boot Wimbush and I cried together on Emily's back porch, although my aunt did not shed a tear and maintained a business-as-usual attitude.

My father was notified by people in the neighborhood that his oldest son was dead. I did not approach him to offer comfort when I saw him outside the pool hall in Rosedale. Neither did he come to me to share any semblance of grief. But I was aware that he had gone to Waterboy's Grill to drink and cry, supposedly over Bubba's death.

"Man, Mr. Slim sure is taking it hard," said my friend Bill Readus.

In my estimation, this was another show put on by my father. The so-called sadness he was purportedly drowning with the cafe's liquor was about as deep as the coastline along the Galveston, Texas, beach at low tide, in my opinion.

The casket bearing Bubba's body arrived a few days later. A borrowed suit enabled me dress up for the occasion. The funeral at Union Baptist Church in Rosedale was direct and to the point. Slim Stewart attended without his wife, Marie. He sat on one end of the church pew, and I occupied the other end. Neither of us acknowledged the presence of the other. A few neighborhood mourners also straggled in to pay their last respects. A folded U.S. flag and a purple heart completed the scene. A quiet peace encircled me as I squirmed on the hard, rickety wooden bench. The solace came not so much from what the preacher said in the short church ceremony but from what the inner voice relayed to me from my mother, Mattie C.: *Jerome is with me, and everything is going to be all right. Don't give up, and don't be frightened.*

We took Bubba to Grace Hill, a little cemetery on the southwest side of town. I remembered Job's dilemma over the urge to curse God for his mountain of torments and miseries. But like Job I would not surrender to instinct. The depression rippling from the latest bad hand dealt to me and my family in the poker game of life did not drown my faith in God nor in the possibilities for a grander future.

———

LIFE ALONGSIDE U.S. 31 by Waterboy's Grill was my main social outlet. Shooting the bull was an activity with low overhead. It was cheaper than going to the movies, for sure. Besides, you did not have to endure the hassle of getting dressed up. It was come as you were. A bath amounted to little more than washing up and spraying on cheap cologne. My whole lifestyle was low maintenance, and earnings at Schiff's and the Jack-O-Lantern enabled me to pay Emily's room-and-board bill. After that expense and other incidentals there weren't really a hell of a lot of surplus dollars and cents to splash around.

Most of the fellows who hung out on the road by the grill were not Mellons or Vanderbilts. They were just plain old guys who, despite the humbleness of their individual circumstances, had access to more resources and material goods than I did. I wasn't really even in a single-parent home. Emily wasn't a parent and certainly not a guardian by any stretch. What income she derived from working in the Lonnegan home was spent on her own food and general lifestyle. I fended for myself whether it was for material support or emotional rigidity.

The persona I displayed at our roadside country club was often a sham. When guys would strut over, talking about meals devoured, I would invariably manufacture my own menu. Chicken, pork chops, or maybe a steak would be the entrees of choice. But the more realistic scenario meant consuming a pauper's dinner of sardines and crackers or peanut butter and water. Of course, sometimes I ate out on the town. In those days, some homes, like Miss Carrie's, and boardinghouses sold plates of food, and if you had enough money, you could purchase a dinner of fish, chicken, and so on.

The grief rippling through me from Bubba's death piled high in my psyche. I concealed my private river of pain from the boys on the road as well as from classmates. Bubba's hard fate became another chunk of emotional driftwood that created two Shelley Stewarts. One was outgoing and thumbed his nose at his predicaments through self-deprecating humor. The other was a quiet soul with a thoughtful inner sanctum. In a true check-and-balance system, the extroverted Shelley shielded the more fragile youth from the pains of the world.

I stole away from Rosedale School early one day and sat on Emily's front porch steps to meditate. The congenial mailman came by and struck up a conversation as he had done on other occasions. He said he had heard I was smart in school. Perhaps, I thought, my intelligence had made this white man consider a conversation with me a tad more palatable.

"You know, Shelley, there's a postcard down at the office that we laugh about," he said.

The carrier's words did not thrill or otherwise impress. I knew that his business was mail and that he had probably touched thousands of parcels in his career; notifications detailing love, death, and mundane communications had been toted around his route. The whole mind-set of the nation's social fabric could be sifted from nondescript post offices across the country. Another postcard was just an extra piece of processed pulp.

"The card said something like, 'To my bro Shurl,'" the mailman added.

Shurl. I sprang to attention at this revelation. This postman knew me as Shelley. Mostly people from my early days called me Shurl or Shurley. I was reeling from the sudden intrigue. Why did the postman stop and talk with me on this particular day? He did not deliver a single piece of mail to Emily's house. There was clearly no need for him to come out of his way and end up on those steps at 2611 Eighteenth Place in Rosedale. This had to be another manifestation of my mother's interest in my life and the lives of all of her sons.

"It's been at the post office for two or three years," he continued. "We can't deliver it because it doesn't have a street address."

The mailman honored my request to see the card and dropped it off the next day as, hopefully, a truly special delivery. When I grabbed the card, it was hot to the touch and radiated a supernatural sensation of heat.

"To my bro Shurl, I need lot help, Sam," the card said in scrawled print. The postmark was clear: Scooba, Mississippi. Where the devil was Scooba, Mississippi? I wondered. But beyond that I knew I had a clue to the whereabouts of my brothers Sam and David, whom I had not seen in a decade. Now in the spring of 1952, I felt like I was closer to unraveling the mystery of their fate than I had ever been. I put the card in my pocket, thanked the mailman, and later went down to the Jack-O-Lantern to work.

That next day I visited Ennis Daniels, the neighbor who had told police that my father and stepmother were feeding us rats. I asked him if he knew what had happened to my brothers. He said he had overheard my stepmother, Marie, say four years earlier that the little bastards had been shipped off to somewhere in Mississippi. But, other than that, he had no other information.

That morsel of information dovetailed with the postcard. I told all my road buddies about the discovery: Jimmy Bonner, Bill Readus, Clack Bullard. They thought the chances of finding Sam and David were about as good as me becoming an usher in one of the all-white churches that dotted the nation.

I walked down to the Greyhound terminal in downtown Birmingham and inquired about a trip to Scooba. Their buses did not make the journey. I went to the Trailways station and learned that the town was on their line and was about thirty miles north of Meridian, in east Mississippi. A round-trip fare

would set me back less than ten dollars. I put the squeeze on pals
for help. I borrowed five dollars from Bill Readus, a dollar from
Albert Milnard, a dollar from Clack, and a dollar from Isaac
Johnson, a driver for Rosedale principal Fess Montgomery. A
buck here and two bucks there.

A trip into Mississippi to find someone could be fraught
with dangers. People told me a black man wandering into the
Deep South state with no specific destination would likely end
up hanging from a magnolia tree with his private parts ampu-
tated. But I figured the knife-throwing skill Bubba and I had
honed at Stringfellow Stables would pull me through. I borrowed and collected about thirteen knives for use as a traveling
arsenal. They included a big military knife called a "Dutch," a
Mexican stiletto, and, for good measure, an ice pick.

On a Saturday morning I awoke with a mission in mind.
I placed a towel under my clothes against my body and used
tape to hold the knives in place. I had also borrowed a pocket
watch from Isaac Johnson, and I stuffed two packs of donated
Chesterfield cigarettes into the trousers. The cigarettes were
an occasional habit I resorted to in order to show off when I
hung around the boys on the road. At the Trailways station I
bought one round-trip and two one-way tickets to Scooba, an
expression of confidence that I would return with my brothers
in tow.

Dressed in an old cap, overalls, and beat-up brogan shoes, I
camped in the rear of the bus with the other black passengers.
Nervous tension buffeted me as I braced myself to do battle
against unseen enemies that might be lurking in the unfamiliar
territory.

The bus roared out of the terminal at 6 A.M., snaked
through downtown Birmingham, and headed west toward
the Bessemer Superhighway. The superhighway was also U.S.

Highway 11, a main thoroughfare linking Birmingham and New Orleans. The federal road meandered through Tuscaloosa, site of the University of Alabama, fifty-five miles away. Beyond Tuscaloosa was Meridian, Mississippi, and about thirty miles north on U.S. 45 and one hudred fifty miles from Birmingham sat Scooba.

Tire rubber caressed highway asphalt as the smell of diesel fuel wafted under my nose and the bus's transmission sang loudly. I was fortified by the inner voice that guided my soul and shouted its closeness in times of crisis or confusion. That communication, I surmised, again belonged to Mattie C. Just as she had directed me to Bubba in Springfellow Stables, I felt that she and a greater divine spirit were now orchestrating this mission to find my missing brothers.

The bus made a dozen forgettable dusty stops along its route through west Alabama. Despite the growth of auto travel, the bus was still a well-used mode of transportation for lots of folks who couldn't afford cars, plane fare, or even a train ticket. Everyone on the bus had their own personal stories, but mine was the only one I gave a damn about at the moment.

At about 11 A.M. we pulled into Scooba, a tiny town dotted with sawmills that was little more than a smudge on the map of Mississippi with an area of 3.8 square miles and a population of a few dozen families. Scooba is located in Kemper County, which was ceded from the Choctaw Indians in 1833. Forestry and agriculture were the major economic stimuli in the county. The hilly terrain in the western four-fifths of the county limited agriculture to small farms, but the flat terrain of the eastern fifth nurtured a plantation economy. Kemper was named for Colonel Reuben Kemper, a native of Virginia, who moved with his brothers Samuel and Nathan to the vicinity of Fort Adams, became a leader of the West Florida Rebellion against

Spain in 1811, and fought under Jackson at the Battle of New Orleans.

"Lord, where am I, and what am I going to do?" I thought, as I disembarked from the bus and asked the middle-aged driver about the exactness of the posted bus schedule.

"Boy, this bus is always on time," he said. "You can set your watch by it. If we don't stop to pick up people, we pick up parcels, but we always stop."

The next bus heading back to Alabama would be leaving at 3:47 P.M. If luck ruled the day, I'd be back for that trip with my brothers. But I never had any doubt that the key to Sam and David's fate was there in the sleepy village. It was the same burning instinct that had guided me to Bubba in the horse stable years earlier.

I scooted out of the station, and the town spread itself out before me in short order. A few stop signs, a feed shop, and a handful of other buildings were sprinkled about, and farmers and workers milled around the area.

The county had seen the birth of one of America's first railroads, the Gainesville & Narkeeta, built in 1836. The area was also the site of Sciple's Water Mill of 1790, the first known water mill in America to use the Leffel Water Turbine. By 1840 Kemper County was one of the largest and wealthiest counties in Mississippi. There were no known Civil War battles fought in Kemper. In Reconstruction times, the county was tagged with the name "bloody Kemper" because of violence between various political factions and gangs of outlaws such as the Copeland Gang and the Murrell Clan. The most famous product of the county in modern times was local lawyer John C. Stennis, who served in the U.S. Senate for many decades.

I started looking for any Negroes I might happen upon. Every time white folks approached, I would kneel down, fiddle with my shoes, and start singing softly an old spiritual, "Hey Lord." Blacks had learned the deception over the years in the cat-and-mouse game played with whites. They noticed that if they started singing gospel songs, nearby whites would seem afraid or disinterested and wouldn't mess with them.

I encountered an elderly black man bouncing down the road in a mule-driver wagon and seized the opportunity to dredge up a clue.

"Hey, how you been doing?" I shouted as if we were old friends. The man wore a mask of bewilderment.

"Don't I know you?" he asked.

"Ain't going to tell you. You ought to know me," I said.

"I'm going to think of your name," he mused.

The dare was meaningless since I knew I had never set foot in Mississippi before that day. My thin cover story was that I was hunting for my two long-lost cousins, Sam and David.

"They got to be living down here somewhere," I insisted. I told him their ages would be about 14 and 12, respectively.

"You know," he responded, "there's two colored boys come here a while back. Up on Alan Johnson's plantation. Up that road there. Yeah, that's them boys, skinny boys. Don't you know Alan Johnson's plantation?"

I played along with the grizzled old man like that truth had been cast aside by a mind preoccupied with more cosmic matters.

"Yeah you right. Alan Johnson's plantation. Sure do know it. How far is it?" I asked.

"Boy, you just like . . . I know who you is. Yo' folks the Coopers."

"I sure is," I lied.

The old man was energized by the falsehood and began to rant. "You tell your granddaddy to pay me my goddamned money," he said. "You didn't think I knew who you was. I knew who you was. The plantation is about a mile or two up the road. You know that."

I thanked him and walked briskly off in the direction he had indicated as the late-morning sun unleashed its gentle rays. King Cotton still held some rights to the throne in these parts. Workers sweated and hoed as they prepared the soil for spring planting; men and women and children labored in an almost robotlike manner. Rows of the fabled cotton plant would soon spread over the rich Southern soil like barnacles clinging to the bow of a rusting ship. Images of slavery danced in my skull even though the institution had been officially disemboweled in the Deep South eighty-seven years earlier.

An electrifyingly surreal air enveloped me as I marched along rows of emasculated cornstalks stripped of their cobs during the previous harvest. Was this a trap waiting for me? Were the workers neutral and disinterested, or were they informers for the plantation overseer itching to turn in a nosy interloper and curry favor? I felt like a sitting duck ambling down the road, so I edged off the path into a cotton field, an arsenal of knives hugging my chest.

I laid down and began crawling toward some workers. I slithered forward several yards, stopped, and got to my knees to survey the situation. There were knots of people here and there who seemed to be consumed with their work. I fell to my belly again and slinked snakelike through the field with a prayer on my lips. Off in the distance I noticed a young man riding a mule. He appeared to be about the age Sam would be. In a crouch, I navigated close enough to discern that he was carrying a bucket of water back and forth among the workers. The youth prodded the old mule toward where I lay hiding but then suddenly began moving farther away.

I would have to act fast and swallow the consequences. Our father, Slim, always used to call us with a loud birdlike whistle, but I never could generate any more decibels than a doorbell when I pursed my lips. So I attempted the next-best thing when the boy moved to within two hundred feet of me.

"Sam! David!" I shouted. "Sam! David!" I repeated.

The youth stopped his mule and looked around, and so did a cluster of workers. I yanked the Mexican stiletto out from underneath my clothing just in case this was a foe. I had not seen my younger brothers since they were little more than toddlers and wasn't sure if I would know them if I bumped into them on the street in Rosedale, let alone on a Mississippi plantation, and this kid was dirty and thin and looked like he needed a good meal.

"Sam! David!" I called again.

This time the rider guided the creature within a few yards of me. It was doubtful that he would know who I was, especially with the old cap pulled down over my ears.

"Your name Sam or David?" I asked.

"I'm Sam," he said.

"Sam what?" I demanded.

"Sam Stewart."

"You got a brother?" I asked.

"Yeah."

"What's your brother's name?"

"You called it a while ago. His name David," he responded.

"Where's he?" I asked.

"He up at the house," he said. "His leg got broke and it ain't healed yet, so he can't work in the fields right now."

"You know who I am?" I asked.

"No, but you could be my brother," he responded. "You

know I got a brother. I got a brother named Shurley and a brother named Bubba."

I peeled the cap off my head with tears cascading down my face like Niagara Falls as the import of the event unfolding sank in. It was hard to put a name on what had happened, but I knew the divine had stepped down from its lofty perch again and made its presence known in the ancient temporal world around me that I could touch, smell, love, and hate. Sam revealed a smile that I had never seen in the time we were together in Rosedale; a pleasant, agreeable, fulfilled look crept across his gaunt face as he tasted the spiritualism of the moment.

"Is that you, Shurl?" he asked, knowing the answer.

Sam related that David had broken his leg after he had fallen off a mule but could hobble. He voiced fears that I, and perhaps all of us, might be killed fleeing from the anachronistic plantation system that amounted to little more than mid-twentieth-century peonage. But it was then or never if we were to escape the town together on the makeshift underground railroad.

I asked Sam how long it would take for him to retrieve David. With no concept of time, he estimated that he could be back by the time I counted to two hundred. He prodded the mule into a trot as I stage-whispered that he not let David know that I was in town.

The hands of time procrastinated as I waited for Sam to return, and the minutes oozed past. In a real sense, perhaps fifteen minutes crept by before I saw the two boys riding toward the place in the field. As they neared, I could hear the pair bantering about the drama of the moment.

"I told you our brothers would find us," said Sam.

"You a lie," said David. "I don't see him. Stop lying."

I rose up from the ground and caught a flicker of recognition on David's face, but sentiment had to be shoved onto a back burner since there was scant time for hugs and tears. This was still a plantation where the overseer probably had stooges or spies. The gateway to freedom could slam shut for all three of us at any second.

"What are we going to do now?" Sam asked.

"Catch the bus," I said, knowing that the bus stop was still a couple of miles down the road.

The borrowed pocket watch posted a time of 2 P.M. The Trailways driver had said that his no-time-to-waste schedule meant the vehicle would arrive at 3:47 P.M. to pick up passengers, parcels, or both. We took off at a fast walk toward town but allowed for David's out-of-order leg. At times he leaned on us or we each grabbed a limb, hoisted him up into the air, and toted him for several yards at a time.

During the rush for the bus line I noticed thatches of woods near the road that would conceal us if we were confronted by any pursuers. I told Sam and David that Bubba had been killed in Korea, a fact they seemed to accept with an irritating dispassion that I attributed to the great span of time we had been apart.

Sam was more forthcoming than David on how they happened to be on the farm. But from the mists of memory, they recalled that a black man had brought them there from Alabama, and they had been scared to death.

"We was slaves, Shurley," Sam said.

Work was second nature for them, whether it was picking cotton, gathering corn for the livestock, splitting logs, or wielding a crosscut saw to knock down timber. They provided youthful manpower for little compensation other than the roof over their heads. Sam revealed that they lived in an old run-down house that lacked indoor plumbing and in which you could look down at the floor and see Mississippi soil. They slept on pallets and killed rabbits and other small animals for sustenance.

We arrived at the town square and stayed out of sight behind a building. The bus pulled up to the store on cue a short while later, and the driver went inside to check for packages and passengers. I told Sam and David to be on the mark to make a dash for the vehicle.

"Go," I yelled on first sight of the driver. We got to the bus shortly after he had returned and taken his seat. I presented the tickets, and we squeezed into our positions in the rear of the vehicle as it lurched toward the Alabama line.

We wound our way to Birmingham up U.S. 11 and arrived at about 7:30 P.M. The streetlights and Trailways station seemed to intrigue Sam and David, whose extraction from slavery evoked reactions in them akin to those of cavemen hopping off a time machine and landing in the middle of twentieth-century technological wonders.

The full effect of what had happened seemed to wash over us after we had ridden the streetcar back to Rosedale and alighted at Spring Park near Union Baptist Church. We convulsed in tears and launched prayers of thanksgiving for being able to find each other and solve a familial jigsaw puzzle created at the hands of our father and stepmother.

Fess's Place offered a place for us to gather our senses and fill up on hamburgers with a few dollars I had on me. Everyone in the place seemed amazed at our reunion, from Kate Williams, the cook, to Boot, who lived next door to Aunt Emily. Word spread like wildfire as folks who had never set foot in the cafe dropped by to marvel at the return of the dirty, unkempt Sam and David.

When we stepped outside, we noticed our father, Slim, who had apparently gotten wind of the siblings' reunion. In true form he took off at a gallop up U.S. 31 toward his home on Twenty-seventh Court.

CHAPTER SEVEN

A Lost Destiny

You CAN GO HOME AGAIN.

The incubator called Rosedale that had nurtured my brothers and me more than a decade earlier was once again our refuge. Our reunion had been cultivated by a workman named fate and harvested at the hands of destiny. This reconvening of kin was so unlikely that I concluded that this event could not be a happenstance by-product of the crapshoot of life but a divine scheme. But survival was not to be celebrated just yet. Even though we had escaped the Scooba plantation, with its harshness and absurdity, Sam and David still needed a lifeline and protection.

The props in their old world were planting and harvesting, sleeping, eating, and illiteracy. This journey to the promised land of hope was pregnant with possibilities and vistas for each of us, but for them to come to fruition was a daunting task. Only little more than a month after Bubba's burial, I was back together with my two youngest brothers in March 1952. I could only regret that the four of us had not been in each other's presence again after Bubba and I separately fled Slim and Marie's house in 1941. What joys and insights we would have shared in a normal childhood were lost in a maze of misfortune. Sam and David's presence dictated brand-new responsibilities for me as I carried the torch passed on by Bubba.

During the time at Stringfellow Stables he had unfailingly taken up the slack for me and done my chores to allow me to attend Irondale School. Now it was my time to look after Sam and David, and the introspective personality of Shelley Stewart would have to become resourceful and productive to pull off this feat.

Aunt Emily seemed surprised and apprehensive to see us when we turned up at the house that evening, pretty much as she had been a few months earlier when she encountered Bubba and me together for the first time in years. This time she was speechless, an odd state for a woman who never seemed to run short of insults. But she wasn't so reticent that she could not make it clear that the two extra boarders would be my responsibility entirely. Emily, like her sister Mamie, unequivocally stated that her womb had never held any children, and she sure as hell didn't desire any surrogates. Reluctantly she acquiesced to the idea that the boys would stay there in the small house. The meager income from the Jack-O-Lantern Supper Club and Schiff's would have to be spread to cover food and clothes for all three of us.

Our menu for the most part was Happy John or potluck. This referred to improvisational cooking in which a modest amount of inexpensive food would be stretched as far as it could conceivably go. We lived most of the week on big pots of black-eyed peas and rice or spaghetti and neck bones. While I had been satisfied with sardines, crackers, Vienna sausages, and peanut butter and water, my two brothers demanded more hearty meals.

Sam and David's wardrobe amounted to the rags on their backs. Kate Williams, the cook at Fess's, provided them with some shirts and other discards to help get by. I got the brothers enrolled in Rosedale School with disastrous results. Principal Montgomery placed Sam, who was about fifteen, in the seventh grade, and David, two years younger, occupied space in the sixth, where, because of their illiteracy, they voiced well-founded feelings of insecurity. The fact they were older than the other children didn't help quell their sense of unease either. Despite my tutoring, I discovered that most days they shot hooky. To cope with their predicament, they seemed to become complacent and gravitate toward other young men who were apathetic about their stations in life. What they lacked in educational fortitude they made up for in physical aggressiveness. If they couldn't beat you mentally, they would prevail with their plantation-cultivated brawn.

My own academic success in school was gratifying but could never spill over to my brothers, and their situations became a source of great consternation. Emily, true to her past history, contributed nothing to our survival. Compensation was expected for anything she did for us. If she washed a tub of clothes for Sam and David, the magic words sliced the air with the shrillness of a traffic policeman's whistle: You owe me.

The angels still apparently sat in my corner in the boxing arena of life, however. Whether it was my mother's spirit or the divine essence of the creator, this force seemed to invade my life at its own volition. That entity again made its presence felt on my way to the Jack-O-Lantern to work one afternoon when I spotted a brown paper bag lying in an empty lot in Pecktown. To squelch curiosity, I decided to investigate its contents, and the revelation sent me reeling. Inside was a virtual treasure, $2,700 in greenbacks. A whiskey dealer's cache, I assumed, had been dropped during a hurried nighttime transaction. Or perhaps its genesis was on the legal side of the law, the cash receipts from one of the nearby businesses. At any rate, I never heard anyone mention the money through the neighborhood grapevines in the black enclave of Rosedale or the white Homewood business district. Perhaps I was morally compromised by not making a more earnest effort to find the owner of the loot, but I doubted if one person out of a thousand would have done any differently. Money was money no matter the source, and I regarded it as a windfall from heaven.

The retail stores in downtown Birmingham seemed to call my name. I peeled two hundred dollars out of the wad of bills and headed for Koplon's Korner on Third Avenue North. The buying safari snared pants and shirts for the three of us and a pair of Edmund Clapp shoes to accentuate my threadbare wardrobe.

"You ain't stealing, are you, boy?" Emily asked, after the sudden appearance of the clothes.

It was my goal to construct a haven for all of us, including Emily since she was still part of my family and the notion of familial ties was becoming increasingly important to me. I heard that neighbors named Finley had bought some property in the adjoining county of Shelby. After checking into this, I used $1,200 to buy eighty-plus acres of land in the rural community of Sterrett. Since I was only seventeen, Emily's name went on the deed, which contained a survival clause naming me as the owner upon my aunt's death. As a safeguard, I had Emily sign a paper stating that I put up the money for the house just in case she wanted to shut me out of the picture entirely and claim that I had no part in the property's purchase. I also bought lumber and told Emily about the plan. Although she was receiving $119 a month from Bubba's military death benefits, she declined to invest in the house. Work began on the modest structure that included three bedrooms, a kitchen, and a living room. Before construction could go any further, Emily's fears froze the project in its tracks.

"Whites don't like for colored to live too fancy," she said. "Colored don't need all that. . . . What you want to live like white folks for?"

Activity at the dwelling rolled to a standstill. It lacked electricity and indoor toilets and was unpainted. But Emily did let me build a hog pen, a chicken yard, a shed for one cow and an outhouse. I went to stay with the Bullards again while my aunt and Sam moved into the Shelby house. I decided to stay in Rosedale because I would be closer to work and, besides, there was no bus or trolley service between Shelby County and Birmingham. David remained at the Eighteenth Place house with an older lady named Miss Pearlie Remberton, who succeeded Emily as renter. Sam enrolled in Columbiana Training School for Colored and used the skills he learned on the Scooba, Mississippi, plantation to plow the land with a mule we bought for thirty dollars. Emily discouraged Sam's pursuit of education and steered him into working around the place like she and her siblings did down in Cordele, Georgia, and this helped his school career fizzle relatively fast.

BY APRIL OR MAY the junior-senior prom was approaching, and I was predictably without a date. I had asked every girl in the two classes and received no affirmative answer. No young lady wanted to be caught dead with Yet, the skinny, homely kid with banana-yellow incisors and an aroma of musk who was yet to have sexual intercourse. Besides, I didn't possess the charm of the football jocks with their cocky swaggers and vacant skulls. The afternoon of the prom was business as usual for me as I strolled over to the Jack-O-Lantern to put in a work shift. Jokes flowed furiously from the bus boys and waiters about my wallflower status. Bill Readus, a.k.a. Tex, had a car, and he and other guys coaxed me to ride down to the Masonic Temple at the end of the shift and peep in at the prom. Their sense of sadism was operating in high gear, but I had to be a masochist for going along with the stunt. The students who spotted me at the door waved, and a few taunted me about being on the outside looking in. It was painful, but I could smell the scent of a scholarship that would even the score.

A strong hint that something was amiss about college came from my adviser and chemistry teacher, Carlotta Harris, who told me that it was a shame that I would not be going. Principal Montgomery had told Mrs. Jackson and others who the college scholarship recipients would be, and my name was not among them, she said. Not one to go on third-hand information, I confronted Montgomery. His answer would gnaw at my already tattered self-esteem.

"Well, Stewart," he said, "you've got good grades, but you don't have the family background and support. You are just not college material."

I was stunned beyond words. A man of academia, who should have been nourishing and cultivating enlightenment in the most barren and hopeless of human personalities, had just, in effect, dropped a ton of bricks on my head. Besides, Mr. Montgomery was my confidante. He had been at my mother's funeral and knew about my rough early life in Rosedale as well as about the time spent in Stringfellow Stables and Clyde Smith's basement. On occasions I had even cried to him about my personal torments and revealed the fact that I had seen a vision of Mattie C. His remarks to me represented a mockery of the trust I had placed in him and were influential in preventing me from laying my emotions bare to another human being for years.

How could we succeed as an underdog race, I wondered, with this type of leadership on our primary and secondary school systems? The black schools were already at a distinct disadvantage in pursuit of socioeconomic and cultural attainment, and this attitude would only serve the cause of ignorance and social darkness.

Montgomery agreed, after my gentle pleading, to reverse his decision and submit my name for a scholarship. I turned my attention toward the graduation rite of passage. Sister Bullard let me wear shoes and a suit belonging to her son Clack. The suit was a blue Kupenshine, and I cried when they entrusted it to me. I strutted in front of the mirror at Clack's house and acted as if I were already marching down the aisle at Friendship Baptist to receive my sheepskin and diploma with a couple of dozen other graduates. Fisk University. Hampton Institute. Tuskegee Institute. Daydreaming came easy as I pretended that I was on my way to some college armed with a scholarship.

Slim and Marie should be told, I felt, that I would be graduating with honors despite Marie's prediction that I would not live to see age sixteen. They should be informed that I was graduating despite my mother's murder, the abuse from Slim and Emily, and Aunt Mamie. The couple was on the porch of their house on Twenty-seventh Court when I found them. Slim never made eye contact with me and sat in monklike silence while Marie glared hatefully. My mother, Mattie, had been with me always, I told them. Her spirit had coached and guided me in a fashion that neither of them had ever attempted during their sorry lives on this side of the great beyond. Their silence when faced with my message was not surprising. Slim and Marie were not orators or even simple conversationalists. What could they say—Marie was wrong to doubt my capabilities? Their unspoken reaction meant nothing to me. My satisfaction had been achieved just by telling them of my accomplishment. I simply turned and walked off the porch, leaving them to stew in their own wicked thoughts.

On graduation day at Friendship Baptist, Mrs. Jackson instructed the seniors on what to do when we received our diplomas. Once our names were called, respective parents, grandparents, siblings, and cousins would stand in the audience. Even for this high school ceremony, relatives had come from as far away as New York City for some of the honorees. No one was there for me. I had not tried to tell Papa Clyde about the ceremony. Perhaps he would have come to see me receive my diploma if I had.

To be sure, there would be eventual teachers in the class and maybe nurses, but the power of those diplomas was limited. It was not unusual in the Negro community to see people with four or five years of college working as elevator operators, laborers, or even Pullman porters. The doors of opportunity were bolted with a chain of racial prejudice, and those who got through to the other side were few, relatively speaking.

Principal Montgomery handed out the diplomas. When my name was called, I strode forward to pick up the sheepskin. Mrs. Mamie Foster, my old mentor, stood up for me and kept me from feeling so starkly alone at the event.

"That's my boy," she said.

The scholarships were announced: Bill Clark, Mary Turner, Ernestine Outlin, and a fellow named Walton. My name was not called, and I felt like I had been kicked in the stomach by a donkey. All of the studying and hard work were for nothing. Principal Montgomery had lied to me when he said he would reverse his decision and grant me a scholarship. Trudging to classes at Irondale, Hudson, Parker, and Rosedale might as well have been trips to a swimming hole to shoot hooky, or day-long bull sessions with the road gang down by U.S. 31. It seemed as if all the nuggets of wisdom and knowledge I had gleaned from books and school might as well have been placed into a potato sack and tossed into the Gulf of Mexico to be carried by the ocean current across the Atlantic and deposited on the coast of Portugal.

The girls were A students and deserved the awards, but the boys' qualifications strained at a sense of merit. Their qualifications apparently stemmed from their popularity since both were just C average students. Bill was a sharp dresser though. Walton was well liked but known to sometimes come to class intoxicated. The snub of not receiving the scholarship was devastating, but the betrayal of trust by Montgomery was equally as painful. He had said I was not college material chiefly because of my family background, and I had been naive enough to share details of my past with a man who had now turned that information against me. Although my confidence in people had been further eroded by the principal, I vowed that I would not let this roadblock prevent me from making something worthwhile of my life.

Money remained an objective since I still wanted to look out for myself and my brothers financially. I inquired about becoming full-time at WEDR but was turned down by the manager as still being too young and inexperienced. I had noticed a snazzy-looking car with New York license plates in Rosedale. On a whim, I sought out the passengers. The three cocky young men flashed money and seemed to know their way around life's boulevards, and I attempted to milk them for information. In a few short minutes they hooked me on the glamour and opportunity of New York City, a place that always seemed to captivate the imaginations of guys eager to roll the dice on the chances of life. They talked about jukeboxes and phonograph records. One mentioned having seen Pearl Bailey.

"Man," said one youth, "the colored folks up North don't take the kind of shit y'all take. We'll kick white folks' asses."

The confidence they exuded and their probable lifestyles

hinted at a pie I wanted to taste. This could be my promised land, and I could become a shooting star of some luminosity. Besides, after World War II, thousands of Southern blacks had headed north to places like Detroit, Cleveland, and Gary, Indiana, in pursuit of more financial leverage with work in industrial plants and such. This could be a pipe dream or, at worse, a deep nightmare, but I would have to find out for myself. I asked them about riding up with them, but they were going to hang around town a little longer.

New York was to be paradise, and somewhere within its boroughs and musty, centuries-old streets hopefully rested a treasure that could ensure greater financial solvency. Certainly, I was teased about not getting a college scholarship, but there was no time to wallow in a sea of self-pity.

Miss Pearlie was kind to David in providing his comfortable lifestyle, but I did not think it was her place to provide for any of us. Sam had left Emily's place in Sterrett and was staying with a fellow named Plookey and his family and was not reaping the material bonanza that David was enjoying. The friction generated by David's comfort and Sam's parallel discomfort was as obvious as the incongruence of a wino rubbing shoulders with teetotalers at a temperance revival. New York City was appealing as the multipurpose solution: a place to clear my head and gain my bearings as well as achieve monetary independence.

The compulsion to jump into the fast-moving social and economic currents of New York left me with a sense of ambivalence. I was not so certain that this would be what my mother would have wanted me to do, but nevertheless, I was still catapulted toward the city. Hopefully, I would make my mark in that land of milk and honey and gain enough money for me and my brothers to start a decent life. Of course, I wanted to show all of those students who had laughed at my clothes and hair and teeth that I could be a success. And, to be sure, now I had a desire to show Principal Montgomery that I would achieve despite the fact that he had given an unqualified person a scholarship that should have been mine.

CHAPTER EIGHT

New York on the Lam

You're too slow for New York."

"Who do you know in New York?"

I had ignored these and other words of discouragement to follow a great notion in the summer of 1952. A ticket on the Silver Comet for a trip from Birmingham to New York cost thirty-six dollars, and I had saved about a hundred dollars for the journey. Two pairs of pants, two shirts, an overcoat, and underwear were in my suitcase, which was tied closed with a rope because the latch was broken. When I climbed into the train coach at Birmingham's Terminal Station, I knew that this could be a fateful trip. This would be my first journey beyond the South's familiar dialects, attitudes, idiosyncrasies, and sensibilities into the unknowns of the renowned northeastern city.

The excursion would certainly be more intimidating than riding to the horse show in Pulaski, Tennessee, with Bubba, Pee-wee, and the Derryberrys. I was saying good-bye to the Birmingham metropolitan area and putting distance between myself and the people who had been significant in my life for good or bad: my father, Slim Stewart, stepmother, Marie, brothers Sam and David, Papa Clyde and his family, and Aunt Mamie and Uncle Henry. The dream of law school had been unveiled as a misguided notion. Hopefully, a new door of opportunity would replace the one that closed with the failure to receive the scholarship.

The journey to New York took about twenty-four hours thanks to a multitude of stops along the way. On first impression, New York seemed to be an underground labyrinth because of the cavernous splendor of Grand Central Station. Travelers and visitors crisscrossed its corridors like termites going to work on the timbers of a rotting harbor wharf. This was the place where trends were launched and social agendas constructed from the wisdom of average, elegant, and grizzled individuals, people who worked hard and lustily for survival through shady and noble means.

Tears welled up as I considered the enormity of the task before me, a youth who would turn eighteen in a few months. Freedom, but now what? Who *did* I know in New York, this so-called paradise where you didn't have to say "yes, sir" and "no, ma'am" to whites? The Silver Comet had deposited me in the Big Apple, but what would be my next step? Papa Clyde used to say, "Boy, if you don't know where you are going, any road will take you there."

The Empire State Building had attracted my attention in news reports, and I understood that the city was a dynamic cultural and financial juggernaut in the nation. But I didn't have any relatives or friends in the metropolis known for its impersonal spirit. The three dudes from New York had mentioned the Hotel Theresa and Harlem, the neighborhood that had restructured its ethnic complexion in the last few decades and had become a haven for Negroes. But I didn't really know how to get there.

Fast trains rushed out of the station into the boroughs and

hinterlands. Some subway cars carried more blacks than whites, and on others the demographics were reversed. A sign on one train read "7th Avenue IRT Uptown." The letters stood for Interborough Rapid Transit. Plenty of blacks were climbing on the subway car, so I figured that this was as good a place to start as any. The train sped out of the terminal as if the Hudson River would boil over its banks if it made its stops a microsecond off schedule.

A menagerie of accents punctuated the air of the compartment. This was the first time I had seen Puerto Ricans and other peculiar-talking people. New York, with its pulsating tempo and hodgepodge of humanity, was a stark contrast to Alabama with its heavy concentration of individuals descended from English, Scotch-Irish, and West African stock.

At 81st Street and 96th Street white passengers were disembarking. Black riders began to exit at 110th Street and then at 118th Street. By the time the IRT sailed to 125th Street and Eighth Avenue, almost everyone started getting off, so I did too.

A vibrant new world rushed forth at the top of the subterranean stairs. I found myself in Harlem, the neighborhood once designated New Haarlem by the Dutch and settled a few centuries earlier. The air was electric with the energy of dark-hued humanity. Refugees from the smothering poverty of Southern tenant farms and the cruel bigotry of Anyplace, U.S.A., had carved out new lives. People fleeing failed marriages, mortal sin, or inner fears were crammed into tenements like one huge extended family. Never had I seen so many blacks driving convertibles. A car almost struck me as I ambled across a street mesmerized by sights and sounds. The Apollo Theater. Club Baby Grand. Hotel Theresa. Sugar Ray's Bar on Seventh Avenue.

For the first time I saw Negroes working as clerks in hotels and shops.

Hunger tightened my stomach into a knot as I ambled along. All I possessed in the world was in my suitcase; my pockets held only thirty-one dollars and some change. It was startling to see Negro men and their white girlfriends or wives driving down Lenox Avenue or Seventh Avenue. I kept expecting to see a police cruiser swing in behind them, stop the cars, and place them under arrest. In Alabama, I knew that such a public display would most likely result in the man being beaten or killed.

New York was a point on the map, but I didn't truthfully know what I was looking for in the city. Besides economic independence, I seemed to possess a craving for something less tangible. Perhaps it was freedom from sitting in the back of buses and the humiliation of legalized segregation. But it was clear that there was separation in the so-called progressive North. There were no colored and white rest rooms, but when people laid down their heads at night to sleep, their neighbors would most likely mirror their own blackness, whiteness, or whatever subculture fit the bill. There was an informal segregation. The separateness was also mandated by economics. You could check into many New York hotels as long as you possessed the money to pay your tab at checkout time. But not that many Negroes could afford to stay in the fancier hotels. So, whereas limitations on blacks were enforced as law in Alabama, in New York, economic constraints helped contribute to a separation of the races that was not written in any musty legal book of codes.

Like a chameleon, I tried to exude an air of confidence and surliness to match the brash surroundings. Think tough, act

My father, Huell Jerome Stewart Sr.

My mother, Mattie C. Stewart

My maternal grandparents,
Willis and Emily Johnson

Me, age thirteen

SCHOOL DAYS 1952-53

My brother David Stewart,
1952

Me as a young man

Me and one big fat snake owne
by the band The Bar Keys

My brother Samuel Stewart as a young man

My brother Huell Jerome Stewart Jr.

Maurice King, me, Daisy Giddens, John Streeter and Jack Randall protesting at the WENN radio station in Birmingham

Zollie and Wilma Derryberry

The man on horseback is Zollie Derryberry (girls unknown)

Me with members of the Butts family, from my mother's side

**My childhood buddies
Boot and Brett**

**Brett again, with another
childhood friend Little Bubba**

**Plukey, another friend
from childhood**

President Jimmy Carter and me in 1979

Me and the beautiful
Gladys Knight

Me and Miss America,
Vanessa Williams

A family portrait of my aunt Estelle and my
uncle Douglas Stewart seated in front of
their daughter (my first cousin) Wynonna
Rhock and her son Hillary Rhock

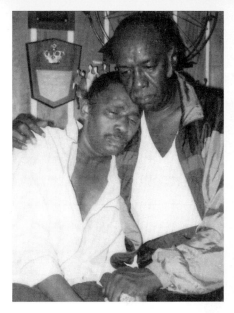

e and my nephews David Stewart Jr.
eft) and Huell Jerome Stewart *(right)*
the hospital bed of my brother David
tewart

Me and my brother Samuel only
two hours before he died

Front row/left to right: Councilwoman Antris Hinton, my aunts
Lonnie Mae Thomas and Odell Taylor next to the then mayor
of Birmingham Richard Arrington Jr.

Back row/left to right: Me, standing next to Councilman
William Bell

Me and Mayor Richard Arrington Jr. during the City of Birmingham Appreciation Day

Me and John Zimmerman, Chairman of 02 Ideas

Picture taken when I received my doctorate of Humane Letters from Miles College, Birmingham, Alabama

tough, and be tough. If I were perceived as a chump, a sucker, or a punk, there would be hell to pay in dealing with the streetwise patrons of the Big City. The education that a lot of these guys absorbed was from crash courses offered only in do-or-die classes taught on the thorny side of life. To walk in their territory, and survive, would mean juggling the thespian talents sharpened in the Playmakers back at Parker Industrial.

Ragged suitcase in hand and rumpled clothes covering my lean torso, I went into an old domicile called the Hotel Cecil. Women pasted into tight, short dresses with ample breasts peeking out from the semi-privacy afforded by plunging necklines meandered outside the hotel. I could only guess how they made a living in the neighborhood of working-class people, but I certainly didn't take them to be librarians. The hotel was managed by a nice-looking fellow with processed hair and neatly manicured nails named Leroy who agreed to get me a bed and room in the quarters. A small, barren room outfitted with a dresser was secured on the third floor of the hotel. I surmised that it had been a mop closet for the janitor in the recent past. The cost was twelve dollars a week.

At least now I had a roof over my head, but I needed to find a way to support myself and pay my rent. The women in tight dresses were ladies of the evening, I discovered. The Hotel Cecil boasted an around-the-clock procession of shopworn and battle-hardened prostitutes and their eager customers.

Leroy could see that I was not as sophisticated as I tried to seem. To help ensure that people would not treat me as a chump, he came up with a ruse. I was to tell everybody that I was on the lam for killing a white man down South. Anyone with such a reputation would not be jerked around and instead would be viewed as a hard-boiled character.

During our conversation, Leroy discovered that I could shoot pool. He got someone to cover the desk for him, and we went around the corner to a pool joint on 118th Street and Seventh Avenue. Leroy may have wanted to see if I was telling the truth about my skills, and he was probably also looking for an excuse to take a break from the hotel duties.

The pool hall was in a dreary-looking building that could have been a store at one time in its life. While the Rosedale pool hall contained three tables, this establishment contained about eight. Wooden benches around the walls allowed nonparticipants to watch or chat. Like the Alabama hangout, this place was frequented by men middle-aged and older. An amiable fellow named Johnny was the houseman for the hall, and he sat in a chair on an elevated platform that was about two and a half feet off the ground and six by six feet in diameter. Johnny was a tall light-skinned man with straightened hair that was called a "do," presumably short for hairdo. I told him that I was on the run for killing a white man down in Alabama, as Leroy had instructed.

"Lots of colored who have killed white folks come up here," said Johnny. "I came from Carolina, and I came damn close to whipping a white man to death for spitting in my mother's face. I changed my name, and I can't go back home. Are the rollers behind you?"

I told him I didn't think the police had my trail yet, but I couldn't be certain. The houseman tried to think of some way to get me settled into the community and start with a fresh slate.

"Can you shoot pool, Bama?" he asked. "Maybe I better not call you Bama since you're on the run. I'll just call you Country."

I affirmed that I could shoot since I had learned to play on Papa Clyde's table and had become skilled in a game of cut-throat, or eight ball. It was one of the simple pleasures of life that had helped occupy my leisure time in those days, and now I would conduct a demonstration. After racking the balls, I commenced to put on a show. Three ball in the side pocket. Five ball in the corner. Pretty soon I had knocked in every ball, which was called running the table.

"Man, Country is slick, a shark," said Johnny.

Johnny saw dollar signs and was enthused when he realized how skilled I was at the game. He developed a scheme with which we could both fatten our wallets. When a patron would wander in for some action, I would engage them since they would assume me to be a pushover because of my youth and Southern background. The strategy was to lose the first game, then offer to play for a dollar. I would then lose again, raise the stakes to five dollars, and gradually increase my skill level and start winning as the money pot mushroomed. When Johnny tapped me on the hand a couple of times or gave me some other signal, that meant it was time to go for the kill. The winnings might rise to twenty-five, fifty, a hundred, or two hundred dollars or more. And many bettors could afford it since a lot of the patrons were big-shot pimps.

It wasn't long before we got a chance to use the ruse. Johnny bankrolled me with a wad of cash to flash around. But looks were deceiving since all I had clutched in my hand were fifty $1 bills, three $5 bills, two $10 bills, and one $20 bill. The $20 bill was at the top of the stack and folded over the rest of the bills. The dollar bills were always at the bottom of the wad.

After racking the balls, I broke with the high ball instead of the Q-ball, which elicited a chorus of laughter from onlookers. Following our formula, I let the man win in a close game.

"Damn," I said. "My luck is bad."

The second game saw me go down to defeat again. However, I won the third game by a whisker. We raised the stakes to ten dollars, and the pigeon nibbled at the bait because he was confident he could recoup his losses. However, I won again, and we raised the stakes to twenty dollars with the fellow still salivating to retrieve his money. We ended up taking that twenty dollars and perhaps another before the guy gave up. Johnny issued me a cut of the winnings.

A while later another confident player came in, and I repeated the formula. At one point we raised the pot to twenty-five dollars, which of course I won.

"Hell," I said. "This is the last game 'cause I got to go pay my rent."

Of course, no opponent wants to know that you are about to walk out of the establishment with *his* money to pay *your* rent, and this makes him that much more hungry for revenge. We doubled the stakes to fifty dollars with the guy remembering that he had beaten me earlier and certain that my luck would run out and he would get his money back. I won again, and we doubled the money to a hundred dollars. He gave up after I took that loot. Johnny issued me my stake, which might amount to about ten or twelve dollars.

It wasn't like passing the Sunday school collection plate at Gaines Chapel A.M.E., but it was a survival tool that I could use until something better stumbled along. The funny thing about pool games was that some guys could not sleep at night for itching to come back the next day to avenge themselves. If any suspected that it was a hustle, their desire for vengeance apparently outweighed common sense. The pool hall characters were like the gunslingers of the Old West. A guy may have been a good pool player, but there was always someone better who was destined to come along and cut him down to size.

Rules of the pool room indicated that a hustler never hustled another hustler, just like a pimp never took advantage of another pimp. The place was a social hangout just like it was in Rosedale, where people could hear gossip in addition to showing off their skills on the table.

Soon I carved out a routine: Get up in the morning, eat breakfast at a soul food restaurant operated by a Chinese family, and then head to the pool room for a hustle. To blend in even further with the neighborhood, I found a fellow to conk or process my hair, which meant combing it with chemicals and pomade until it developed a straightened look. Johnny wore the style and so did Leroy, the hotel manager. It seemed to be a sign of hipness and suaveness. And we were in good company. Not only did run-of-the mill Negroes sport the look, but it was also popular among such luminaries as Nat King Cole and Sammy Davis Jr. Of course, this was before the days of the black racial pride movement of the 1960s and Afro or natural hairdos.

It was rare that you would hear someone say they had been born in New York. Besides plenty of transplanted Southerners, you, of course, found people with their roots snaking from all over the world chasing the scent of the same fleet-footed quarry—opportunity. Blocks and blocks of row houses contained a melange of ethnic pedigrees. In various sections of Harlem alone you would find Puerto Ricans, Cubans, and West Indians. On Sugar Hill there were middle- and upper-income Negroes. A person could literally move one block away and you would never see them again.

The simple differences between New York and Alabama were

glaring. Tenements did not lend themselves to porch sitting or raking yards. You could also ride a subway with newspapers that seemed to fit the environment. Unlike broad sheet papers, the smaller dimensions of tabloids like the *New York Daily News* allowed you to read them on the train without disturbing anyone else's personal territory. In New York City you did not invade people's parameters like you did in the South. Alabamians would most often speak when you saluted them on the street. In New York it wasn't kosher to gleefully ask somebody, "How are you doing?" If you did, they would look at you as if you were nuts or maneuvering for a favor, or worse.

After I spent a few days hustling, Count, a native North Carolinian who frequented the pool hall, told me about a room for rent in the boardinghouse in which he lived on 113th Street, a few blocks away. A tall, likable man who always wore a wide hat and drank from a bottle that bore the emblem of a snake on its label, Count assured me that the proprietor was a highly respected churchgoing lady named Josephine.

The house contained three bedrooms, a bath, dining room, and kitchen, but only the room and bath would be in the deal. I was introduced to the woman whom many called Sister Josephine because of her church involvement. A stout woman about sixty years old, she sported a slight trace of a West Indian accent, and a few strands of hair directed attention to her chin. Many days she could be seen pushing a basket and walking her small dog down the street to the market. We agreed upon a payment arrangement for the room, which was an improvement over the Hotel Cecil, and I moved in immediately.

The grayish-looking building was well kept and tidy. Pictures of the Virgin Mary holding the baby Jesus could be seen when you passed the door to Josephine's room, which was at the

front of the building. Candlelight radiated over a beautiful Bible
that rested on a coffee table in the hall. The room was very warm
since it only contained a skylight and no window. My door was
the only conduit for a fresh air current, so I opened it to catch a
breeze to relieve the stuffiness. I had not noticed that Josephine
was apparently prone to sitting in a chair on the front porch
looking out over 113th Street. After an afternoon's slumber, I
awoke to discover that the bed covering was lying aside and my
genitals were exposed. I am not sure if I had kicked the covers
off or if they had been removed, but I was embarrassed to real-
ize Josephine had a clear view of me from her vantage point on
the porch. I quickly closed the door to my room.

Later, after I had dressed, Josephine cooked a meal for me in
an undertaking that I knew was not part of my fee. The woman
disappeared while I was eating, but when she returned to the
room I was flabbergasted. She was now wearing a see-through
gown, no bra or underwear. The gray-haired woman then escorted me to her beautiful bedroom, which contained a huge
sofa, chairs, and a vanity mirror.

"I will take care of you, but I am going to have to have this,"
she said as she unzipped my trousers and threw them over a chair
and took off my shirt. Josephine then proceeded to perform oral
sex on me, an act that blew my mind. We progressed to the
world of full-fledged sin before the afternoon was over, and my
virginity was now a condition of the past. New York was now a
true turning point for a man who most girls had ridiculed over
the shame of poor teeth, hair, and hygiene. If only my Rosedale
School nemesis, Melvin Cook, could have seen me making love
with a woman possibly three times my age. He couldn't laugh at
me anymore, or could he?

"You don't have to pay any rent to me," said Josephine.

"Don't worry, I'll take care of you. You're mine. Can you drive? Maybe I'll buy you a car."

Her offer was beginning to sound like music to my youthful ears. A woman who could double as a surrogate mother was willing to give me my heart's desires as long as I stayed around as her play toy. The offer was almost too good to be believable, but there she was in all of her Caribbean, matronly splendor.

Josephine was true to her word and provided me with money and clothes. I went over to 125th Street and purchased stylish fashions in the form of nice slacks and shirts. Josephine always wanted me to make sure the pants were tight though. Although I knew some people would call me a gigolo, Josephine was getting the arrangement she requested. I was her lover in exchange for certain gifts. This wasn't the most noble endeavor, but it helped ensure survival in the predatory environment of New York.

The welfare of my brothers was always a concern throughout this time. But I felt that they were somehow better off than I was. After all, they could go up to almost any house in Rosedale at supper time and announce that they were hungry, and chances were they would be welcomed at the table. That warmth was not so obvious in the frenetic pace of New York.

With money on my mind, I sauntered down to Columbia Square to A-Good Employment Agency to find respectable labor. Broadly, I claimed that I was qualified to do most anything they had to offer. So the clerk came up with my first job outside of Alabama: Palace Metal Works in Brooklyn. I rode to the end of the IRT line and then walked about three miles before I arrived at the place where metal kitchen cabinets were produced. All I had to do was spray paint the items. Before it was over, however, the units looked like the work of some semi-talented, abstract artist. The curtain dropped astronomically fast on my Palace job.

But the A-Good people were indeed good. They dug up another endeavor for me at Anchor Plastics over on Long Island, which was an even longer IRT ride. The company made such items as straws and tubes for medicine. I graduated from cutting plastic to assisting in mixing chemicals by pouring granules into a hopper after supervisor Joe Dilby told the manager, a Mr. Fisher, that I was smart. Loot from the pool hall winnings and Anchor Plastics also permitted me to expand a flimsy wardrobe with new shoes, and Billy Eckstein shirts with rolled collars fleshed out my attire. Now I was even further, it seemed, from the days of wearing the Derryberry brothers' hand-me-downs.

The flamboyant Shelley who had his roots in the Parker High talent show and sack boy days at Yeilding's store was ideal for New York. I used the gregarious camouflage I had used on WEDR and WBCO radio shows in Birmingham, which had its inception in the pain and misery extracted from Mattie C.'s death, the beatings from relatives, and the subsequent homelessness. This personality would not be too slow for New York City. After all, that Shelley displayed a hip, devil-may-care kind of attitude, and what was New York City if not free spirited with a conformity-be-damned mind-set? The clubs and streets and pool halls were where I perpetrated, that is, pretended to be something that I was not. Cigarettes and social drinking were also props that I used in an act that hid the inherent immaturity of a nearly eighteen-year-old youth who toted around an incessant inner torment.

THE BRAND-NEW MINTON PLAYHOUSE was next door to the Hotel Cecil. Many afternoons I would drop by to catch a show.

All of the well-known jazz musicians and distinguished nationally known entertainers waltzed through at one time or another. It was nothing unusual to see Count Basie or Sammy Davis Jr. show up as a headline act at the place. And it was remarkable to see how whites like musician Louis Bellson, the man who was to marry singer Pearl Bailey, could mingle and be accepted among blacks at the playhouse. The city, for certain, had its prejudices and biases, but the contrast between New York's interracial mechanics and the strict segregation of the South was rather surprising.

Willie Bryant, known as the "mayor of Harlem," and Ray Carroll would broadcast live on radio station WHOM from the window of the Club Baby Grand on the corner of 125th Street near the Apollo Theater. Bryant was a mulatto who could easily pass for white if he had wished to do so. Carroll was a white man. This was the first time I had seen an integrated work operation. Some nights I would walk up to their booth and watch them at work in the hotel. They were incredulous when I related that I had been on the air at WBCO and WEDR in Alabama. The pair said Negroes were not allowed on the air down South, and decided to have some fun with me.

"Ladies and gentlemen, we got a country man, a farmer from Alabama, who wants to go on the air," Bryant told the listening audience.

The earphones fit comfortably on my head, and I leaned into the microphone and went into action.

"Hello, New York!" I bellowed with enthusiasm. "Now let me tell you something. If ya'll want to know how to do this thing, understand. Just take it easy g-r-e-a-s-y."

Carroll and Bryant were dumfounded as the country bumpkin pressed on with his patter.

"Hello, New York. My name is Bama from Bama. Aw-w-w let's go Harlem," I said smoothly as I introduced a record.

The phone started ringing urgently as listeners told the pair that whomever they had let on the air, "He sho' is bad!" The disc jockeys were impressed to the extent that they allowed me to sit in occasionally and do my own thing for a few minutes at a time. Now I was back in my natural element, and just the pure excitement of being on the air was cathartic and helped me to gel with the fast-paced, razzmatazz atmosphere of Harlem.

In the meantime I enrolled at the Cambridge School of Radio Broadcasting, a small outfit in downtown Manhattan. Classes consisted of using a control board and tape machine, and instruction was offered in news delivery and writing advertisement copy. The fee was twenty-five dollars, but the school's obligation was to place you in a job and you could pay the fee out of your salary. My radio experience impressed the instructors to the extent that I was allowed to coach other students on how to project their voices for broadcasts. Also, I shared my insights into the advertising axioms: introducing and selling the product; I tipped students on what ads would and would not sell in practice exercises. Another lesson learned, at least for me, was that the South did not possess an exclusive lock on bigotry. This happened when a student blurted that he did not take the class to be taught by a person of my racial heritage. The insult did not infuriate me because I did not figure that his words diminished me as an individual.

Young women my age caught my eye at the Club Savoy, which featured jazz great Sonny Thompson. The club contained a bar about thirty-five or forty feet long on one side of the room and another one half that size on the opposite wall. Huge lights shaped like balls hung from the ceiling. Women in provocative dresses carried themselves in a manner different from Southern women. These New York women were more aggressive and didn't mind approaching a man they found attractive or interesting. Just looking at the females only magnified the situation I was in with Josephine, a woman I was ashamed to take out dancing.

Casual drinking, smoking, and flirting consumed most of my time in the club. I became proficient at performing dance steps like the jitterbug and the camel walk, and integrated dances from down South into my routine. All of this amounted to projecting an air of false bravado. It was an art that you had to learn and was similar to the ability to stand down on the road in Rosedale and shoot the bull.

A predisposition toward acting as reflected in my venture with the Parker Playmakers probably helped me establish the facade. For instance, in the club the less you said, the more attention you drew to yourself, and you were never so conspicuous as to stare at the women or even the bright lights and thereby betray your naïveté. Usually I would smoke a cigarette, buy a few drinks, and strike a certain pose to suggest confidence and awareness. And one thing you learned was you never asked a guy where he had been; it opened up too many dangerous possibilities, and most New Yorkers kept their lives to themselves anyway. Sometimes I would inquire into the whereabouts of a particular dude for the hell of it or to make it seem like I was really in the thick of the action.

I became familiar with the lingo that separated the hip from the parochial. For instance, I knew that if a fellow had a "piece of wood" that meant he had a Fleetwood Cadillac. The guys also had another saying: "If you are rich and want to get poor, get yourself a '49 Ford and a no-good whore. If you are poor and want to get rich, sell the car and make sure you get rid of the bitch." Often, to enhance the charade of being a hip Harlem swinger, I would mimic other guys. Sometimes, when I prepared to leave the bar, I would say, "I've got to go check my traps." This was parlance for a pimp checking in on prostitutes or a hustler checking on the progress of a scam. Most of the time I would excuse myself and merely jump on the subway to downtown Manhattan and go sightseeing.

However, not all of the talk in the club was dripping with underworld connotations. Many people were in the establishment discussing legal business deals. Others were talking about wonderful husbands and wives or exchanging details about love affairs that would have been better left unspoken.

On one excursion to the club my adventure lasted until the early hours of the morning. When I glimpsed Josephine standing in the window as I exited the cab, I knew I was in for a cat-fight.

"I should just blow your goddamn brains out," she shrieked, waving a revolver in my face as I approached her door. "You ain't gonna take my money and hang out with those bitches."

Smothering my fear, I stood my ground as she ranted the chant of a woman scorned.

"You don't know who the hell I am! I cut a man's throat. Here it is in the paper. And I didn't serve a day in jail for it either."

Sure enough, the yellowed newspaper substantiated her claims in 42-point Bodoni type. Her name was listed as the assailant in a domestic incident of a few years earlier in which a man's throat had been sliced. To take the wind out of her sails, I told her that there were women at the Savoy, of course, but that I had just spent my time grooving on the music and didn't leave with anyone, which was the truth.

The next day, when Josephine stepped out for a while, I gathered my belongings and moved away from her possessive grasp.

I had met a fellow on Seventh Avenue named Ike Phyall who worked as a dishwasher for the Hotel Theresa, which was where Cuban premier Fidel Castro would stay when he visited Harlem in the early 1960s. Ike, who had a penchant for good, cheap wine, told me about a vacancy at 2076 Seventh Avenue above a restaurant and bar owned by Sugar Ray Robinson, who was then the middle-weight champ of the world. The front room over the bar was available since no one liked it because of the noise from the tavern below.

After moving into the quarters, I discovered I had a front-row seat to gawk at the big-shot personalities who frequented the place. Sometimes I would holler out the window at Sugar Ray or his driver, Little Johnny, who chauffeured the champ around in a pink Cadillac. Johnny was no celebrity, but he wore a certain glamour by association. But bona fide celebrities did drop by, like Pearl Bailey, her fiancé, musician Louis Belson, and singer Sarah Vaughn. These were people whom I had only read about in magazines or heard on the radio before I hit New York. Sometimes I surrendered to the impulse and mingled with the crowd like I did at the Club Savoy and the Minton Playhouse.

I had perfected my social skills to the extent that I even crashed a party for Pearl Bailey and Louis Belson at the Birdland Club in Manhattan. A few hearty but phony salutations like "How ya been doing?" and "I haven't seen you for a while" made the most complete strangers think that I was a forgotten acquaintance. The ability to converse on many levels, thanks in part to a proclivity for reading, helped me to fit in with the conversations at the club just like I had done at the Club Savoy.

A growing respect began to emanate from the people in both clubs. Sometimes people would ask me about my opinion on some issue with a question like, "Hey Bama, what do you think?" Oftentimes the conversational clamor along the bar would drop to almost a hushed silence as other patrons listened for my answer. This, of course, made me feel good and boosted my ego. A fellow who was taunted because of his clothes and hygiene at Irondale, Parker, and Rosedale schools was now associating with the so-called beautiful crowd. I would have been tickled if some of my old school detractors could have caught a glimpse of my new environment. The irony of the situation was not unappreciated.

But the moment I departed from the clubs, I faced the same loneliness and depression that was a constant companion for me. No one in the establishments suspected that I cried privately every day because I was starved for love and a sense of family. Daily, without fail, I would ask my mother if I was following the proper course about matters large and small. "Mama," I said, "what am I supposed to do? I know you are with God and with me too." Her presence offered solace and cushioned me from the pain that flowed from the secular world around me.

Count, the pool hall patron, introduced me to his sister, a woman named Vera who lived in an apartment up on 145th Street in Sugar Hill, a middle-income black community. This woman, like Josephine, was my senior but only by several years. She was built like a high-salaried model, although she actually only worked in the Manhattan garment district. I'm not sure what she saw in me, but I moved in with her at her request and continued my shift at Anchor Plastics. Our agreement was that

I would bring her my check from the plant and she would buy groceries and dole out my allowance of five dollars a week. Why I agreed to such humiliation is enigmatic; perhaps it satisfied my need for a feeling of domestic life.

About five or six weeks into this arrangement I came home one evening to find our apartment door latched. Vera shouted through the door that a nearby box in the hall contained my clothes.

"You don't live here no more," she yelled from the other side of the closed door.

I reminded her that I had faithfully turned over my check and had given up a perfectly good room above Sugar Ray's place at her coaching. Her whole behavior was stupefying and aggravating. Women were still a novelty for me, and perhaps I just didn't understand their workings, then being only eighteen and having been deflowered a few months earlier by Josephine. Apparently, she had squirreled away parts of my Anchor Plastics paychecks and had no more use for me. The whole scenario made me livid with anger.

"I don't give a damn about your money," she said. "You don't live here no more. And get away from my door with all that noise."

Someone was walking up the apartment steps as the scene played itself out. Vera had called the police, unbeknownst to me, and two hulking New York City officers rode up to the place where I stood in the hall like a wounded deer. She informed them that I was trying to break into the dwelling she had shared with me. Despite my protests and that I had only a dollar in my pocket, the policemen sided with her and ordered me out into the chilled night air with a cardboard box full of belongings.

A gentle snow had begun to caress the New York streets as I gathered my shattered senses and hopped on the IRT for a ride with no special destination in mind. I stayed on the subway all night long, and the rumble of the cars along the track evolved into what audiologists call white noise, a bland background of vibrations bouncing off my frigid eardrums.

The New York trip was not really what my mother had wanted me to do, and now I was paying for my disobedience with a failed relationship and more unhappiness to add to my usual malaise. Ideas about rewards and punishment, death and redemption flowed through my mind. Again I thought, like I had in Papa Clyde's basement, about my mother's crucifixion at the hands of my father when he knocked her into the pecan tree, and my own near crucifixion at the cruel hands of Aunt Emily. Now I was suffering again, but this time as the immediate result of a fractured romantic relationship and, in a larger sense, because I had rejected the inner voice that had always guided me. What would I do now—leave New York and admit that I had failed to conquer the Big City? Lyrics to an old spiritual that has become one of my favorites came to me: "There's something within me that holdeth the rain. There's something within me that banishes the pain. There's something within me that I cannot explain. All that I know is that there is something within."

At daybreak I was instructed off the train by a conductor and toted my bag and brooding to ground level. I noticed a group of men walking into a shelter on Broadway in Manhattan and followed them to the respite offered by a hot meal and cot, which allowed me to contemplate my options.

Here I was again seeking refuge like I had done in Stringfellow Stables and Papa Clyde's basement. I knew my life had not changed appreciably since I had left those earlier environs except that now I had a high school degree and my law school dream had been shattered, but I could boast modest experience with women. Here I was in the company of men down on their luck and struggling with their own failures and deep disappointments. How long, I thought, had they been slipping and sliding along on the paths of life without a solid foothold on financial, emotional, or mental stability? Would I become a permanent denizen of shelters in my mission to make something of myself and show Principal Montgomery that he was wrong about cheating me of the scholarship? The abuse at the hands of my father, stepmother, and aunt was awful enough. Now my mental distress had been increased thanks to my own ignorance about the wiles of a particular woman and because I apparently did not follow the wishes of Mattie C., who was somewhere in a superior yet spiritual dimension.

All along I knew that there was no future at Anchor Plastics. Radio was closer to my heart, but I did not want to raise the suspicions of Bryant and Carroll at WHOM by hanging around the broadcast booth too much. I worried that the tale I had let spread about my fugitive status would catch up with my boast to the disc jockeys that I was a big-shot radio personality in Alabama, and the result would be a catastrophe for me. The story had achieved such credibility that a policeman in Harlem had sidled up to me one day and said, "We know who you are." He then admonished me to keep my nose clean so that the New York law would not have to jail me for any local offense that would uncover my identity as a murderous fugitive.

It seemed I had been exploited by Josephine, by Johnny the pool room maestro, and by Vera. In the case of Josephine and Johnny, the action may have been two-way since in the first in-

stance I was receiving free board and in the second I was bene-
fiting from the pool hustle. But how could I have been so
gullible to have been used by Vera? Of course, I was naive, but
to be smacked in the face with the truth was almost too much to
bear. Sometimes the swirling torrents of rage taunted me to go
back and kick her door in and confront her face-to-face. But reason won the match by a millimeter. A hard lesson of life had
come my way about how people can use each other. Maybe I
wasn't much better with the pool hustle I had run, but no one
had put a gun to those suckers' heads.

The next morning I began wandering the snow-swept streets
again and continued to do so all day, steaming mad inside because I had been jilted, and chilled outside by the northern air.
My choices began to come into focus. Josephine would probably
have welcomed me back. And the world of pool hustling, pimp-
ing, gambling, or even thievery was at my fingertips. No scholarship was in my grasp, and law school aspirations had been
exposed as a pipe dream. That was to have been the tool with
which I would work to navigate the system on the legitimate
side. But when one avenue is suppressed, others, more dishonest
and less conventional, seem to grow in seductiveness. It would
have been easy to be like the has-beens at Ratkiller's Shoeshine
Parlor—men who had let tidy, illegal fortunes slip through their
hands like grains of sand washing away from an Atlantic Ocean
sandbar. In Harlem I had even happened across the three guys in
the sporty car that I had met in Rosedale. Their success had
made me want to dive into the New York bustle and find my
own riches. However, it turned out these fellows were actually
gangsters who had accumulated their material success using underhanded techniques.

That dimly lit road of unethical enterprises was not really

my bag, and pool hustling aside, I could not walk any deeper into the shadows of the underworld. Signing checks on the front as boss of my own company remained a motivation, and I certainly wasn't doing that at Anchor Plastics. I knew I had to maneuver toward a more constructive lifestyle, something that would make Mattie C. proud and provide real income to improve the stations of Sam, David, and myself.

As night fell, I ended up back at the shelter where men were packed as tightly as in a nineteenth-century slave ship crossing the sea from Africa to the Americas. Lying on a cot, I considered who I might contact for help, but that would be extra difficult in view of the fact that it was a Saturday night and the snow had made travel messy. If only there was someone who could rescue me like I had done for my brothers. Mama was there in a spiritual sense, but no person was available in the physical realm. Another night in the shelter gave me an answer to the quandary. Monday morning I walked down to Columbus Circle and saw a billboard inviting guys to join the air force and proceeded to the air force recruiting office to enlist.

In that fall and winter of 1952 the Korean War still churned as the U.S. poured men and munitions into the effort. Bubba was among the million-plus U.S. casualties, but I was not going into the military to avenge his death. I went for a sense of security. The mental aptitude test to weed out misfits was only a formality. I was to proceed to Maxwell Air Force Base in Montgomery, Alabama, and afterward head to basic training at Lackland Air Force Base in San Antonio, Texas.

Riding on the L&N Railroad's Hummingbird for Maxwell via Birmingham, I licked my wounds and assessed my maturation. Somehow, during those six months in New York, I had crammed knowledge that would have taken years to accumulate and process if I had stayed in Rosedale. All in all, I was walking away from my first months in Harlem with gems of knowledge about life that I would never have gotten if I had won that college scholarship to Tuskegee or Howard College. The Cambridge School of Broadcasting was a pleasant diversion, but I was more knowledgeable than most of those in the classes and ended up acting as an adjunct instructor and was leaving New York before I could see what type of job the school could help me obtain. But the "University of Harlem" represented my freshman year in the school of life, and I would have to give myself a good mark for riding the flow of the city's tempo, surviving the place, and not ending up mortally wounded and bobbing facedown in the Hudson River. For every experience engaged, we should walk away more refined and erudite, if not more polished. Now I was more discerning about human personality and the quirks and foibles and deficiencies that lie under the surface of civility and decency, hidden but ready to scramble forth to inflict damage to the psyche.

CHAPTER NINE

The Stockade Shuffle

THE L&N HUMMINGBIRD spirited me back below the Mason-
Dixon Line and into Terminal Station in downtown Birmingham. I did not feel compelled to go over the mountain into
Rosedale and look up my brothers since I had not really made it
big yet. Nancy's Hotel was around the corner from the air force
recruiting office so I took a room there. I was going to serve my
country and gather enough dollars for the three of us to have
economic stability. Hopefully, this would be the beginning of a
better life for the Stewart boys. They were the only family to
which I felt close. They did not know everything about the way
the wheels turned inside my mind, but they had at least a superficial understanding of my personality because of our shared
heritage on Slim and Marie's back porch.

Uncle Sam was willing to shell out seventy-two dollars a
month to help me achieve a solid bedrock for long-term survival
for all of us. Hopefully, this military venture would finally allow
me to send money home to them, something I was not able to
do in New York since my Anchor Plastics paychecks and pool-
hustling money were barely enough for me to survive on and,
during one period, were being managed by the exploitive girlfriend Vera.

After a bus trip to Maxwell near Montgomery, and more paperwork, we recruits flew into Lackland. We arrived about 3 A.M. and were herded into barracks. Out of a few dozen recruits, only about six were black. Dozens of male strangers laid down to sleep under the same roof as if we were a tribal family. It seemed that we had no sooner transversed the realm of deep sleep than a thunderous commotion raced through the building like the German blitzkrieg.

"All right, you sons of bitches. Get your sorry asses up," a voice thundered. "I'm not your mama or your daddy. And I'm sure not your girlfriend so don't try to screw me."

Rising up in my bunk, I directed a reply to the barracks interloper, who stood ramrod straight in his starched uniform, with scowling face and furrowed brow topped off by the requisite military cap.

"Man, you better shut up that damn noise," I said, disoriented and clueless about the identity of the circus barker.

The other guys were scrambling out of their bunks as I lay there. Simultaneously, the man strutted over to the cot where I lay prone and thrust his nose within an inch of my own.

"I'm gonna court-martial you. Don't you know who I am?" he said.

His identity was of no major concern to me, and I warned him that his dogged intrusion in the barracks was bound to trigger a tooth-and-claw fight between the two of us.

"I'm gonna break you down!" he yelled, as images of Aunt Emily spewing the same declaration at me in Rosedale, Alabama, more than a decade earlier galloped forth. Animal instincts ordered me to retaliate, but it dawned on me that I was now in the organized, disciplined world of the U.S. Air Force, and not on the streets of Birmingham or Harlem. So I informed the sergeant that I felt he could address me in a more respectable manner.

We all ended up outside the barracks with the sergeant steaming mad and nipping at our heels like an angry Rottweiler. This keystone cops routine seemed like a wake-up call for fraternity boys stumbling through pledge week. But this frat boy was here to stay, no matter what the dude with ill manners, Sergeant Smith, had in mind.

Among the first items on the day's itinerary was marching to the mess hall for chow and then over to a building for hair styling. The air force barbers cordially asked each man how he wanted to be trimmed. Everyone had their particular style: take a little off the top and close around the sides, or easy on the sideburns, for instance. But everyone, to a man, climbed out of the chair with the same scalped, military buzz cut.

The Lackland base planned to work on us like the Sloss Furnaces and Tennessee Coal and Iron plants back in Birmingham processed iron and steel; a raw material went into the place, but, under optimum circumstances, a more resilient, valuable product would be belched from the factory. We drilled, learned rules and regulations, and did push-ups and calisthenics until we dreamed about them.

The air force was our family now, and Sergeant Smith, although he professed not to be our mama or daddy, came close to filling those roles for a lot of us. At one point I even related to him the miseries of my early childhood, including my mother's death, the beatings, and life in the horse stable. Sergeant Smith, to my astonishment, broke down and started weeping before we both dropped to our knees for a word of prayer; apparently his shrill military bark was worse than his human bite. I understood that the sergeant merely was doing his duty with his rough talk and insults, and I discovered I had made an impression on Smith that drifted beyond the rocky moments of our first encounter on the base. He took me aside one day and said that because of my six-foot-three height and my intelligence I would make a good leader. Every squad wanted to be the best in drills and overall performance, and I had already told Smith that I thought our unit was capable of distinction. He began to allow me to lead the men as we marched from the exercise yard or other areas on the base.

"Lift your head and hold it high. Flight two thirty-two is passing by! Honey, baby, now!" we chanted as we marched in step.

The blacks incarcerated for various infractions would entertain themselves with what was called the stockade shuffle. It was a colorful form of marching in which enlistees would lift or kick their legs high and move their arms in an exaggerated fashion as if they were digging at the air with a shovel and using skill that a seasoned Broadway trouper might envy. Conceivably this bit of choreography alluded to work on an old-fashioned Southern chain gang. Sometimes, in our leisure hours, black airmen who weren't captive would engage in the dance to help defeat the tedium of the prisonlike environment.

After I had led several drills and was, in effect, squad leader, there were grumblings among some of the white airmen. During a confrontation in the barracks, a Caucasian from the South told me that where he came from, all blacks did was mop the floors and were lynched when they got out of place, and he wasn't about to take orders from the likes of me. Before I was aware of my actions, I'd decked the guy, and his pals rushed forth, as did an equal number of Negro airmen. Fists started flying. The air force police came running into the barracks to break up the scuffle and inquire about its roots.

"That guy called me a nigger," I said.

"Well, you are a nigger," the AP said. "Now hit me."

Of course, since he was wearing a sidearm, it would have

been useless to test the officer. Besides, I knew I could beat the system in other ways.

In late 1952 and early 1953 the military was just becoming visibly integrated but was still noticeably bowing to the god of segregation. President Harry Truman had signed Executive Order 9981 on July 26, 1948, establishing a policy of equal opportunity for the armed forces with no regard to race, color, religion, or national origin. But, like the Emancipation Proclamation, it was several years before words evolved into tangible results that could be seen and experienced by everyday folks.

The air force was still very segregated, although the Korean War was greasing the wheels for the use of more black personnel in combat units. But it was known that no matter how well Negroes did on the aptitude or skills test, they more often ended up in lower-status "black" jobs. It was rare for Negroes to have clerical positions; they were more likely to be confined to the supply service or to the motor pool as laborers rather than as mechanics. Frequently they were relegated to kitchen patrol or latrine duty. Several black career men, I noticed, still did not wear any stripes on their sleeves after seven or eight years in the service. Also, there was little entertainment for blacks unless they possessed a taste for country music.

I began to question the fairness of the whole setup at Lackland (which was most likely a microcosm of the military); it undermined the widely espoused U.S. principles of democracy. Negro activist was not the label I was pursuing, but I felt like this was a human rights issue. The conditions at the base seemed to diminish the noble principles for which America had been established. After all, my brother Bubba had lost his life in Korea at the hands of a sniper, defending the concepts of freedom. Air force recruiters had promised me that the military had no tolerance for bias and discrimination.

Military officials said that I would have to go to school at Francis E. Warren Air Force Base in Cheyenne, Wyoming, after boot camp in order to qualify for a trade specialty. After six weeks at Lackland, I was transferred to Warren, where the training schools were packed and I had to wait for a slot to become available. Of course, I persisted in being vocal about the jobs to which blacks were assigned, promotion limitations, and the scarcity of entertainment. In the meantime I was still sending money back to Rosedale each week in care of David. Neither brother was doing anything consequential; they engaged in odd jobs such as caddy work at the Hillcrest Country Club, so the money was sorely needed.

At Warren I was an assistant day clerk in the orderly room. This involved keeping track of airmen's records and their whereabouts on the base. For this work I received a high evaluation. A gruff sergeant told me I had gotten the job partially because the brass wanted to keep an eye on me. Some blacks asked me why I would not leave well enough alone and stop bellyaching about post conditions, and a middle-aged Negro sergeant tried to persuade me not to rock the boat. The man was the personification of Harriet Beecher Stowe's Uncle Tom character. Whites would regularly tell insulting, slur-filled jokes in his presence, and he seemed to make a point of laughing loudest of all at the demeaning punch lines. Needless to say, his admonition to me was ignored.

The incident that brought me to the attention of the brass was a USO dance. Since our social needs were ignored, I decided to gather a bunch of black airmen and proceed to the base affair. We went against a major ancient U.S. social taboo when we danced with some of the white women in attendance. This, of course, raised eyebrows among many of the white airmen. I was showing the same spirit of defiance that I had displayed when I moved the board on the segregated streetcar against the driver's wishes back on the Number 22 Boyles/Tarrant City line in Collegeville.

It wasn't long before I was summoned to see the base commander, a colonel. He asked me my views of the base and, believing that he was earnest, I told him I did not feel the black airmen were receiving a fair shake. Also, I shared my past including the events surrounding my mother's death and my own abuse. The colonel wanted to know if I had ever received a psychiatric evaluation, which of course I had not. A few days later I was ordered to report to the base hospital. A psychiatrist asked me about my life and the operations at Warren. According to the physician, I seemed to possess excessive anger against whites and asked an inordinate number of questions. His assessment was that I was deeply depressed and ordered that I be admitted for electric shock therapy, or EST.

"No other coloreds are asking all these questions," he said. "Maybe this treatment will calm you down."

The words did not particularly alarm me because I had never heard of electric shock therapy. When I asked if I had a choice, I was told that I was government property, and subsequently my wishes did not matter. In the mental ward there were airmen who were apparently veterans of combat in Korea, but I had no idea if their demons were war related or flowing from some other secret, malicious torment.

The next morning I was placed in a wheelchair and taken into a room in which there were five or six hospital personnel. The white-coat-wearing employees then jumped into a ritual that they carried out with familiar efficiency. Straps were placed on my arms and legs. After this a salvelike material was smeared on the sides of my temple and on my ankles. Then they produced contraptions that radiated the cold sensation of metal touching skin, which they attached to my head and lower limbs. Suddenly, I squirmed in apprehension of the unfathomable busywork undertaken by the nameless individuals.

"Wait a minute," admonished an orderly as two large men fell across my legs and my abdomen, respectively. "You are not going to remember anything."

The psychiatric ward crew forced my mouth open and inserted an object that was to keep me from biting or swallowing my tongue, I presume. Within seconds a searing pain rippled through my head as the voltage surged through my body. Now I knew what it was like to be sent to the electric chair. But the differences were a matter of logistics. In the Warren Air Force Base hospital, I was lying prone instead of sitting upright, and the voltage was mercifully less than that used in capital punishment.

Throbbing pain danced around my head for hours after each EST session. Apparently, the voltage was increased after each treatment. Back in the ward, I talked with a pleasant, well-spoken Negro airman who said he had been receiving the same treatments for months. He said he did not know why he was subjected to his electric shocks, but he felt that it was an inhumane tactic being used in a civilized culture. I discovered that I was no lone ranger in my protest against bias in the military. A few other black airmen were in the hospital ward receiving EST and other treatments because ostensibly they had not "adjusted" to life in the service. But the real reason, I surmised, was to silence our voices raised in an effort to rock the military's boat.

The doctor returned and asked me how I was feeling, but my gut told me the query was more rhetorical than sincere. He stated that I was bordering on schizophrenia and that I had to dismiss my dreary childhood and learn to accept life for what it was. Also, he inquired if my views had changed, if I now realized that I had probably imagined the unfair treatment of blacks on the base and the inadequacies in the system.

The words of Clyde's stepdaughter, Mary Sue, floated into my consciousness from a decade earlier to augment my stand. "Shurley," she said, "if you know you are right, don't let anyone tell you you're wrong." Views I had the day before were still embedded in my thoughts, I said. Problems for Negroes did exist, and it would not do any good to pretend to have altered my beliefs.

Consequently, the doctor scheduled me to be brought to the room every other day until I completed the first twelve-session series. After a week's intermission, a second series was executed. Another followed that group, which meant I had been "electrocuted" thirty-six times.

At no time did I feel that I deserved the treatment I was receiving, and I knew full well that I was not mentally ill. The device of electric shock was clearly an expression of the power of the military to do as it wished with its personnel. It seemed that the continuum of torture was persisting. I had been hung up and whipped by Emily, and now I was beset with this sadism. In the first sense I was my aunt's possession to be abused, and in the second, I was the government's property for misuse. Whether my treatment was at the hands of an individual or the establishment, both experiences smacked of evil manipulation and a twisted desire for dominance.

I was later shipped to Geiger Air Force Base in Spokane, Washington, and was given the job of handling records for F86-D fighter planes. I had to log key information about fuel use and flight time. For a man who supposedly needed shock treatment, this job seemed to be mighty responsible. Also, I accepted the bet of a sergeant who said I could not launch the idle base radio station. Using my skills from Birmingham and New

York, I simply went into the studio, dusted everything off, turned the microphones on, and began broadcasting. The same white sergeant later was given a promotion and placed in charge of the station.

At Geiger I corralled the Negroes to go to a dance where we ended up dancing with white women again. Halfway through one song the music suddenly stopped and everyone was told that the evening had drawn to a close. I knew that we had challenged old mores again, but I was also aware that all whites were not hung up on miscegenation. A white airman at Geiger had invited a black fellow to go out for the evening with him and his girlfriend plus a blind date. The date turned out to be a white female. Nevertheless, there was enough anxiety raised in the dance hall for the music to die that night.

The Spokane City Club was a ritzy, exclusive establishment downtown. I happened by one afternoon and asked two waiters outside about possible employment. Since they eyed me as a dubious candidate for work, I coaxed them to let me audition. After answering their questions on the makeup of various entrees, I put on an exhibition using my Jack-O-Lantern skills of loading trays and balancing them in the air as I walked ramrod straight across the dining room floor. After I was hired, the funds I accumulated from the few evenings' work was useful and added to the pot of money that I could share with Sam and David.

It was while working at the club that my right leg started to radiate pain. When I reported to the Geiger base hospital, my records were retrieved and the prior shock treatment was noted by a physician. His diagnosis was that the pain was the aftermath from the large attendant lying across my legs trying to keep me still during the EST. The doctor then committed me to the hospital's psychiatric ward. This was quite a surprise since I had only gone there to inquire about leg pain. I suspect this was a chance to further silence me that the base officials could not pass up.

I strengthened my resolve that I would not let the hand of the military break my spirit. If I was government property, I would still be my own man. The officials who hatched the scheme to torture me with my first shock treatments and now committed me to a mental facility were not living the ideals of the forefathers who breathed a spirit of freedom in the U.S. Constitution and helped set the tone for America as a beacon of liberty. But I vowed the aberration of the shock treatment would not destroy me; that which does not annihilate only makes the individual stronger and more determined, and this was my reaction to the EST.

Magazines like *Life* and *Look* never showed up in the psychiatric ward, which left me with a void. An empathetic nurse began bringing in books for me after I told her about my craving for literature. After observing me for a while, she ventured that I seemed out of place. That was a welcome opinion, and I urged her to tell the hospital officials her views. Her reply was direct: "You want to see me end up in this place?"

The next stop was Madigan General Hospital at the army's Fort Lewis in Tacoma, Washington, where I remained in the psychiatric ward. By the summer of 1954 I had settled into the limbo of the mental hospital. In early August I received word that Slim Stewart had died at age forty-six on the first day of the month. I would learn from his death certificate that alcohol poisoning was the blame. During his final days, I discovered, a friend had taken him to a voodoo doctor in Rosedale in an effort to slow his inevitable demise. This was the man who had helped precipitate so much inner angst, and his passing barely disturbed me. I was filled with neither sadness nor joy at his death but something more akin to indifference.

The air force released me for the funeral, and I was to proceed to Eglin Air Force Base after the furlough. The first leg of the journey was a plane ride from nearby Fairchild Air Force Base to Chanute Air Force Base outside of Chicago. A bus ride took me to Chicago where I was to board the Hummingbird for Birmingham. As I put one foot on the train steps, however, thoughts of Mattie C.'s death tiptoed out of the recesses of my memory as well as images of the beatings and the fried rats. I backed away from the train, turned and walked down the street to a liquor store, and purchased a pint of whiskey. A nearby flophouse provided a respite where I checked in and drank myself to sleep.

Slim Stewart had been in the ground a full day by the time I arrived in Birmingham. I resided with the Bullard family in Rosedale and tracked down Sam and David. David was still staying with Miss Pearlie, and Sam had been gravitating between different Rosedale households after getting fed up with Emily, who still lived in Sterrett in the house we had started building. I scouted out WEDR and told the manager that I would probably be out of the service soon and was told the station could use me.

At the end of the ten-day furlough, I headed to Eglin Air Force Base where I was admitted to the mental ward. After a few days, a psychiatrist who was second in command of the unit came by to discuss my records. He revealed that I had been labeled "chronic schizophrenic—severe." A thoughtful man, he told me I did not fit the criteria for the diagnosis and deduced that the U.S. Air Force had dealt me a bad hand in their bureaucratic poker game. To free me from the pernicious sport, he stated that he would recommend that I be released from the service with a medical discharge under honorable conditions. Uncle Sam and I were going our separate ways after eighteen months of cat-and-mouse shenanigans.

The military experience deposited a sense of ambiguity in my soul. Enlistment in the air force wasn't bad if you considered the escape it provided for an Alabama youth bent on assembling some well-needed cash. Butting my head against the air force establishment also served to cultivate my give-'em-hell, say-what-you-will radio style to a greater degree. If you could take on the air force, with its entrenched attitudes and operations, you could tackle anybody. But the shock treatment was grossly unfair to me, and the general bias was eminently unfair to everyone, including the air force since it cheated itself of the talents and skills of people who happened to be black. Since those days, I presume, the military has gone on to take the lead in making itself an inclusive branch of government.

CHAPTER TEN

Timber! Let It Fall!

Birmingham HAD A REPUTATION as an entertainment center in the 1950s, and the black business district around Fourth Avenue North downtown was considered a mecca for leisure. It was nothing for Atlanta blacks to ride the train to Birmingham, see the fantastic Birmingham Black Barons play ball, and go to clubs and restaurants downtown. Also, three black-oriented radio stations in the metropolitan area—WBCO in Bessemer, as well as WEDR and WJLD in the city center—contributed to the glamour.

By 1954 I was ready for another stab at Birmingham and its radio market. After my rocky tenure in the U.S. Air Force, I returned to WEDR, AM 17.50, in the Forniss Building downtown (where I had worked in my high school days) and talked to Ed Estes, the station manager. Pursuant to the conversation we had had when I was on furlough for Slim's funeral, he dangled a thirty-five-dollars-a-week job, which I quickly accepted. The station bosses crafted a 12 noon to 1 P.M. daily show, and I poured my energy into the flippant, bombastic character that served as a disguise for the tortured, grief-stricken individual who wept every night in the seclusion of his room.

"Good googly-woogly! . . . Timber! Let it fall! . . . I'm hurting you, baby!" I groaned into the microphone. Even though I was back on the air, and harbored a grudging affection for the broadcasting craft, tucked away in my ultimate heart was the desire to be more than a performer or showman. I had watched Papa Clyde wheel and deal in his enterprises as a developer, restaurateur, and motel owner. And Earl Stringfellow, the stable owner, directed his own operation with smooth efficiency. The moral of their stories was that it would be more rewarding to be the driver of the bus than the passenger. Station ownership was my ultimate goal, but I knew I had to crawl around the airwaves before I could walk over them as a master.

WEDR was superb as a source of income, but economics dictated that I still needed to supplement my paycheck with a second hustle. I found work as an elevator starter at Newberry's Department Store in the heart of downtown at Third Avenue North and Nineteenth Street. A starter was not the same as an elevator operator, most of whom were black women. Newberry's, like many Southern department stores and businesses, designated the freight elevator for the use of Negro customers, although whites would sometimes ride if the other compartments were full. Starters essentially directed the customers to both the freight and passenger elevators. Sometimes, he would take command of compartments when the regular operator was on a break. The showmanship I had sculpted through mock sermons as a preacher in Papa Clyde's basement and as a sack boy at Yeilding's paid off again in my job as a starter.

"Step right up, ladies and gentlemen," I stated in carnival barker fashion. "On the first floor you'll find . . ." The names of merchandise rolled off my tongue in staccato fashion as I indexed items such as women's and children's clothes, shoes, jewelry, and whatever else was featured in the store inventory.

"Watch your step, please," I would say, with more than a hint of theatrics.

After cranking out an hour's shift, I would dash out of the store for the 12 to 1 P.M. program on WEDR, which was about five blocks away on Fourth Avenue North between Fourteenth and Fifteenth Streets. Sometimes my introductory music would be playing as I slid in the door, simultaneously shifting personalities for the program.

"Timber! Let it fall . . . The mighty burner is here," I roared and proceeded to raise the devil with my antics.

People certainly must have wondered who the hell that crazy dude was on the radio. I would do stuff no one else had done, such as read mail on the air. I developed the ability to introduce a record with such fervor and intensity that the listening audience might imagine that the artist was crooning from the studio control room itself. An appeal to women was essential to my modus operandi. I reasoned that once I lured the females into the web of listeners, the men would follow. Consequently, much of my radio banter was peppered with flirtatious come-ons.

"Hey b-a-a-by, how you doing, b-a-a-by . . . Talk about it, baby . . . Hey sweetheart," I would purr suggestively.

Empathy with the plight of black women was paramount. While I coached black men to step up to the plate of community leadership, I would acknowledge that finding a man with a decent job might be difficult. The overwhelming majority of the good jobs—in engineering, clerical work, journalism, and the like—were considered white folks' jobs, except for those in the fields of teaching or preaching. Women responded to the pitch, and several fan clubs sprouted up in the area such as the Asbestos Chicks, a group of high school girls from the Tallapoosa Street area on the east side of Birmingham. The group consisted of Joyce Parker, Big Ada, Vera Brown, and Catherine Burk. The asbestos tag referred to the fact they "couldn't get burned," whatever the devil that meant, and I would toss their names around often on the air in appreciation for their support.

If it's true that the kind of car a person drives reveals his or her personality, then the vehicle I bought was tailor made to fit my radio persona. A black 1947 Plymouth decked out in leopard skin upholstery was my set of wheels; I even used black fingernail polish to paint over the inside dome light to promote a romantic, or even eerie, effect for fans. The car, a junkyard on wheels, broke down often and was soon put to pasture. Its successor was a two-door 1949 Pontiac Streamliner on which a friend had installed a huge horn operated by a fifty-pound canister of air that was placed in the trunk. A wire running from the dashboard triggered the attention-demanding gimmick. Once even that car broke down, and the Asbestos Chicks had to push me out of the middle of the street.

The style I culled from preaching sessions in Papa Clyde's basement shone through in my broadcasts. Since I had read the New Testament twice forward and once backward at the Smith house, I was as familiar with its passages as the most upstanding Southern Baptist preacher, black or white. It was not unusual for me to intersperse the radio dialogue with biblical verses while commenting on community and world issues. "Let he who is without sin cast the first stone," I might say, coupling the phrase with a point I was attempting to get across.

Although much of my delivery was couched in humor, the underlying message was often serious. On May 17, 1954, the nation witnessed the historic *Brown vs. Topeka* school integration ruling from the U.S. Supreme Court. The following year, in 1955, seamstress Rosa Parks refused to relinquish her seat to a white passenger on a bus in Montgomery, the first capital of the Confederacy. While the term *civil rights* was not in vogue, my heart was with the cause of social justice. I insisted that we needed to rearrange our thinking and push for the front of the bus. This attitude complemented my grassroots philosophy that the masses should take precedence over the classes. Negro doctors and lawyers had to ride in the back of the bus just like the rest of the minority community, I said, and there was no room for class distinction and division in the campaign for the promised land.

By and large, I did what I could to foment the rumblings of freedom with my pronouncements on police brutality, the need to register to vote, and general social inequities. Even Eugene "Bull" Connor, the former broadcaster with the Birmingham Barons who had graduated to the post of city commissioner in charge of the police and fire departments, was a target for me. Connor was notorious for his dedication to upholding the tradition that mandated separation of the races, and he did so with much vigor. To many, he was the expression of white Birmingham's love affair with the quintessential Old South and the subservient roles mandated for blacks over a span of generations.

Sometimes on my program I took potshots at Connor's "redneck" or "KKK" policemen for beating the devil out of some hapless Negro male. Police brutality was a chief concern in Negro communities across America before the formal civil rights movement was recognized by the national media. It was no secret that blacks had been fair game for the Birmingham police across the years. The police department's Car Number 3 was notorious during the 1940s and 1950s because its occupants had a strong reputation for whipping Negroes. The car was nicknamed the Black Cat because there was a miniature feline doll hanging on its rear license plate. The officers in the car would randomly stop a black male pedestrian and ask him to lean into the car window. Then they would roll the window up on his neck and hit him about the head with blackjacks, which were small clubs with rubber handles and a hard inner core at the other end.

Police were also noted for other humiliating tactics. During the days when there were few black hotels, a lot of people would use so-called lovers' lanes, which might be an alley, a vacant field, or a less traveled road, for sexual escapades. Black men would tell stories among themselves of how police staked out the rendezvous spots waiting to catch couples in compromising positions. If the woman was attractive, and if either one of the individuals was married, this would be a chance for the officer to have sex with the female as a form of blackmail. To avoid being charged with indecent exposure or summarily hauled off to jail, the woman would have to submit to what was essentially rape while the man watched.

A similar situation occurred at rooming establishments that doubled as shot houses like Marie's in Smithfield and Mama Dueth's near downtown. Police would raid these places and again conduct a form of sexual extortion. They also used a pickup man who would collect money on Saturday or Sunday. Usually, to remain open, a joint would pay from fifty to two hundred dollars a week. The men who operated these businesses always wore the best suits and oozed prosperity.

My radio delivery in attacking these and other social injustices was so unrestrained that people would invariably describe my style in one sentence (which has been polished for politeness): "That Negro is crazy."

For blacks to talk on the radio was almost an act of insubordination back in the 1950s. It was fine to be seen as jovial and happy-go-lucky, posing no threat to the traditional image of blacks as served up by Hollywood and the general media, but to deliver a message that might portray blacks as having a hint of intelligence or moral fiber was seen as a perilous threat to the dominant culture. On WEDR my advocacy of economic self-determination and commentaries on social issues apparently did not suit the appetites of many whites. One day listeners started calling the station telling us that we had begun losing our signal. A phone call I made to a Mr. Kirkpatrick, the engineer at the radio tower located near Elmwood Cemetery, did not alleviate the situation.

"We're losing power, Mr. Kirkpatrick," I said.

"I know you are," he responded in a dry voice.

"Well, what's going on?" I said.

"There are some folks out here, some Klansmen, cutting the guide wires," he said.

"Can't you do anything to stop them?" I entreated.

"Nope. I can't do that . . . 'cause I'm one of them too," he said.

The tower collapsed a few minutes later, and the station went off the air for about five days until a temporary tower with a weaker signal was constructed.

After about three months on the air, the show gained momentum, and I was considered a big-time personality. I persisted with my mix of music, outrageous banter, and social messages. For instance, sometimes I would rap about the ancient color caste system that had percolated into the black consciousness from the steamy bedrock of slavery when the so-called plum jobs were staffed by house servants who were usually light-complected blacks, while the brethren whose skin contained more melanin toiled out in the cotton fields. Of course, countless images in the media holding up blue-eyed blondes as the ideal had brainwashed Negroes and whites alike about the nature of beauty and transformed a subjective concept into one that stood in the pit of objectivism. I satirically summed up the touchy subject in a popular catchphrase.

"If you're bright, you are right; if you're brown, stick around; and if you're black, get back."

The listening audience was charmed by my outlandish, flamboyant, and outspoken approach to broadcasting. Slowly my popularity grew, and WEDR management expanded my airtime. Shows were broadcast from 6 A.M. to 8 A.M., 12 to 1 P.M., and 3 P.M. to 6 P.M. In addition, I had begun getting requests to play at platter parties, which were forerunners to discotheques. This allowed me to add thirty or forty dollars a week to my income.

One of the places I played was George Moore's Club in Leeds, where I was featured every other Saturday night. The club consisted of a lounge that could hold about eighty people. A stage in a rear room probably could accommodate another hundred people, many of whom sat on benches around the wall. Not only did I play music, but I was also combination pep-squad leader and flirt. I would often wear tight pants and shirts open enough for my chest to show. I would change clothes during intermissions in the performances. Each time I returned to the stage, I would have on tighter pants and eventually, perhaps, no underwear. That would have the similar effect as a woman wearing a tight blouse and no bra underneath. Basically, I was selling myself as a sex object for the female fans.

I prided myself on being able to introduce records with great fervor and intensity and simultaneously orchestrating the emotional involvement of the audience in the songs.

"Do you feel all right tonight?" I asked in a slow conversational tone. "You gotta find somebody to touch tonight," I continued. "Here's B. B. King, ladies and gentlemen . . ." Then I began singing.

Sometimes I would pick up my guitar, sing, and act as if I were strumming the instrument. By that time, audience members would have leaped into the spirit of the evening, and many would be dancing and cavorting around the room in the relaxed social atmosphere.

The charisma that resonated from my on-air character apparently made me appealing to the female fans. After some of the platter parties, I would find nude women in my car or backstage at different establishments, and they would say, in effect, "Look what you can get." At WEDR women also would occasionally show up and disrobe before, after, or during the broadcasts. Although I didn't get involved with these women, the unfounded rumor that I was a ladies' man laid the groundwork for the on-air name that someone saddled me with—Shelley the Playboy.

The morning show featured a roll call with students from around the metropolitan Birmingham area phoning in to trumpet their school names. Shelley the Playboy fan clubs were started at black high schools such as Ullman, Parker, Hayes, and Western-Olin, and at white schools such as West End, Ensley, Woodlawn, and Mountain Brook, and even at the University of Alabama at Tuscaloosa.

When females called in, whether white or black, I would always address them as "darling." Or I would say, "I love you madly, baby." Police Commissioner Connor began referring to me as Shelley the Plowboy, and the tunes I played he called "jungle music." He urged whites to be vigilant lest I be the precipitating force in "y'all's pretty little white girls going to bed" with Negroes.

The fear of interaction between Negro males and white females had always been a special point of hysteria in the South. An incident that highlighted the emotionalism the subject elicited occurred when I was walking downtown and students from Phillips High asked me for my autograph. A white girl didn't have anything for me to write on so she pulled her skirt up above her knee and I wrote: "Best wishes. I love you madly." Four or five police cars showed up, and an officer cursed me and said I needed to get back to "Niggertown." Outside of Ratkiller's Shoeshine Parlor I encountered a group of fellows and told them that the police had accused me of "feeling on a white girl's legs." The guys seemed to regard me as a hero for stirring up a fuss with such a transgression, whether it was true or almost true. But as a phalanx of police cars showed up in the black business district, the little gaggle of admirers instantly vanished like cold butter in a hot skillet.

One morning I went to work at WEDR and discovered the letters KKK written in the blood of some unfortunate animal. It could have been the work of the infamous diehards, or perhaps it was the calling card of narrow-minded wannabes. After I mentioned my discovery on the air, people came by to gawk, and the *Birmingham News* sent a photographer. It was my chore to scrub away the letters representing the racists who were trying to wash away my independent streak and the Playboy's messages.

Voting was a right I fully intended to use as a sword to try to vanquish the injustices of the world around me. Aunt Mamie and Uncle Henry never voted, but I knew this was going to be something I would pursue despite the notorious poll tax and other hurdles Negroes had to circumvent. Birmingham's W. C. Patton led the National Association for the Advancement of Colored People's nationwide effort to get blacks registered. The Democratic Party suited me because Franklin Roosevelt always seemed more levelheaded and fair when it came to dealing with so-called Negro issues. I turned twenty-one in September of 1955 and resolved to go down and register to vote at the Jefferson County Courthouse.

A rope divided the registration process into white and colored sections. The written test consisted of a few general history questions and was relatively simple. Afterward I got back in line to take the oral test. A white fellow ahead of me in the line was asked by the clerk, "What was the Declaration of Independence signed with, an ink pen or a feather?"

"A feather," the man answered.

At my turn, the same clerk or registrar noted that I had passed the written test. She then asked me about the nature of the instrument used at the historic signing.

"A feather," I said confidently.

"I'm sorry, that's wrong," she said. "You did not pass."

After waiting several months, I returned to the courthouse, repeated the process, and passed. Voting became an exercise I would often use to ensure that I tossed my two cents into the workings of the United States' heralded democracy.

Rebecca

True love is the cornerstone of radiant happiness, fulfillment, and peace of mind in the human spirit. Marriage was something I knew I wanted, but I had not truly tasted the sweet nectar of a loving relationship by the time I ambled to age twenty. Encounters with women were still novel experiences and were created largely by the popularity I enjoyed as Shelley the Playboy, which had given me more access to them. But none of the so-called groupies had electrified my soul and spirit. The woman who seemed to lure me toward a complete sense of adulthood was Rebecca, a student at Daniel Payne, a small black college in the northwest sector of Birmingham operated by the A.M.E. church.

A buddy, David Grant, an employee of Southern Funeral

Home, said a young woman he was dating at the college had a friend they wanted me to meet. Grant was a fun fellow, and sometimes he and I would sleep overnight at the funeral home just for the heck of it. But he seemed sincere when he said this was a woman he thought I might like. She was eighteen-year-old Rebecca Ruth Jones of the Covington County town of Andalusia in southern Alabama.

A startlingly beautiful mahogany-looking young woman, Rebecca impressed me with her pleasant, easygoing personality and quest for education. Whether the itch was actually lust or love, it didn't take long for me to feel that I had fallen for Rebecca, while she was apparently enamored with my celebrity status. After a whirlwind four-month courtship, we were married in May 1955 on her mother's porch in Andalusia. She moved out of her dormitory and into my room at Mrs. Nelle Tarver's boardinghouse, several blocks north of downtown.

Immediately, Mrs. Tarver seemed to resent the presence of another female, and we limited our interaction with the landlady by basically confining ourselves to one room. The strain was akin to being cooped up in a hamster cage. Besides, two adult folks needed a kitchen, and I always had a soft spot for down-home Southern cooking like collard greens, fried chicken, pork chops, and grits. That deficiency alone made it imperative that I find us a real home.

Income from work as platter-party host and WEDR record spinner helped me to develop a comfortable lifestyle. I had quit the job as an elevator starter at Newberry's store after a few months. As I became more popular, I was sought after for platter parties in cities like Tuscaloosa, Alexander City, and Talladega. This enabled me to save about $1,800, which I planned to use toward a mortgage.

A new middle-class subdivision was under development in

the southwest Birmingham neighborhood of Titusville, about three miles from Rosedale. It was called Lincoln Park, and much of the terrain had formerly been a large farm owned by the Lusco family. The house cost $12,000, and I told the Realtor that I was the owner of the impressive-sounding Shelley Stewart and Associates. A GI loan was approved, and we moved in about three months after we were married. This was the first place that I could take a bath in and that I could call my own—804 Center Way Southwest, a modest structure with a living room, kitchen, bath, two bedrooms, and a den. Now the distance from the Stringfellow Stables and Papa Clyde's basement seemed even more profound.

During 1955 I began to broadcast from my home. This was unprecedented for a Negro personality, although at least one white announcer, Joe Rumore of WVOK, went on the air from the basement of his residence. Another status symbol I achieved was a new 1955 red and white Ford Custom Liner that I bought from Marion Crawford Ford on Third Avenue North for $1,800.

A respectable portion of my energy went into making the marriage work since my own tattered family history loomed like a specter. Rebecca, however, seemed to be caught in a hair-raising tug-of-war between two people: Shelley Stewart and Shelley the Playboy. The beguiled creature could not understand why her husband did not act like the performer twenty-four hours a day, which is to say, ebullient, finger-popping, jive-talking, and gregarious. While I frequently declared my love for Rebecca, she never managed to express a hint of a reciprocal emotion. Whenever I questioned her about the reticence, the response was succinct: "I'm getting there."

The formidable task of Rebecca having to deal with alternative egos in one individual was something I could not fully appreciate at the time. Rebecca was fond of the Playboy, but the conservative, low-key, introspective Shelley Stewart was apparently more than she could stomach. That individual preferred solitary drinking rather than liquor-sogged parties; throw rugs as opposed to Persian rugs; catfish, chitterlings, and ham hocks over caviar. He was a 100 percent, honest-to-God sucker for reading, spading dirt in the yard, fixing the plumbing, and painting walls and cupboards. If this dichotomy was indicative of a schizophrenic personality like the air force had claimed, then so be it.

Although I had told Rebecca about my mother's slaying at my father's hands and the beatings I had incurred, I hesitated to divulge the tortured side of my personality and was afraid to let her see me shed tears. The quiet solitude of the car served as a personal chapel where I would weep daily from ancient sadness and offer prayers that God would shower our marital union with love and harmony. It was still imperative that I succeed in marriage where my father, Slim Stewart, had failed catastrophically.

It also became apparent that Rebecca seemed to be bothered by the adoring female fans whom I would greet with a generic "Hey, baby" or "Hey, sugar." This approach was the signature of the Playboy that created an image that obscured reality. Although I never pursued these women, no wife wants competition for her man from one real rival or dozens of harmless ones buzzing around platter parties, street corners, grocery stores, or at worst, ringing the front doorbell. Soon women were telling Rebecca lies that I had had sexual relations with them. Usually, it turned out these were women I may have greeted on the street or, frequently, had never laid eyes on.

Other issues began to dissolve the foundation of our marriage. Rebecca felt that I dissected the hours in a day and left her with minuscule crumbs of attention after WEDR, platter parties, and sock hops were considered. Also, the fact that Rebecca stated after we were married that she did not want children and was not physically able to bear them also contributed to the marital drift in no small measure. Perhaps if our courtship had been longer, we would not have left so much of the relationship to chance in the realm of personal compatibility.

My brothers Sam and David were the catalysts for some of our discontent. They were known for drinking, fighting, and hanging out in unsavory places. Whenever I would round them up and bring them to our home, I was annoyed by the coldness that radiated from Rebecca. As soon as they had ended their visit, she would begin mopping, spraying, and dusting as if exterminating residual germs left by a dying victim of the bubonic plague. If they visited the house on their own, she restricted them to the carport entrance. Often we would just remain outside shooting the bull rather than activate Rebecca's almost obsessive-compulsive cleanup routine.

Rebecca's attitude regarding my brothers irritated me especially since she felt she had to remain close to her own family and wanted us to drive to see them in Andalusia at least once a month after I had purchased the 1955 Ford Custom. Her family was beset with its own brand of problems, and she was loyal to the cadre that included her mother, Nellie; an older brother, Jacob, who had been in the army during the early portion of the marriage; a troubled teenage sister, Edith; and a younger, jobless brother named Mac. Rebecca, without my blessings and on different occasions, invited both brothers to stay with us, and they did so for months at a time without contributing any money to offset household expenses. Her sister also came to live in our home at one point in an attempt to massage her high-strung personality, but a rebellious nature prevented her from accepting discipline, at least from me. After a few months of friction, she packed her bags for Andalusia and was destined to commit suicide a few years later.

Sam, David, and I continued to socialize and hang out together whenever possible. As their schedules permitted, they continued to accompany me on my platter party engagements at clubs and various organizations. They would help me set up equipment and act as security outside the front door of the clubs.

My shows at George Moore's Club became particularly popular events. Sometimes, thirty or forty people would pile onto the backs of flatbed trucks on the west side of Birmingham for a fifteen-mile hayride to the establishment. Fans from all points on the compass headed to the club, and Moore's place would end up with five or six hundred people some weekends trying to occupy space that was designed for perhaps a third of that number. Packed like cattle in a Chicago stockyard, patrons would perspire profusely and even faint in the room. Promoters would shy away from booking big acts like B. B. King on the weekends that I performed for fear that I might cut into their revenues. I sometimes negotiated a fee scale of seventy cents out of each dollar taken into the show, which meant that I would receive the entire profit from ticket receipts and the management would make its money from alcohol and food sales.

The performances were Shelley the Playboy in his finest form, but they were still a mask for the somber, tortured Shelley Stewart. In a real sense, my heart was not in these shows. Aside from the fact that the events were only props for the Playboy, there was another reason that I secretly disliked them. The mixture of bloated crowds combined with the demon of alcohol often made events of leisure magnets for violence that took the form of fistfights and cuttings.

An unforgettable incident occurred on Valentine's Day in 1957 at a platter party for adults that I hosted at Brighton High

School in the Birmingham area. That night about three hundred people were present in an auditorium that should have held only a hundred. Carl Perkins's "Don't Step on My Blue Suede Shoes" was playing. The song was considered a crossover, which meant that, although it was sung by a white artist, it generated appeal among blacks. Several patrons in the crowd were performing that Bear Mash Stomp, a dance created by people from a Birmingham neighborhood of the same name (the neighborhood was later displaced by the county's hospital for the indigent). A man in the crowd wearing blue suede shoes was dancing when another man performing the Bear Mash Stomp made the fateful mistake of stepping on his footwear.

"You mother . . . !" the offended patron yelled.

Suddenly, I could see the offended dancer raise a knife above his head and plunge downward, hitting the hapless victim in the neck. Blood spurted everywhere after the blow, which apparently struck the jugular vein. The victim started running toward the exit, and I followed him. Outside, he ran a few yards and embraced a tree. I grabbed his arms in an effort to ease him to the ground and attempt to stop the bleeding. The man slid to the grass, and onlookers began praying for his well-being. Almost instantly, the nameless stranger was dead, his blood covering my shirt and the clothes of a few other bystanders.

On another occasion I was about to perform at a place called the Green Gable in the Oxmoor Valley. Sam was outside preparing to handle security duties and was talking with a friend of his named Dump. A patron came up and exchanged words with Dump over some issue. Sam tried to calm the situation and demanded that the two men end the disturbance. The angry man told my brother that the matter was none of his business, pulled a revolver, aimed it at Sam's head, and pulled the trigger. The gun misfired. Seconds later the gunman focused on Dump again. He pulled the trigger again, mortally wounding Dump in the chest. We placed him in a car and frantically rushed to Hill-man Hospital. Dump was pronounced dead on arrival at the medical facility. This incident further soured me on the platter-party circuit.

———————

REBECCA AND I DECIDED to take a trip to a town in northern Florida that featured glass-bottom boats. I had heard from my father's sister on the south side of Birmingham that my grand-mother, Rosa Lee Stewart, lived in Phenix City, down U.S. 280, which was the highway we would be taking to see the boats. On the way, I detoured into Phenix City and sought out my grand-mother, who lived on Bank Street in an old, unpainted house near the government projects. She was a dark-skinned, tobacco-chewing woman with long, thinning hair wearing a trademark apron. From her chiseled features, she could have been a blend of Negro and one of the East Alabama tribes of Indians. She was known as Mama Rosa among whites and had been the house-keeper and cook for several families including that of Albert Pat-terson, the state attorney general candidate who was gunned down on June 18, 1954, while campaigning on a platform that included a pledge to clean up Phenix City's renowned vice and corruption. His son, John Patterson, took his father's place and won the attorney general's post and used it as springboard to be-come governor of Alabama in the late 1950s. He would be at the helm of government when the integrated Freedom Riders were beaten at the Montgomery bus terminal in May 1961. While Rosa Lee had been a domestic, her late husband, Alonzo, had been a foreman at a cotton processing plant in Phenix City. To-gether they had produced ten children, some of whom, she would say, ranked among the biggest fools in the entire world.

I decided to play a game with her to see if she could recognize who this stranger was.

"You could be one of Huell's boys . . . I don't know which one," she said.

That degree of recognition from my grandmother uplifted my spirits and seemed to regenerate me. A child who had lost his mother at age four had now become a man hungry for any real sense of family. This was my father's mother, and although I had blamed him for much of the agony in my life, the satisfaction I received from the recognition of Rosa Lee Stewart, my blood kin, was rather remarkable. This was my grandmother, not the mother of a killer. That was the dominant view I would take of her. I introduced Rebecca, and after lingering a few minutes, promised to keep in touch and then resumed the trip to Florida. Now my cup of life had not runneth over, but with this knowledge of a grandmother, I knew that it was at least half full.

THE MATRIMONIAL HOUSE OF CARDS Rebecca and I had erected started to falter more noticeably on Mother's Day in 1957. That morning began with me coughing and wheezing and feeling like a person teetering under the weight of a horrid tropical disease for which medicine has produced no known antidote. The symptoms I exhibited had actually bedeviled me since the night before, when I had had to abruptly end a platter-party show at Smitty's Place, a club in the former mining camp of Powderly in western Birmingham.

I protested when Rebecca insisted that I drive her to Andalusia, but she peppered me with accusations that I did not like her family. I acquiesced after she promised that she would drive and I would be able to rest at her mother's house. About a half hour later on U.S. 31, I lost consciousness. In a listless daze, I regained my senses at Nellie's house under the analytical but vacant gaze of an old white doctor who sported the unmistakable fragrance of alcohol and halitosis. At his behest, we would not leave Andalusia until the coolness of the evening, but other than that, he offered no diagnosis or cure for my condition.

Back in Birmingham a neighborhood physician, Dotson Curry, was summoned to our house. His words pulled no punches. "My God, this man is dying," he said. "Get him to the hospital now."

With a temperature hovering at 103 degrees, I was admitted to Holy Family Hospital, where I was diagnosed as suffering from double pneumonia. After a few days of treatment at Holy Family, I was discharged but still caught in the throes of an unholy family saga when I returned home.

Both my wife's mother, Nellie, and her younger brother, Mac, came to live with us during the latter part of 1957. The woman and I had always been on cordial terms. In fact, she acted as if I was the greatest manifestation since sliced bread, principally, I presumed, because she thought I was rich by comparative standards. The liquor I kept in the house was accessible to her, and she indulged quite liberally; her frequent states of intoxication were accepted by Rebecca. However, after about a month of harmonious coexistence, a confrontation ensued that added momentum to the marriage's dismemberment. Nellie voiced resentment at Rebecca's preparing food for the household and went into a liquor-lubricated rage.

"She ain't got no business cooking for you," Nellie said to me with her son Mac at her side. "We are going to put your ass out."

The words resonated like brass knuckles raking across the tympanic membrane. Allowing my wife's family to reside in the house was gracious enough. Now her relatives had crossed the threshold of propriety and good sense and were mad that my own wife was cooking for me. Angered beyond speech, I grabbed a .38 caliber revolver from its resting place in a bedroom drawer and chased the trio out of the house. Eddie Bates, a neighbor, calmed me down with an appeal to reason, but the episode represented my in-laws' exit from the house and helped hasten Rebecca's departure from my life.

John McClendon, head of the McClendon-Ebony Broadcasting chain, wanted me to help sign on his new radio station, KOKA, located a few hundred miles away in Shreveport, Louisiana, in 1958. Rebecca and I rented out our Titusville home and moved to the town where we stayed in the Sprague Street Hotel. A barber in his mid-thirties named Perry suggested I should check out a lovely three-bedroom house in the community that was available for renting. The brick house was just as attractive as he had promised it would be, and both Rebecca and I fell in love with the structure, which was not far from the radio station. After a few days the utilities were turned on and we moved in.

The first evening in the house Rebecca and I broiled a couple of steaks, rinsed the dishes after the meal, and put them in the sink since Rebecca was going to wash them the next morning. After counting our blessings over our new home, we turned in for the evening. A bloodcurdling scream jolted me from a dream world in the middle of the night, and I rushed into the kitchen to find Rebecca in hysterics. She pointed to the sink where I noticed that the white dinner plates had turned a dark brown and seemed to be alive. On closer inspection, I could see that they were covered with roaches. Above our heads, the ceiling seemed to wiggle too because of scores of the grimy insects. They had been hiding when we first entered the house, but apparently the scent of food and dirty dishes was too tantalizing to be ignored. They now covered cookies on the counter and were visible in every room of the house.

The next morning I called the landlady to tell her about our experience. "Oh yes," she said. "There is a small roach problem that I forgot to tell you about."

Perry, the barber, and his wife, Bonnie, who also cut hair, said we could stay with them in their two-bedroom apartment. One reason that I agreed to the arrangement was that I had noticed how well the couple got along, and I was hoping that some magic from their relationship would rub off on Rebecca and me. They did not charge us rent to live there, but we contributed to the household expenses.

Cy Steiner was a man I met in Shreveport during this period. A personable and likable individual, he was selling ties in a department store on Texas Street and addressed me with the courtesy titles of "sir" and "mister," which was uncommon in those days. At my urging, I told Steiner to come down to KOKA for a job. Although he had no experience in radio and sales, he was hired the next day on my recommendation.

Since my services gravitated toward the highest bidder, I accepted more money to come back to WEDR after a few months in the Shreveport market. After I left Louisiana, I invited Steiner to try his hand in Birmingham. Weeks later the salesman came to Birmingham and was hired on my recommendation at WBCO in Bessemer. I developed a close friendship with Cy and his wife, Nancy, and Cy and I would talk several times a week on the phone about different aspects of business and life in general. Sometimes we would get together for drinks at his Southside apartment or my home in Titusville. Neither of us foresaw the groundbreaking business path our relationship would reap years later.

Professionally, I was in top form back in Birmingham, which seemed to again magnify the deficiencies in my marriage. Rebecca had not wanted to return to Alabama. It seemed we were back thrashing about in a marriage that had turned to quicksand. The main issues continued to be her jealousy over fans' attention and her inability to understand the wallflower Shelley Stewart. During this period, a male friend of hers named Billy, an older man, was at the house one day when I arrived from work. He chastised me, alleging that I did not treat her with respect and appreciation. For some reason, I never asked Rebecca if their relationship represented a mentor-to-protégé arrangement or something more amorous. Perhaps this was out of indifference or a desire to turn a blind eye to a possibly glaring weakness in our union. In the late spring of 1958 I came home to discover that Rebecca had vanished like a leprechaun.

Several months after Rebecca had moved out of the house, a middle-aged woman showed up at the WEDR station while I was on the air. The woman's words were startling. She accused me of having impregnated her daughter Gwen during the period after Rebecca had left. I denied the allegation because I could not remember the incident. Then she beckoned her daughter from the hall, a woman in her second trimester, and my dormant memory began to stir. The young woman now looked different, but I said yes, sexual intercourse had occurred between us after a platter party in West Blocton. I remembered that after the show someone told me that a nude female was in my car waiting to demonstrate her appreciation. The robustness of youth presented this as a golden opportunity that I did not ignore, most likely because Rebecca apparently was no longer in the picture.

I told Gwen and her mother that I would be willing to do whatever was necessary to support the child after it was born. With that the two women vanished as abruptly as they had appeared, and I was aware that a transient moment of pleasure was now coming back to haunt me.

CHAPTER ELEVEN

Kick That Mule

Pᴇʀʜᴀᴘꜱ ᴀ ᴍᴏʀᴇ ɪɴᴛᴇɴꜱᴇ ᴄᴏᴜʀᴛꜱʜɪᴘ would have short-circuited the negative energy that torpedoed the relationship between Rebecca and me. Then maybe we would have seen past lustful urges or romantic, idealized notions. But after staying in Birmingham for several months following her departure, I decided to change scenery and pocket more money in Jackson, Mississippi, at WOKJ, which was owned by John McClendon. Rebecca, I figured, had probably gone back to Shreveport, the town she had reluctantly left months earlier after I had helped sign on KOKA.

McClendon also owned KOKA; KOKY in Little Rock, Arkansas; and WYOU in Tampa, Florida, and was apparently in the process of purchasing WBCO from Jess Lanier in Bessemer, designating it WENN, and moving it to Birmingham. He was one of the handful of whites that dominated the black radio market, or dollars, in the eastern United States. Others were Stanley Ray, chief of the group whose station call letters always ended in OK and whose stations were situated in such cities as Memphis and Louisville, and the Rounsiville broadcast group that stretched from Ohio to Florida. None of the entrepreneurs was allowed to own more than seven stations. Black on-air personalities in these chains included people with names such as Diggy Doo, Hotsy Totsy, Eddie OJ, and Hot Rod Hubbard.

Without hesitation McClendon hired me as a broadcaster for the Mississippi outlet. Most of my belongings were packed into my white 1957 Holiday Oldsmobile, which boasted my signature below the door. With a do-rag around my head to hold my processed hair in place, I rolled into Jackson, the Crossroads of the South, at about 11 P.M. one night in the latter part of 1958.

Mississippi was a state of which I had seen very little since I had rescued my brothers from the Scooba plantation in 1952. Now a misfortunate turn deposited me into a white neighborhood where I came face-to-face with every black man's nightmare. Flashing blue lights alerted me that a Jackson police cruiser was on my tail. It was my observation that many black males harbored a hidden anxiety over the possibility of ending up with a bullet in the head fired by a lawman in those days of blatant racism. Police were a reflection of the white community and consequently were their agents in upholding the customs, practices, and mores of the civic structure. Their hostility toward Negroes was legendary in many states, Southern and Northern. While life with Papa Clyde had helped me to understand and relate to whites, I knew that a simple traffic stop could escalate quickly into disaster, even for me.

Prefacing his remark with the obligatory racial slur, one of the lawmen asked me what was I doing prowling around a white neighborhood and whose car had I stolen.

"My name is Shelley Stewart," I said in response to his foul words.

"Oh, you are a smart one," he said. "We ought to kick your ass . . . we gonna hold you."

The mental exercises Bubba and I had practiced at the stables came into play. We had trained ourselves not to show any fear as part of a self-defense curriculum that also involved learning how to throw knives and ice picks. It was our conclusion that the horses at Stringfellow Stables possessed personalities and intuition that could sense fear or confidence. If we revealed fear in the presence of the large animals, we believed that we could have been seriously hurt if they decided to kick or bite. Similarly, I deduced that any fear in the presence of the officers could push them over the edge of restraint.

The officers rambled around in the car and found a near-empty bottle of whiskey under the backseat. They handcuffed me and put me in the patrol car, which was, in effect, a cage. The police impounded my vehicle and hauled me to the drab city jail. After the steel doors clanged shut, I breathed a heavy, heartfelt sigh of relief that I had not been summarily executed or, at the least, suffered a cracked skull at the hands of lawmen who could have easily been Ku Klux Klansmen during their off-hours.

The jail was populated with all the usual suspects: vagrants, winos, and violent offenders. A toilet amounted to a hole in the floor into which inmates would urinate and defecate. When a man finished his business, he would yell for a guard, or trusty, to pull a handle outside the cell in order to flush the so-called commode. An inmate would yell "Kick that mule!" and the waste would be jettisoned down rusty sewer pipes.

Coincidentally, a trusty was excitedly talking about a new dude that WOKJ commercials had been promoting as coming to the airwaves.

"Man I can't wait for that guy to get here. That disc jockey is going to rock Jackson," he said.

The trusty was incredulous when I confessed that I was the

personality everybody had been waiting on. I explained that I had a rich white man's phone number in my pocket and that the jail was not going to be my quarters much longer. I went to sleep that night with the anonymous vagrants and roustabouts, using my shoes as my pillow.

The next morning I called McClendon and informed him of my predicament. Within a few hours the station owner, a small-statured middle-aged man with brownish hair, paraded into the jail to bail me out and bellowed that this was Mississippi and I needed to mind my p's and q's. I went on the air that afternoon and respected his request that I not mention the jail incident. But I never vowed to remain silent about the jail on any *other* day.

McClendon got ample mileage out of the encounter with Jackson's finest and said he would have loved to have seen my lanky frame and long legs squeezed into the backseat of the patrol car. That image was the catalyst for a brainstorm for him about what my radio alias should be: Daddy Long Legs. I agreed but hedged at using *Legs* as part of my name because I just didn't like the ring of it. McClendon remembered that I had mentioned in Shreveport that I had lost a brother, Jerome, in action in Korea and said he would call me Jerome Long in lead-ins to news segments on the program and during off-air time.

After securing a seven-dollars-a-night room at the Edward Lee Hotel, I was ready to do my thing on the radio again. That afternoon I glided onto the airwaves of WOKJ with my trademark banter and audacious delivery.

"Good, googly woogly . . . Hello, Jackson! . . . I'm Daddy Long," I shrieked.

Immediately, I launched my commentary on social issues like I had done in Birmingham under the glazed gaze of Bull Connor, the rabidly antiblack police commissioner. In Jackson, as in Birmingham, remarks on significant issues were often couched in comical delivery. I took swipes at the absurdity of segregated society and issued warnings for Negro men to walk on the side of caution when dating some of the light-skinned, mixed race, or so-called Creole, women in the area who could be mistaken for white. Of course, police brutality and voter registration were also part of my radio agenda again.

McClendon saw red when he heard my broadcast and predicted that I would get everybody at the station killed by fire-bomb-tossing night riders. He urged me to tone it down a few decibels, but I reminded him that this don't-give-a-damn attitude and delivery was what had made me so hot in Birmingham and Shreveport. Activism was always my second nature, and I aligned myself with organizations and individuals struggling for black justice such as Charles Evers, brother of Jackson NAACP leader Medgar Evers, who was to be gunned down by Byron De La Beckwith in June 1963.

On one broadcast I wondered aloud whether there were any black policemen patrolling the streets of Jackson. Before the program was over, two Negro officers showed up outside the station and gave me a thumbs-up sign while I was on the air. But to me these guys were "fake" since they were not allowed to arrest whites.

As my reputation grew, strangers would compliment the program and Daddy Long's performance. Earl "Buster" Davis, the respected proprietor of People's Funeral Home, liked the show and had let me rent a tidy two-bedroom apartment unit he owned on Bell Street for eighty dollars a month. Surprisingly, about a week after I had set up residence, Rebecca surfaced in the neighborhood. She was boarding with a family that lived nearby. Tense and on edge, she assumed I was stalking her and wanted vengeance because she had dematerialized into the southern landscape. I tried to assure her that she was mistaken and used the encounter to plead for reconciliation. Her recalcitrance against mending fences only convinced me that I was arguing a lost cause, and I resolved not to pour any more energy into patching up the marriage. Rebecca soon left Jackson for Shreveport, and we both knew a formal divorce was inevitable.

Daddy Long strode with respect across the airwaves of Jackson. I always loathed the term *disc jockey* and considered myself an on-air personality rather than just a record spinner. The showmanship interlaced with humorous but purposeful commentary placed me in a category too burgeoning for the term *DJ*. Radio station WOKJ was a microcosm of the Jackson, Mississippi, society in a hierarchal and cultural sense. All the on-air personalities, including Reverends Spencer and Newsom, were black, of course, but the entire sales department, who received the fatter paychecks, was white and used a separate rest room. Also, the blacks were expected to wash windows, clean floors, and take out the trash, jobs I told McClendon I would not do. This stance, to be sure, grated on the nerves of manager Al Evans.

The true plantation nature of the station did not express itself to me until a specific incident unfolded. Word spread around the office one day that McClendon was holding a party at his upscale home that evening, and I overheard several radio personalities say they were going to show up. McClendon, in passing, asked me whether I was going to be there, and I answered affirmatively, feeling that a social invitation from the station boss signaled that I had finally arrived.

With suit pressed and shirt starched, I drove over to the McClendon home for the soiree, which was attended by the elite in Jackson's business and political community and even included the mayor. Elegantly coiffed white matrons and their suited gentleman escorts mingled in the living room. I began interacting with the guests, some of whom reluctantly shook my hand when I introduced myself. Reverend Spencer was preparing drinks at the bar, and I ordered a scotch and a sandwich. He looked at me oddly, but I considered his bartender role as some manner of moonlighting. In short order, McClendon rushed over with the chalky look of a man who had been staring into the jaws of a great white shark and pulled me aside.

"Jerome, didn't they tell you? You were supposed to serve as a waiter," he gasped. "Go get you a jacket."

Apparently, I said, we had gotten our channels of communication clogged up and there must be a misunderstanding because I wasn't about to revert to my Jack-O-Lantern days.

"I'll talk with you tomorrow. Get the hell out of here now . . . you don't want to get us all killed," he said.

The event only crystallized the discontent I felt over the station's management. McClendon called me that night and voiced his dismay at my actions regarding the "Guess who's coming to dinner" escapade at his residence.

"Jerome," he whined, "I know you are strong on your people and folks, and it's great to be accepted—"

I interrupted at that juncture, determined to rebut his lecture with my own self-assertion. "Mr. McClendon, I don't want to be accepted; I want to be respected," I said, adding that service as a white-jacketed waiter was not a part of the job description.

The flap set the stage for an opportunity to vent the black staff's displeasure with the humiliation and inequities inherent in the WOKJ operations. Although the other black employees had voiced discontent about policies out of management's earshot, they had never confronted McClendon directly. I was tapped as the group's spokesman for a meeting that would finally clear the air about the Negroes' treatment.

When I told McClendon that we wanted to meet with him and voice our grievances, his round face turned beet red. An afternoon meeting was arranged in McClendon's office, and all seven black employees showed up for the gripe session. Like a plantation "boss Negro" confronting the overseers, I rattled off a series of complaints and irritations: segregated rest rooms, extracurricular menial activities we were expected to perform around the office, and the fact that there were no blacks in management at the station and virtually no opportunities for promotion at WOKJ.

After listening patiently to the monologue, McClendon asked me whether I had exhausted the list of complaints. Feeling that I had adequately and eloquently stated the general mood of the staff, I rested my case.

"Well, Jerome, you are one of the newest staff members here," said McClendon. "Let's hear what some of the others think that have been around here awhile."

One of the black employees who had been quite vocal about the conditions in conversations with me and others was asked his opinion about the setup. He offered that, on second thought, maybe things around the station were not so bad after all. As it stood, he really had no problems with the way WOKJ operated. One by one, the other Negroes answered with the meekness of lambs in a pride of lions while station manager Evans smirked. The situation at WOKJ was not as bad as I had made it out to be, they chimed.

"Well, Daddy Long," said McClendon, "looks like you are the only one with a problem."

At that point, I exploded like an errant rocket at Huntsville's Marshall Space Flight Center. All of them were nothing but a bunch of black so and sos, I charged. The fellow who had done all the bellyaching behind the scenes objected to my insults, which escalated my anger to the point that I threatened to beat the hell out of him. Evans used my volatility as a chance to tell McClendon that my employment at the radio station needed to be abbreviated, and besides, I was disrespecting my own people with the tirade. McClendon opined that at least I had sufficient backbone to speak out, and with that, the session evaporated. Later that evening McClendon called me at home and offered his paternalistic advice. "Jerome, the next time you come forth like that, make sure you have it all together," he said.

———

THE CHANCE ENCOUNTER WITH Rebecca in Jackson only convinced me of the hopeless plane to which our relationship had sunk. A door was closing on a once-promising experiment of love that had malfunctioned like a feebly constructed high-school chemistry-lab formula. But almost at once, another passage opened toward a relationship that showed much potential.

Josie Mae was a well-built, prissy, handsome woman a couple of years my senior who shunned alcohol and drugs. She was up front with me about her profession as one of the leading thieves in the state of Mississippi and revealed that she had been trained in the craft by her mother, Big Liz, a woman weighing over three hundred pounds. She had a gift for communication in the guise of a fast tongue and was always armed with a Bible.

One of the first questions Josie asked was about my church denomination. She was Catholic, while I was a lifelong Protestant, like most of the relatives on both branches of my family tree. We would often go to Mass at a local church or have break-fast at one of the restaurants near Lynch Street and absorb the knowledge in magazines and books together. Her taste was for business and economics, while my favorite subject was history.

Josie Mae's goal was to open a dress shop since she felt she knew the preferences of customers because of the insights she had gained as a thief. Radio station ownership was my ultimate aim. Josie Mae said that she didn't figure she could ever steal enough to make her dream of shop ownership come true. And I didn't think I could make enough personal appearances to furnish me with sufficient capital with which to buy a radio station. So, frustration over career advancement was a matter that we had in common.

Further, it seemed our hearts were not totally captivated by our undertakings. I actually saw radio and platter parties as mere means to the end of ownership, while she possessed a disdain for the shoplifting that she had used as means of survival. Stealing was degrading enough, and Josie Mae hoped that she could soon leave the endeavor behind. But for her, the ethical and moral implications of the situation could not overpower the material benefits of felonious acts.

Although she was a good-looking woman, Josie Mae had drawn the line at prostituting her body. But some people thought I was her pimp because of the flashy clothes she had given me with manufacturers' labels like Botany 500, Hickey Freeman, and Three G's. The clothes represented a different world from the days when I had borrowed suits to attend my brother's funeral and graduation exercises back in Rosedale or wore old clothes given to me by the Derryberry family at the Stringfellow Stables. While most likely the duds were stolen, I winked at the situation because it was my observation that the economics of the times and shortage of quality jobs for Negroes forced some to resort to things they would not consider otherwise, such as operating liquor houses or even selling their bodies or stealing.

One of Josie Mae's most charming characteristics was her empathy. Slowly I began to share more details about my rugged childhood, and I noticed that as I talked she would dab at her eyes with a handkerchief. Despite her thievery, I felt Josie Mae was an otherwise decent woman who was caught up in the quest for survival.

Josie Mae, I discovered, was supposed to be the girlfriend of a snappy-dressing restaurateur and alleged trafficker in stolen goods named Woodrow. Although she was a waitress in the eatery he owned, she assured me that she saw no future of any consequence with the man and that their relationship was mostly casual. Apparently, Woodrow, a married man in his early forties, felt otherwise, since he approached me on the street one day and inquired about my intentions with Josie Mae. His entreaty was akin to a male lion sniffing out a competitor to gauge his strength in a possible fight over a lioness, and he even inquired about the beautiful silk suits she had given me that cost from three hundred to five hundred dollars.

Even though I was only in my early twenties, I realized that if a woman chose to be with one man over another it was her prerogative. I felt no fear that Woodrow was going to attempt to push matters to a violent level. Woodrow declared that he didn't want to go tooth and claw over the woman he called Jo, but he admonished me not to mistreat her and stated that I should be proud to be arm in arm with the best thief in Mississippi. Woodrow and I more or less kept our distance after that encounter.

Josie Mae and I complemented each other; we both sparkled

with celebrity status in the town. She was considered a prize because of her renown as a thief, and I was valued because I was the popular Daddy Long on WOKJ.

Josie's skills as a booster, or thief, were legendary and alluring enough that thieves across the state of Mississippi and elsewhere wanted to conduct capers with her. The world of hustlers was a self-contained business. Teams of rogues would scope out some of the finer department stores in Jackson. In a period before high-tech surveillance, a man or woman would go in and bunch up a section of men's suits or women's dresses. The store clerk would then be distracted by what was called a blocker. A woman wearing a loose-fitting dress would then stuff as many suits or dresses as possible underneath. Most times the scheme worked flawlessly, and the thieves were rarely caught. The word was that the clothes were discounted and sold to individuals in the upper crust of Jackson's white society. A five-thousand-dollar fur, for example, might be marked down 50 percent before it was peddled.

The hustlers even erected training seminars for potential recruits in a local hotel. It was an impressive operation complete with a clothes rack filled with old clothes on which the instructors could demonstrate the technique of marking or bunching up items for snatching. A related class showed people how to stuff clothing between their legs and walk without resembling a pigeon-toed oddball.

Josie Mae was a heartfelt love that was not to flower, and our relationship represented a journey on a street heading to nowhere worthwhile. She ambushed me with startling news one day that she had violated her probation after being arrested for shoplifting in a store in Louisiana and was to report to Angola State Prison for completion of a sentence. I estimate that if not for this event, Josie Mae and I eventually would have settled into a life of domestic tranquility. I drove for hours one weekend to see her at Angola but was turned away at the door for lack of the right paperwork. After that I never tried to connect with Josie Mae again.

CHAPTER TWELVE

Chattahoochee Kinfolks

JUST GIVE US ONE YEAR," the broadcast executives said.

Mary O'Shields and Eathel Holley were radio managers in Atlanta and felt they could make a respectable showing with their own station in the Phenix City/Columbus, Georgia, market at WOKS. The station sat on the north bank of the Chattahoochee River in Alabama but was licensed in Columbus.

Phenix City is the only Alabama municipality using the eastern time designation as opposed to central standard time. The area, with its foundation in cotton and textiles, is a few miles west of Fort Benning, Georgia, site of a large U.S. Army base. Residents of the town would amble across the bridges to textile mills in Columbus. The town was struggling to redeem itself in view of its history in the 1940s and 1950s when it was beset with gambling, prostitution, and clip joints. It had been the site of the Bamboo Club, the Bama Club, and Ma Beechie's Swing Club, which was reportedly famous for exotic dancing and prostitution. Some in Phenix City can recall that during World War II soldiers attracted to the town would roll in on buses with paychecks in their pockets and end up intoxicated. One resident remembers members of General George Patton's 1st Armored Division and the 82nd Airborne Division engaged in a lengthy free-for-all on the Fourteenth Street Bridge. On the crest of summer in 1954, Albert Patterson, a Phenix City native running for attorney general on the platform of cleaning up the city, was gunned down in a political assassination. The next day the town was placed under martial law, and the National Guard rolled in to revoke liquor licenses, smash slot machines, and chase off prostitutes.

A venture in a new market presented a chance for me to shuffle the painful memories of Rebecca and Josie Mae onto the back burner. The radio world was my oyster, and Phenix City was as good a place as any in which to ply my skills after having left Mississippi. Besides, my father's mother, Rosa Lee Stewart, lived there, as did other relatives. To be clutched in the bosom of family remained a tauntingly elusive desire.

Rosa Lee Stewart still chewed tobacco and wore an apron all the time. I had not seen her since Rebecca and I had detoured off U.S. 280 to find her a few years earlier on our way to the glass-bottom boats in northern Florida. She had been well respected for her integrity among the black and white communities and was still known to many of them as Mama Rosa. At her advanced age, she had mostly retired from work in the Patterson household.

"Where you gonna live, boy?" she inquired when I showed up at her small wood-frame house on Bank Street.

Next to her humble dwelling was an empty three-room house owned by an aunt, Marie Jackson, and it would be no problem to squat there until I could settle in with the flow of the community, she said. Rosa Lee admitted she had heard some of the details about my mother's death. She had actually visited Slim and Marie's house when we were living on the back porch but somehow had come at a time when Sam, David, Bubba, and I were out scouring the neighborhood. Many aunts and cousins knew the conditions under which we lived, but none had seen fit to step up to the plate to alleviate the situation.

"You got a heap of relatives, sonny boy," she said. "Some are messy and may not like you. There comes your sister now," my grandmother said.

A twenty-something woman named Lera came staggering up the steps in an apparent alcohol-shrouded fog. Rosa Lee warned her that she was skating along a slippery road to an early grave. Lera asked me for a few dollars with which she could purchase a bottle of wine, a request I summarily denied. The fact that her first words would be about money were not disappointing or surprising. This symbolized her lifestyle, and I accepted the situation as a fact of life.

This was the first inkling that I had a sister, but I recalled that two young men had once materialized at Slim and Marie's house like interlopers from a parallel universe. They had been identified as Slim's other sons, obvious mementos of a virile youth. When these boys were younger, the story goes, Slim would travel with a son from Birmingham to Phenix City, or vice versa, on his primary mode of transportation between cities—the freight car. He would tie a sack around his neck, put a son in the sack, and hop in a boxcar on the L&N train that ran through Birmingham and past his family's house in Phenix City.

Slowly, word spread that I was in town, and kinfolk by the bushel showed up. Aunt Lonnie Mae Thomas, my father's sister, arrived with her children, a girl named Yvette and a boy named Sherold. Another cousin, Venira, a schoolteacher, and her husband, Jasper, a waiter, made an entrance. Cousins Brenda Knight and Margaret, who had been raised by Rosa Lee, were expected to make appearances. Now, it seemed, I had relatives up to my armpits. This situation struck me as a union of relatives rather than a reunion. Earthy folks who I had never known existed were now to be part of my life; I had longed for family rather than kinfolks, but this was a start.

We cut the fellowship meeting short since I had to be at the WOKS station for the 3 P.M. broadcast. Aunt Lonnie Mae went with me in hopes of landing a job at the place, which was a brick house that had been converted. The control room was situated in what was once the kitchen, and the office was in the back of the building, decorated with "Welcome, Shelley the Playboy" signs in strategic locations.

"Get ready, here's Shelley . . . He's a playboy . . . he's my boy . . . make him your boy too," went the theme song sung by the Poppies. I jumped into a fast-paced monologue about the town and the fact that I had relatives living there, which was to help build an empathy with the listeners. Commentary coated in hip-minded humor was dished out as I hit a comfortable rhythm in the four-hour-long program.

That evening I discovered that my relatives had a penchant for Gilby's gin. Venira, Margaret, and her husband, Leon, dropped by the house armed with a couple bottles of alcohol. Brenda showed up in time for the toast. In minutes the liquor had been devoured, and there was only a residual trace visible in the bottles. Margaret and Leon excused themselves from the parley and returned shortly with corn whiskey. The partyers' consumption of the beverage laid the groundwork for loose tongues and unchaperoned inhibitions as relatives verbally assaulted each other.

"You ain't seen a damn thing yet. You don't know your kinfolks, Shelley," said Venira.

The next morning, apparently sobered up from the cutthroat atmosphere and liquor consumption of the previous evening, Venira dropped by before she was to go to her teaching job and fixed breakfast. It was a nice familial touch that I appreciated.

Back on the air later that day, I unleashed a barrage of jive laced with nuggets of homespun wisdom and music spun on a turntable.

"I wish all you married women would stop calling me," I joked on the air. "You haven't seen me, and you don't know me."

The kinfolks and their intimacy with liquor were fair game. Targets included grandmother Rosa Lee, who swore that the little bottle she sipped from contained nothing more than brown water. On the serious side of the banter, I pointed out the need for blacks to register to vote and commented on current events that blipped across my radar screen. Calls to the station soared during my first days on the air, as businesses bought advertising space for the broadcasts. Motorists would often drive by during the broadcast and wave and toot their horns. Even soldiers from nearby Fort Benning called in requests for songs.

Phenix City was a place I had hoped to find myself and craft out a sense of belonging. Rosa Lee, Lonnie Mae, Margaret and Brenda and Venira were the hub of the new relationships, although they were not above cashing in on my name for a little social recognition. The liquor consumed at our family bull sessions continued to unlock frustrations and hidden resentments to which humble people are sometimes prone. Even I was not immune to put-downs and comparisons to a successful cousin, William Stewart, who resided in Mayfield, Illinois.

"You think you are better than us, but you ain't shit," a cousin said. "You ain't got a damn thing. What are you doing living in this place if you got so much?"

The exception to the rule was cousin Margaret, a woman five years my senior. She sold whiskey out of her Frederick Douglas apartments to supplement her maid's income. She and her husband, Leon, had adopted a daughter and son. Margaret cried when I poured out my soul about my particularly difficult early life. Now, she said, I was her brother, and anyone who hassled me would receive a remarkable beating.

Sock hops or platter parties were staples of the entertainment venue, and each week I was booked to appear at a club, organization, or school. Police would escort me through the throngs of teenagers hungry for grooving experiences. At South Girard High School about a thousand youths showed up for an event. The modus operandi would be to play records like "Just a Matter of Time" by Brook Benton, converse with the audience, and even sing tunes myself.

A Mr. Cook, owner of the Club Lavanna, approached me about conducting a party on a Wednesday night in February 1959. The event was overflowing with customers who swayed and bounced to the music. A song by the Fiestas reverberated around the room and ricocheted off the ceiling and floor with acoustical dexterity. I caught the eye of an attractive woman sitting with her girlfriends, and I lip-synched along with the music.

"You are so fine . . . you are mine," I sang as she slipped down in her chair under the weight of embarrassment.

During an intermission I went over and introduced myself. Her name was Lucille Lemon, and she was a schoolteacher in Phenix City who had graduated from Fort Valley State College in Georgia. She stated that her biological father, a man named Lemon, had divorced her mother and gone on to marry another woman. After his death, the stepmother married a man named Beavers. Lucille's natural mother was no longer a part of her life for some reason, and she now regarded her stepmother and stepfather as her essential family.

Lucille and I seemed to click and began dating. Cousin Venira, of course, asked Lucille why a schoolteacher was keeping company with an "ignorant ass" radio personality, a statement with more than an atom of irony since her husband, Jasper, was a waiter. At any rate, the vaguely dysfunctional nature of her family represented a common denominator between us.

Not long after my relationship began with Lucille, I received a notification from the state of Alabama that Gwen's mother was pursuing a legal action against me, charging lack of support for a child, Sheldon Collins. This was the first I had heard from the women in more than a year. I felt it was imperative to let Lucille know the whole story, and, predictably, she faced the news with understanding.

I went to a state human resources agency to meet Gwen's mother in West Blocton and told the officials that I would do anything I could to support the child and even take him to live with me, but the grandmother began ranting and raving.

"I want your money," she screamed. "I don't want a damn thing from the SOB but his money."

The hearing quickly disintegrated, and I would not pursue the issue until weeks later. I knew that I had an obligation to Sheldon and wanted to fulfill it. The specter of my own father lurked in my mind as an ideal example of what a parent should not be. I wanted a clear distinction between my behavior and his. Besides, I knew Mattie C. would have wanted me to own up to responsibilities regarding my child and her grandchild.

The Birmingham radio market still appealed to me, and I wanted Lucille and me to go to Birmingham as man and wife. We were married in Phenix City in November 1959. By this time, John McClendon had purchased Bessemer's WBCO, changed its call letters to WENN, and moved it to a storefront building at Eighteenth Street North between Fifth and Sixth Avenues North. Reluctantly, Lucille agreed to move to Birmingham into a Fountain Heights apartment building. Almost immediately, Lucille became pregnant, and I knew that I would have to hustle if I wanted the child to have a decent lifestyle. I went to work at WENN on January 3, 1960, for $125 a week. I would also augment my pay with platter parties.

The club or organization sponsoring the party usually could expect from two hundred to three hundred patrons who paid about fifty cents each. My cut of the action was about seventy cents out of each dollar, which meant I pulled in from $70 to $150 per party. Often, I would not get home from these events until late at night or early in the morning. Financial security aside, the parties and radio broadcasts shredded quality time with my wife.

Later Lucille and I traveled to West Blocton to Gwen's mother's ramshackle house. The woman and her husband were raising a half-dozen children of their own and about five or six grandchildren. Lucille said the baby, Sheldon, resembled me, and I did not dispute that. We brought the child to stay with us for a while and took him back to Tuscaloosa County after a few weeks when his grandmother began raising hell stating that she wanted the boy and money. We again considered adopting him because of the congested conditions in which he was living, but his grandmother still would not consent. Also, I discovered that funds that had been sent for Sheldon were redirected to other children in the house. On other visits to the dwelling, the grandparents greeted me with such belligerence that I broke off contact lest the situation escalate to physical violence. The boy and I were to have little contact after that for many years. Gwen's mother, a volatile woman, was eventually stabbed to death in an altercation in Tuscaloosa County.

CHAPTER THIRTEEN

Rocking the Boat

IN JUNE 1960 I walked straight into the acrid smoke of Southern racism. The chameleon of racial suppression was endemic to most of the nation and adopted many forms from the blatant segregation of the South to the subtle but notoriously effective economic and social constraints prevalent in the rest of the United States. But the ace in the hole was the Ku Klux Klan, which often did the dirty work while genteel Southern society merely winked or turned its head in a gesture of blissful ignorance. Born under the guidance of Confederate General Nathan Bedford Forest, a soldier whose motto was "to get there fustest with the mostest," the Klan had long been a harbinger of terror for many Negroes. The national headquarters of a major Klan faction was situated in Tuscaloosa, some fifty-five miles away from downtown Birmingham.

The summer of that year was the perfect backdrop for an exhilarating sock hop at Don's Teen Town in Jonesboro near Bessemer. Operated by Ray Mahoney, the hop attracted about eight hundred white teens who danced to what many of their elders called race music or jungle music. My brother David and friend Wallace Montgomery helped me set up the sound system and amplifiers for the event. The party presented an opportunity for the middle-class, neatly dressed youth to dance and let their hair down.

The event also attracted the attention of reactionary elements; dozens of carloads of Klansmen and Jefferson County sheriff's deputies massed outside the building. It was not clear if the lawmen were there to preserve the public safety or act as understudies to the Klan, but I suspected the latter. A fight broke out between the teenagers and the thugs, which allowed us to escape. We sped down the highway and holed up in the driveway of a house in Lipscomb owned by a friend, Mary Mason. Disguising ourselves as laborers, we talked our way through a roadblock on the Bessemer Superhighway. We arrived that evening at my apartment and found gun-toting strangers around the place. Radio station WSGN had broadcast a report that I had been killed by Klansmen after the sock hop.

A reporter for the *Birmingham News* showed up at my residence, and voices in the crowd grew menacing. The journalist asked me if I planned to return to the air, and I said that I would. In the next day's paper it was erroneously reported that I had stated I would never play for a white audience again. When I went back on the air at WENN, there were armed men staking out the station to make sure that no segregationists attempted to finish the job that the racists had attempted in Jonesboro. As a postscript, I did play before a white audience the following week at the Tutwiler Hotel.

————————

FATHERHOOD WAS AGAIN APPROACHING by the summer of 1960. Our apartment in the Fountain Heights neighborhood consisted of two bedrooms, a living room, and a small kitchen. We converted the second bedroom into a nursery complete with bassinet and infant paraphernalia. Anticipation and excitement over the birth made the nine-month gestation seem like an eternity. This was my first real chance to prove that I would not be the same kind of useless father that Slim Stewart had been to me and my brothers. A daughter, Sherri, was born in Holy Family Hospital on August 28, my mother's birthday. This child born twenty-one years after my mother's death seemed to represent Mattie C.'s hand in the scheme of my life again. The words her spirit spoke a decade earlier when I saw her ethereal form as I sat in the outhouse at Aunt Mamie's home flowed into my mind: "Know that I am with you and in you."

The child was a joy to behold and served to enhance the relationship I enjoyed with Lucille. This was my flesh, blood, bones, and perhaps even my soul being extended for another generation. Certainly, I had fathered Sheldon in a one-night stand with Gwen, but I was not raising him as my child. This baby would be under my care for me to feed, change her diaper, and help blow her nose. As she matured, I could teach her how to ride a bicycle and provide her with the education of which I had been cheated when others got the scholarships at Rosedale School nearly a decade earlier. Real fatherhood in its best sense had arrived that summer.

By 1961 I was going full throttle at WENN, which had moved to the 1500 block of Fifth Avenue North. Across the street was Kelley Ingram Park, which served as a buffer between the station and the Sixteenth Street Baptist Church. The nation had just elected John Kennedy to lead the country into the New Frontier, and the civil rights movement had begun to heat up on the heels of the Greensboro, North Carolina, lunch counter sit-ins and the Freedom Rides from Washington, D.C., that ran a gauntlet of violence when they reached Anniston, Birmingham, and Montgomery in May 1961. The firebrand Reverend Fred Shuttlesworth, a graduate of my alma mater, Rosedale School, and Edward Gardner, director of the Alabama Christian Movement for Human Rights, had helped to accelerate activism on the local level. And, of course, I used my radio pulpit to push for change at the voting booth.

Clyde Smith appeared at WENN in the early 1960s with a small boy, Clyde Jr., in tow. It had been years since I had seen him. Of course, the rock house was gone; this was a fact I discovered after I had detoured on my way to Leeds for a platter party at George Moore's Club in the mid-1950s and gazed up the hill from U.S. 78 to see an empty spot on the landscape. He and Mama Bessie had split up, and she and Mary Sue had gone their separate ways. Papa Clyde had remarried and was the father of a son and still developing subdivisions and operating restaurants. Never an emotional man, he shook hands with me, and I expressed pleasure at seeing the man who had literally saved my life in the 1940s. Our meeting was short, but he voiced pride in my statements on the air regarding equal rights and for the fact that I was standing up for something in which I believed. I don't know what Clyde's sympathies were regarding the civil rights struggle, but I never attempted to classify him as a liberal. To me he was simply a decent man who seemed to believe in fairness for the individual. After our brief conversation, Papa Clyde disappeared into his own world again, but I still possessed fond memories and grateful sentiments for the world we had shared together in the 1940s.

WENN WAS PRESUMABLY A PROFITABLE operation for McClendon-Ebony Broadcasting, but it was far from utopian for the African Americans working there. Whites filled the better-paying jobs as ad salesmen and technicians. The salesmen would draw a 15 percent commission off commercial time sold. The atmosphere was reflective of Old South culture, and an attitude existed to make the black employees feel "less than." At the old Eighteenth Street WENN office there had been only one rest room that everyone used, but the Fifteenth Street location featured an unlocked toilet in the hall that was unofficially designated as being for blacks. Another rest room in the back of the building near the manager's office was the one whites used and required a key. The humiliation of the setup became even more obvious when Daisy Giddings, the black traffic director, was occupying "our" rest room when I had to relieve myself. I kicked the lock off the white rest room door, used it, and told the station manager that we were not going to tolerate that situation.

While the black personalities were clearly the backbone of the station, any respect was begrudgingly shown. The managers were often hostile and terse, sometimes refusing to answer black staffers' simple questions or prefacing a remark with "What the hell do you want?"

Personality conflicts catapulted WENN through a menagerie of bosses within a time span of a few years. They were sent in from other stations in Memphis or Little Rock and included Eddie Phelan, Jim Loftin, and Carroll Jackson.

During Jackson's reign, the staff came up with its own solution for the persistent stream of objectionable bosses. We arranged a meeting with McClendon and told him our thoughts on who we felt would be more palatable: Joe Lackey, our office manager, a mild-mannered man whom most of us liked. Although Joe never said he was in favor of or opposed to integration, and never socialized with Negroes, we felt he would be fairer than the others, more decent, and not openly bigoted.

"Joe!" McClendon shrieked. "Joe Lackey? Him?"

Lackey could be seen sitting at his desk fiddling with papers on the other side of his office glass, apparently oblivious to the rooting section he had engendered. We reiterated our position that we felt that Joe seemed to be a man with whom we could work in relative harmony.

"You mean to tell me . . . ," McClendon began. "Joe has no experience in sales. He just handles the books and financial reports . . . Him?" With that he stalked out of the room, slamming the door behind him.

Lackey was promoted to the position, however, and became a more dapper dresser and even traded in a ragged old Ford for a new Buick Electra 225, or, as it was informally called, a Deuce and a Quarter. He knew what the blacks would not tolerate and was aware that we had rallied for him and that we expected to be able to count on him in a pinch.

BY THE EARLY 1960s, my brothers Sam and David and I still spent time together when they aided me at platter parties or just plain socialized. And they still stirred up trouble. Sam, because of his temperament, was even accused of cutting a bread delivery man whom he claimed was flirting with one of our cousins, Lorene. While Sam was creating mayhem in Smithfield and elsewhere, David seemed to be trying to outdo him in his parallel world of Rosedale. Almost every other weekend I was going to the city jail to post bond for one of them on some complaint citing public intoxication or violence.

Sam had married a churchgoing, hardworking woman named Norris in 1959. They lived in a shotgun-style duplex on Graymont Avenue, not far from Legion Field where the University of Alabama's Paul "Bear" Bryant was building a record as one of the winningest coaches in college football with his Crimson Tide gladiators. Sam worked at a metal shop nearby, and sometimes he would drop by WENN with his drinking buddies. His job capsized after he let drinking interfere with his work. His occupations represented a hodgepodge of endeavors and ran the gamut from metals plant worker to killing chickens at a Jasper poultry factory. Even the fact that he and Norris had begun having children did not slow down his drinking at places like New Gary's and Parkview Inn downtown. Sam, possibly because of the alcohol that allowed his personal demons free rein, had also drifted into beating Norris and ignored my admonishments on the matter.

David, of course, was not able to qualify for any substantial vocations either and knocked around at anything that could bring in a few dollars. A chef's job was one of his most profitable endeavors.

He who lives by his fists will certainly nearly perish the same way. Fighting finally caught up with David. He had finished caddying at Hillcrest Country Club on the eastern side of town when a bunch of guys caught him on their Woodlawn territory, whipped him severely, and left him in a culvert. After taking weeks to mend in University Hospital, David began driving through Woodlawn trying to find the assailants so he could render his own brand of street justice.

One day Sam came by WENN to visit me, shoot the breeze, and appeal for what amounted to drinking money. Three or four other guys also came into the station since it was not unusual for fans to drop in off the street. Sam struck up a conversation with the guys, and they mentioned they were from Woodlawn. He, in turn, stated he was from Rosedale.

"You know a dude named David?" a fellow asked. "Man, me and some of my partners caught him on our turf and beat the hell out of him."

Sam, surmising that fate had brought our brother's attackers to within his grasp, played it cool and said he thought he knew where David hung out. Ostensibly, he told the guys that he would take them there so that they could perform an encore beating. I sat at the control board broadcasting with less than fifteen minutes before my afternoon show would be off the air. Sam walked close to me, winked, and let me know that downtown was on the verge of heating up.

"I am gone, brother," he whispered. "I think I got one of them."

Sam and the guys went down to New Gary's place where they were going to wait for David to show up, but Sam got to a phone and tipped our youngest brother off that he had found his attackers and would attempt to stall them.

Not long after I ended my broadcast, I heard a commotion of police sirens. Looking out the window, I saw patrol cars speeding in the direction of New Gary's on Seventeenth Street. David had apparently shown up at the joint and identified at least one of the guys as having been among his Woodlawn assailants. Sam and David stabbed the guys, some of whom were apparently innocent and knew nothing of the precipitating incident. The men survived their wounds to the best of my knowledge, and no one around the club would identify my brothers, who fled the scene before the police arrived. Without question, I did not approve of their behavior, but attempting to change the leopard's spots on the duo seemed nearly impossible.

Sam and David, although they were generally cantankerous, would throw a punch quickly for one reason in particular: if you talked ugly about our mother, Mattie C. A practice that blacks called "playing the dozens" occurred when someone insulted your mother. But most of the time the phrase "yo mama" would do just as well or better if you wanted to trigger a fight among some blacks. Usually I would take such a comment in stride, but a person was taking a great risk with his own safety if he made such a remark to my brothers.

One day Sam, David, and I were out riding and were about to travel down over Red Mountain into Birmingham. I was driving, David sat in the front seat, and Sam had the rear seat to himself.

"You know," said David, "I don't believe us and Sam have got the same mammy."

"Don't talk about my mama," Sam growled.

"Hey, she's my mama too, ain't she?" David responded.

"Well, you talking about my part," said Sam. "Man, ya'll are some dirty SOBs."

By this time, we were going forty miles an hour heading down Red Mountain. I looked to the rear just in time to see Sam shove the door open and jump from the car. He hit the ground and rolled several feet. Luckily, there was no other traffic in our immediate proximity. In a panic, I turned the car around at the bottom of the hill and sped back to where Sam lay bruised, but conscious and shaken. We drove him to University Hospital where he was treated and released.

"Don't nobody talk about my mama," said Sam as we left the hospital.

Otis Redding

The South, particularly Birmingham and Atlanta, were launching pads for many songs hatched from the talents of black musicians in the 1950s and 1960s thanks to the radio airwaves. Atlanta boasted J. B. Blayton Jr.'s WERD, the first black-owned radio station in America, and Zenas "Daddy" Sears's WAOK. Once a record took off in Birmingham's WENN, WEDR, or

WJLD, its success would have an impact on the Atlanta market. Distributors in that city would note the volume of sales in Birmingham, and this made it easier for the disc to receive airtime in Atlanta. It would take a relatively short time for a song to achieve hit status across the country after its Southern debut.

Otis Redding was one of those golden-voiced Southern singers that became icons in U.S. pop culture in the 1960s. He had been born in Dawson, Georgia, on September 9, 1941, but raised in Macon where he worked as a roofer and was later to be influenced by Sam Cooke and Little Richard. I first met Redding when he was on his way to the Fame recording studios in Muscle Shoals as the bus driver for Johnny Jenkins and the Pine Toppers in 1962, although some reports erroneously say they recorded at the Stax studios in Memphis. The group had traveled from Georgia and stopped at WENN to socialize for a short time. It was common for people in the disc jockey business to have connections with all kinds of musicians, famous and obscure. Redding sang two songs of his own at the end of the Fame recording session, and one of them, "These Arms of Mine," launched his career.

Months later Otis was set to perform at an anniversary program in my honor that was given at the Club Eldorado in a former mining camp community called Powderly. At curtain time the show almost did not go on as scheduled. Otis showed up so intoxicated he could hardly keep his footing. Atlantic Records promoter Joe Medlin, a former vocalist with Buddy Johnson in the late 1940s, saved the day. After we could not get Otis sober, Joe took the stage and belted out a few numbers and kept the continuity of the program intact. The next morning I gave Otis a brotherly tongue-lashing and told him his conduct was unprofessional and not appropriate for a man of his talent.

ARTHUR GEORGE GASTON, USUALLY KNOWN as A. G., was a special man for the fact that he had pulled himself up by his own bootstraps to become possibly the wealthiest black person in Alabama. A native of Demopolis in the state's Black Belt, he had used homespun business acumen to weave a respected dynasty consisting of a funeral home, insurance company, and Citizens Federal Savings Bank. But like many people with money and power, he had an elephant-sized sense of his own worth. This became clear when I visited the Gaston Lounge one afternoon for a drink. He waltzed into the establishment, and the men in the room stood in reverence as they always did and said, "Hey, Dr. Gaston, how are you doing?" The businessman usually acknowledged their greetings and proceeded to a table. This time he walked over to the table where I was drinking a beer and eating a sandwich. He asked me to get him a sandwich and beer also, which I did, and he then sat down for a conversation.

"Shelley," he said, "I notice that whenever I come into the room, you always remain seated and never say a damn thing. Why is that?"

Obscenities flew from my lips as I called the man every uncomplimentary description I could muster in preface to explaining my rationale for not standing up as if the Queen of England or the King of the Zulu nation had just graced the room.

"I'm spending my money in your lounge . . . you are a man, are you not?" I said.

"Wait a minute Shelley," Gaston said. "I knew there was something about you that I liked. You have got backbone. Everyone of those Negroes over there has borrowed money from me or is beholden to me."

Determined not to seem in any way obsequious to the senior citizen, I rattled on in the spirit of candor.

"Even if you had helped me, I still would not stand up," I said. "I gave you respect by spending my money in your business."

Now Gaston knew what manner of man he had encountered. Perhaps he figured me to be bold, or even insane. During this episode I had demonstrated to him that I felt I was his equal in personal value if not in financial trappings.

This, of course, would not be the last of my interactions with Gaston. The Fountain Heights apartment seemed to be closing in on Lucille, Sherri, and me to the extent that daily life was growing physically uncomfortable. I discovered that Gaston was using bricks from a demolished funeral home to build a small subdivision of attractive houses in the northeastern area. With an air of brashness, I went to his office in the Citizens Federal Savings Bank building and told the civic leader that I was going to buy a house in the area in which his son, a local dentist, and a plumber had homes. The fourth home, which was under construction, would be mine.

"Shelley," he said, "you know those houses cost seventeen thousand dollars apiece. How are you going to do it?"

"You are going to loan me the money," I said. "Didn't you say I had more backbone than any man you had ever met?"

The businessman, after further attempting to throw water on my plan, relinquished and told me to go down to see his lawyer, Philander Butler, for the loan. Butler, confused, told Gaston that it would be unprecedented for his insurance corporation to loan money for a mortgage. Usually such transactions flowed through Gaston's Vulcan Realty or Citizens Federal Savings Bank.

"Philander," Gaston said, "just draw up the damn paper-work."

The executive drew up the papers with the Gaston firm as mortgage holder. After the house was built, we moved out of our cramped apartment to more suitable quarters.

To supplement my income I leased space at 1607 Fifth Avenue North around the corner from WENN and prepared to open Shelley's Record Mart. I stocked the place on consignment; that is, I would sell whatever I could and return leftovers to the company. The sign in the shop window caught the attention of Joe Lackey, who asked me about it. I confirmed that it was my establishment. The next afternoon, after I had finished my broadcast, Shelley's Noon-Flight, Lackey approached me and told me that station owner John McClendon had said that I could not work for the radio station and own the store too.

"Why?" I asked.

"Because no one else does it," Lackey replied.

"There's something wrong with this," I said, and reaffirmed my plan to open the business.

Later that day I returned to the station for my 3 P.M. show. I noticed Lackey was still in his office shortly after 5 P.M., the time he usually left for the day. At the conclusion of the program at 6 P.M., he came over and said McClendon viewed the business as a conflict and feared I would become too independent. He had a check in his hand in anticipation of my final answer, and again I refused to give up the store.

"Here's your check," he said. "If you change your mind, you can come back to work."

The whole scenario was, of course, an outrage. Those in the all-white ad-sales crew were raking in 15 percent commissions, and even Lackey was receiving 10 percent of gross radio advertisement sales rather than a standard salary.

Across the street was the Gaston Lounge, and I went there to unwind and break the news to the lawyers and business types assembled. The word spread apparently with the speed of Halley's Comet. That evening I received a surprising phone call from Otis Dodge, manager of WJLD, which amounted to a job offer at his station. It was startling since Dodge had said he could never work with a man that showed my activist spirit. The unseen progenitor of grand schemes had stepped into my life again. Perhaps here again was my mother, Mattie C., influencing Dodge so that I could jump back into a radio job so quickly.

The next morning I went on the air at WJLD and shocked the devil out of the listening audience. The first perk showered on me was a fifty-dollar-a-month raise. Again, I understood that this was chicken feed when juxtaposed against the reenumeration the whites were receiving in radio sales, management, and ownership.

The idea of bringing me into the WJLD fold belonged to Mrs. Rose Hood Johnston, the station owner who had taken over full operation of the radio outlet upon the death of her husband, George. WJLD was more conservative than WENN. A policy was on the books that said on-air personnel could not get involved in promoting the civil rights movement during the broadcasts and that any so-called public service announcements had to be approved by Dodge. These were rules that I planned to regard as tissue paper. It seemed that the McClendons and Dodges of the world were satisfied when black personalities were acting contented and dancing in the slave quarters, so to speak. But I vowed that I would always pursue the naked truth while dispelling the well-dressed lie.

Others on the staff included Johnny "Jive" McClure, who played rhythm and blues, and Deacon Willie McKinstry and Truman Puckett, both of whom handled gospel music. At least

the on-air staff was integrated since Puckett was a white man.
Erin Connolly was the top salesperson, Patti Wheeler and Judy
Howell worked in the office, and Bob Delander was the engi-
neer.

Three days after I went on the air, I was served with an in-
junction stating that I was violating a contract with McClendon
that supposedly stipulated a disc jockey could not immediately
transfer to another local station after leaving WENN. WJLD decided to fight the suit, and in the meantime I stayed on the air.
Johnston Broadcasting lawyers argued in court that McClendon's claim was invalid because I was, in effect, fired from
WENN. The judge agreed and stated that WENN had no legal
reason to hinder the record shop.

WJLD was then located on Red Mountain. I persuaded
Dodge to set up studio equipment in my record shop, and I
broadcast from there. Working conditions at the station were
cordial for a while. The environment among the whites began to
chill noticeably after a few weeks. It was most obvious when I
would make simple requests of the engineer, Delander, such as
asking him to check the sound system, and the appeals would be
ignored. Dodge finally revealed the source of the aloofness when
he asked me why I did not address the white staffers as Mr. or
Mrs. or Miss as in Mr. Bob and Miss Judy. I told him that as
manager I felt he deserved a courtesy title, as did Mrs. Connolly
and Mrs. Johnston, both of whom were old enough to be my
mother. But I did not see the necessity of using the title for the
others, especially Judy, who was only a year or two out of college.
If anything, as a leading radio personality, it would be more
appropriate for the others to call me Mr. Stewart, or even Mr.
Shelley.

Dodge went into a rage at the uppity attitude I was shoving
into his face and launched into a diatribe.

"Damn it," he said. "Who do you think you are?"

I stood up, and at six feet three inches, I was almost a foot taller than the man.

"You are not going to get in my face," I said.

Dodge climbed up on a chair in an effort to gain a psychological advantage over me. "It's kinds like you that are causing all of these problems down here in the South," he said.

Not be outmaneuvered in the confrontation, I climbed up on my chair and repeated my position on the issue. Dodge grew even more mercurial and seemed to almost bite his lip to keep from shouting out a racial slur. The ranting and raving had attracted the attention of Mrs. Johnston, who dottered into the room, arms folded, to sort out the situation. She listened with the attentiveness and dispassionate interest of an elementary school principal trying to settle a school ground fracas.

"Well, Otis," she began, "Shelley is respecting you by calling you Mr., and he is respecting Mrs. Connolly and me. I think it's very kind of Shelley." There was nothing wrong with the way I addressed the other employees, she said. Apparently she did not want to alienate me any more than a farmer would would want to tick off a prize-winning Angus bull used for stud purposes. I would continue to bend the time-honored rules of Southern etiquette.

———

THE QUEST FOR FREEDOM had begun to snowball in Birmingham by the early 1960s. Civil rights leaders wanted to invite to Birmingham a young minister who had made an impact in Montgomery with his leadership during the bus boycott that helped break the back of segregated bus systems across the South. The Reverend Martin Luther King Jr. was pastor of the state capital's Dexter Avenue Baptist Church and known for his erudite manner and intelligent leadership. Some black preachers and businesspeople were already wary of firebrand activist Fred Shuttleworth's confrontational style and feared that he would get folks killed. These same voices of discouragement from the ministerial and economic arenas were now none too pleased that reinforcements in the guise of King were being summoned to help Negroes cast off a century of accommodation to subordination to Birmingham's white supremacist power structure. It was my position in statements on the air that all willing to whittle down the status quo of segregation and injustice for Negroes should be welcomed.

The Reverend Martin Luther King Jr. was a man who was crafted in the bosom of destiny so that he would provide an articulate voice for millions of disenfranchised black Americans. Although I had met him a few years earlier in Montgomery, I saw him in action one morning during my tenure at WJLD when I was outside my record store that sat across from Kelley Ingram Park and the Sixteenth Street Baptist Church. The park and church would become focal points for protest rallies and were in the shadows of City Hall, three blocks to the east. King came striding up with a small entourage consisting of two men whom I came to know as civil rights strategists Reverend Andrew Young and Reverend James Bevell.

"Which one of you is Shelley?" Young asked.

"I'm Shelley," I said as we shook hands.

"I heard you this morning," King said. "You are quite a personality."

The minister had heard about my broadcasts from his turf in Montgomery about a hundred miles to the south of Birmingham and said he appreciated the work I was doing providing information for the burgeoning movement to attain equality for Negroes.

"Well, we've got some talking and walking and work to do this morning and get more people involved in the cause," he said.

King said he was going to go to the whiskey parlors, pool halls, and cafes that dotted the nearby bustling black business district to recruit people for the struggle for human rights. This was rather startling to me since most ministers would shy away from being seen in unsavory places where alcohol was served or pool was played specifically because of the rather rough-hewn clientele the places often attracted.

Wishing him well, I watched as King and his two companions strode down to Seventeenth Street and Fourth Avenue North and disappeared around a corner.

About two hours later, still at the record store and between broadcasts at WJLD, I looked to the east to see a surprising spectacle. King was at the lead of a chattering throng of about fifty or sixty people that he and his two lieutenants had collected during their door-to-door campaign in the area. It was reminiscent of the day when people followed me as a pied piper on my long walk from Collegeville to Parker Industrial School in the late 1940s. While the trek to school was almost a social excursion, this parade of humanity had smelled the rose of freedom from their vantage points in the thorny garden of segregation and discrimination, and they wanted to hear more about how to clutch that sweet flower to their breasts.

As the crowd slowed, King said a few words to me and others gathered outside my store.

"Birmingham is a hard city," said King. "You have got to deal with the masses and then try to bring the classes."

This, of course, was a facet of Papa Clyde's own perspective, a viewpoint that I had adopted as well. It's best to favor masses of people over classes of people.

King was a great orator and a skilled tactician, a man who was devoid of an overbearing ego. However, I did not know that this subdued, thoughtful preacher with his emphasis on nonviolence would achieve the revered yet deserved role in American society that he eventually did.

During April and May of 1963 the push for integration of schools and department stores was reaching a fever pitch. Dr. King and other black leaders had chosen Birmingham as a focal point for the civil rights struggle partially because of the organizational infrastructure hammered by local battle-hardened soldiers in the quest for justice. The swift currents of history had brought Birmingham to the crossroads in the fight to tear down the formal walls of segregation, although many knew that the individual attitudes that supported the social phenomenon would die hard.

Birmingham had a long history of mean-spirited treatment of Negroes. It was routine for a store clerk to summon the law on customers who were considered smart or uppity. Consequently, the black person would be knocked senseless once the police arrived. The brutality of the law officers complemented sundry humiliations such as relegation to the back of the bus and segregated store elevators, lunch counters, schools, and just about every other component of life where there was anxiety over the races interacting.

My record store near Kelley Ingram Park represented an orchestra seat from which I could view the human drama. It was known that King and his lieutenants were being watched and monitored by the city police headed by "Bull" Connor. An abandoned hallway connected my shop with the law offices of J. Richmond Pearson. King and others would sometimes drop by ostensibly for small talk and then sneak down the hallway to meet with Pearson and arrange strategies for the nonviolent offensive. I became known as "the man with the passage."

The radio personalities filled a vacuum in that they represented the few media advocates of breaking down the walls of segregation. In ancient Africa the chief form of communication was by drums. The beat from that instrument resonated across grasslands to fall on the ears of attentive villagers and spoke of urgent news and casual information: births, deaths, and perhaps preparations for hunting parties or even war parties. Historically, the black community could not depend on the traditional white-oriented media to disseminate information on the struggle since most of them in Birmingham and the South did not support the civil rights quest. Like most Southern and many Northern media outlets, papers like Newhouse's *Birmingham News* and Scripps Howard's *Post-Herald* did little to pave the way for integration, possibly either because of financial risks or their adherence to cultural tradition. Black radio stepped into the breach left by the papers and television stations like Newhouse's WAPI and WBRC, then owned by Taft Broadcasting.

The radio station became my device of communication to an even greater degree. Basically, I pushed the scholar W. E. B. DuBois's concept of the talented tenth, a minority within the black community shackled with the altruistic notion of serving the greater community and relegating self-interest to second tier. I attempted to help persuade more members of the black middle class to get involved in their own future by joining in demonstrations, and continued spotlighting inequities for minorities, like I had done for years. In some quarters I became known as the "talking drum" for the role I played in bridging the communication gap for the black community.

Dodge pressured me to put a sock in my mouth over the free-spirited delivery and attitude I displayed.

"Mr. Dodge," I said, "I am a man, and my people are suffering. I would rather eat shit with a toothpick than stop the fight for freedom. Fire me." Entertainment without education is misinformation, I said, and warned that the movement would not evaporate because of the station owner's opposition.

The ranks of protesters began to expand with the youthful bodies and indomitable spirits of more and more children from schools like Lincoln and Parker High School. They were motivated and fearless and would walk undaunted into paddy wagons and school buses to be hauled to the city jail on Sixth Avenue South or to the old Rickwood Field baseball stadium.

I and other radio personalities like Tall Paul White and Erskine Faush of WENN began using codes to help civil rights demonstrators outmaneuver Bull Connor's police department. It was common knowledge that the police employed informants among the civil rights demonstrators. One of our challenges was to distract the police so a phalanx of demonstrators could attempt to integrate lunch counters in the department stores like Woolworth's or Newberry's.

An agreed-upon song would be played on a signal from a leader such as the Reverends King, N. H. Smith, and Andrew Young. It could be anything from "Wade in the Water" to "Yakkety Yak." Once a protest leader sent a messenger for White, Faush, or me to play the tune, people would walk from New Pilgrim Baptist on Southside to a downtown store. They would always be launched in pairs and at intervals so as not to draw attention. Meanwhile, demonstrators near Kelley Ingram Park would rush toward the police and begin taunting them. "Ain't nobody scared of your jail," the protesters would chant.

This technique riled the police up, and it was repeated over and over for about thirty minutes to allow the other teams to make it to the downtown rendezvous. By the time police caught on, there would be two hundred to three hundred protesters at a store.

Sometimes we would use codes to alert listeners to the times of a certain meeting or demonstration. This was executed with the help of a sort of double-talk.

"Well, let's check the time," I might say. "All right now. It's a 3 o'clock . . . No, it's not 3 o'clock, it's 9 o'clock." The message was that the time for a planned meeting or gathering would indeed be at 3 P.M.

Another radio message might use a person's name. "Hey, you know I saw Reverend Gardner up on Sixteenth Street?" I would say. This meant that some event was scheduled for the Sixteenth Street Baptist Church, such as a rally. The technique used by me and other radio personalities was a form of communication to help the drumbeat of freedom beat louder.

The music industry should be credited with coming to the aid of the civil rights movement. An incident outside my record store helped to galvanize the industry's commitment to the cause with real dollars. During a day that had seen rallies near Kelley Ingram Park, policemen would periodically sweep through the area in an effort to harass and intimidate protesters. One day an officer came down Fifth Avenue North swinging a billy club and shouting orders that sent many bystanders scurrying. "All you niggers get off the sidewalk," he yelled. By the time he got to bystander Joe Medlin, the Atlantic Records music promoter was bound and determined to stand fast.

"I am not moving any damn place," said Medlin, who was about six-feet-four. "This is one damn Negro that is not nonviolent."

Record promoters were an intrinsic part of the music industry circuit. Many of them, like Medlin, were intimate with the communities in which they traveled since they often stayed in neighborhood boardinghouses. He followed the tradition of Dave Clark, a promoter who worked for Don Robey, owner of the first black-owned record company in the U.S., Duke Peacock Records.

In an expression of moral and physical support, I went over to stand next to Medlin. "I don't think you want to talk to him like that," I said. "He is not going to move."

The officer, flustered at the confrontation, ignored us and went on down the sidewalk and resumed rousting others. Medlin, tears flowing in anger, was dumfounded at the barbarism of those who supposedly represented law and order. He used my store phone to place a call to legendary music pioneer Jerry Wexler at Atlantic Records in New York. Wexler had played a pivotal role in developing Alabama's Muscle Shoals into a major recording center and was to enjoy a career producing albums for the Drifters, Ray Charles, Aretha Franklin, Willie Nelson, and Bob Dylan.

"Police are swinging billy clubs," he said. "My people need help down here. You've got to call up some of your rich-ass friends and get some money here."

The record executive listened attentively, and the conversation ended. The music industry knew that it owed much of its success to black consumers whose purchasing power had contributed to the musical girth of companies like Stax and Atlantic and Motown. A few minutes later Leonard Chess, president of Chess Records, called and said he and others would be arranging for money to be sent to civil rights organizations operating in Birmingham.

Birmingham's struggle that pitted a restless quest for rights against the lethargic movement of the establishment culminated in the September 1963 explosion at the Sixteenth Street Baptist Church that claimed the lives of four precious, innocent black girls. I was called to the scene and arrived before rescue workers could remove their mangled bodies from piles of brick and plaster. I thought about another bombing, Pearl Harbor. In that instance, many were ashamed that Americans had been caught off guard. But now those with any semblance of a conscience were embarrassed at the climate in Alabama that had made the church blast possible.

MEANWHILE, THE TURBULENCE of the civil rights movement reflected the turmoil of my brothers' lives. Sam continued to hunt me down to request money to the degree that it became an unfaltering habit. One day in 1963 he came by WJLD and began pestering me to give him two hundred dollars. I was going to Bessemer for some matter, and he climbed into my car, still jabbering about money and accusing me of thinking I was superior.

"I am tired of this bullshit. You can go to jail and rot," I said.

"There's a truck going to Texas," Sam said. "If you stop that truck, I'll get on it."

Exasperated, I decided to call Sam's bluff and pulled alongside the eighteen-wheeler bearing Texas plates that had been barreling along ahead of us on Third Avenue West. By honking my horn and flashing my lights, I got the driver to pull over to the side of the road. We asked him if he would accept a hitchhiker. He told Sam he was welcome to ride with him to Texas, and my brother climbed aboard the vehicle.

"You can kiss my ass," Sam told me. On that note, they drove off toward U.S. 11 and west toward Texas. Sam's wife, of course, had no idea of his actions. All he had was the clothes on his back, and I certainly had not given him any money. Norris needed rent money, so I helped her with that obligation.

About a month and a half later I received a postcard from

Gila Bend, Arizona. Sam had gotten someone to write a message that stated that the truck had dropped him off in Dallas, Texas, and he was now walking to California. Within weeks he had made it to the Los Angeles area. Six months later Sam sent for his wife and two children.

———————

THE PRICE OF SUCCESS can be inordinately steep. This was the conclusion I reached after a couple of years of marriage to Lucille. We had moved from the Fountain Heights apartment into the comfortable house in the A. G. Gaston Estates. The joy of raising Sherri together was quite rewarding, and I continued to hustle with the radio job, record store, and platter parties to provide a comfortable life for our family. We even brought one of Lucille's sisters, who was about eight or nine, to live with us to remove her from the poor living conditions she endured with my wife's mother in Atlanta. However, the girl could not tolerate discipline, and we took her back home after a couple of months.

The high profile I enjoyed as Shelley the Playboy made me a sitting duck for resentments from various quarters. Through conversations with different fellows, I detected that they seemed to envy my success. Women fans voiced annoyance over the fact that I had married an outsider, a woman from Phenix City, and brought her back as queen of the manor.

During the fall of 1962 we discovered that Lucille was pregnant. For some reason she considered aborting the baby, but I insisted that the child would be born. By June 1963, a son was delivered, but Lucille did not want to call him Shelley Jr. She instead labeled him Shelley Lamar and nicknamed him Kip.

Although we had moved into better quarters with the relocation to A. G. Gaston Estates, the marriage had grown gradually more tenuous. Some of the dissension was promulgated at the knee of jealousy over imagined romantic rivals, as had been the case with Rebecca. Different women, some of whom were Lucille's friends, began to fill her head with lies about my supposed infidelities. A woman might come up to her and make an outrageous claim in this regard apparently since the myth of the swinging Shelley the Playboy was more seductive than the pedestrian lifestyle of Shelley Stewart.

What had been a carefully crafted mask to help sublimate old pain had taken on a life of its own in the minds of members of the public. "Aren't you Shelley the Playboy's wife?" a person might say. "Well, he used to go with my sister." These allegations helped to erode the marriage, and so did other malevolent issues.

Rumors began circulating that Shelley Lamar was not my biological child. "Mama's baby, daddy's maybe," was how the taunt was phrased around town. I refused to confront Lucille with these allegations and felt that no matter what, I regarded Shelley as my son and would love him no less even if he were not my offspring. Regardless, this contention did contribute to the quiltwork of tensions and anger in our marriage.

Financial problems began for me about 1964 and centered around my record store and lousy accounting practices. My accountant, T. L. Crowell, had overstated my inventory in the business to make me "look good," and consequently the store's profits were exaggerated. I was handed a $39,000 tax bill from the Internal Revenue Service, and a lien was placed on my radio station salary.

I learned later that Lucille had called the government and told them I had underreported income from platter parties. The fact that I had probably underpaid taxes for this income was partially based on ignorance and reliance on the informal pay system involved in the compensation for services. Often I would receive 70 to 100 percent of the ticket profits with little or no paper trail. It was akin to a vendor who takes the money and runs. The funds I received from the club engagements was viewed as income to balance the scales of justice within my career. After all, no matter how popular I was on the radio, my salary was always from $110 to $125 per week with the majority of profits flowing to white station owners, managers, and sales staff. The money from the parties, which could sometimes reach as much as five hundred dollars an engagement, made the glass ceiling that stifled my radio earnings more palatable.

I discovered that word of my financial situation had leaked to white politicians. Soon tax agents began calling or visiting the owner or promoter of each event at which I performed and freezing my income. This represented a coup de grace, a fatal blow for me in that my earnings were drastically reduced.

Now the world was closing in on me from multiple directions. Marital frictions and now financial pressure were forcing me to take the most traumatic step I could take—separate from Lucille. As a man whose original nuclear family was so treacherously torn asunder with the death of my mother, this new fragmentation of kinships would be no Sunday stroll through Central Park. But the unremitting tensions in my life seemed to dictate no other path.

CHAPTER FOURTEEN

St. Louis Blues

MARTY BROWN, MANAGER OF KATZ in St. Louis, Missouri, called and offered me a job following the death of radio personality Dave Dixon, who had been killed in an auto accident. This would be a coup for me to go on the air in a major market like St. Louis, although the Playboy could have gone any place to work on the strength of his popularity.

French fur traders from New Orleans founded St. Louis on Spanish territory in 1764, and it was named for Louis IX, the Crusader King of France. The explorers Lewis and Clark had set out from St. Louis to chart the Louisiana territory in 1804. Now, 160 years later, in 1964, I was using St. Louis as a launching point toward hopefully more solid financial footing and peace of mind.

My '63 Buick Wildcat, with its balding tires and clanking valves, rolled into St. Louis, a town that sits on a bluff eighteen miles south of the confluence of the Mississippi and Missouri rivers. I had fled Birmingham, hounded by financial and marital discord. The mortgage holder on our home in A. G. Gaston Estates apparently foreclosed sometime after I left, and Lucille and the children ended up in Columbus, Georgia.

Professional time was divided between a 6:30 to 9:30 A.M.

KATZ program and Earl Neal's Chatter Bar where I performed on Wednesday and Friday nights. The radio show became popular, and typical performances at the Chatter Bar would draw 120 to 150 people into a place that was designed to seat 75. Patrons enjoyed the records I played and my antics, which included climbing up on the bar and singing songs, screaming and yelling and hollering. The crowd would get worked up to a fever pitch. Joyce, a middle-aged divorcée, was a regular customer. She had children and grandchildren, but she liked to sugarcoat her troubles with the sweet numbness of liquor. We were birds of a feather; the tax burden and shattered second marriage had pushed me into depression, and I too was using alcohol as my lifeline.

After chatting one day at the club, I gave her a ride to her Westside home since she had no car. Joyce offered me the use of the damp, dreary basement of her comfortable house until my finances improved. The basement was constructed with an entrance that allowed me to come and go without disturbing the people upstairs. Of course, the symbolism of returning to live in a dreary basement like I had done in the Smith house during the late 1940s did not escape me.

So, Joyce and I became partners. Drinking partners. My Wildcat helped her get to different places around town, and her love for liquor meant I had someone with whom I could indulge in the spirits, whether it was in her home's breakfast room or at the Chatter Bar. No romance raised its head between us except for our mutual affection for the bottle. A low point occurred when the Wildcat was repossessed, but a dealer who happened to be a fan cut me a deal on 1964 Plymouth Fury despite a bank account that had all the luster of discarded silverware.

Although Earl Neal's Chatter Bar was one of my frequent haunts, the drinking would start before I crossed the threshold of the tavern. The morning radio show began at 6:30 A.M., and I would often take a drink before I went on the air. This meant I was humorous and informative but functioning on six cylinders rather than eight. After I left the airwaves, I would consume liquor in the car and wait eagerly for the Chatter Bar to open at 11 A.M. Ronnie Gregory, brother of famed comedian Dick Gregory, was an occasional visitor to the bar, and I became friends with him and his family.

Although suffering private torments, I was still relatively successful making two hundred dollars per week from KATZ and as much as three hundred a week from performances at the Chatter Bar and, less often, the Palms nightclub. However, this financial stability soon became as flimsy as a skyscraper built on the muds of the Florida Everglades. After about six weeks in St. Louis, I went in to pick up my paycheck and discovered that the long arm of the IRS had reached into my pockets again with a new lien on my wages. This government action crippled my ability to send money to the children, pay my rent and car note, and "look good" with fashionable clothes. Also, I had to meet my obligation to pay fifty dollars a week rent to Joyce after she began charging me for rooming in her basement. The IRS apparently did not know about the platter-party income, but those funds were consumed by another insidious force. My fee from performing at the Chatter Bar would nearly vanish through simple arithmetic. A seventy-five-dollar payment for a performance minus a seventy-five-dollar bar tab left negligible take-home money. Soon I stopped paying my $110 monthly car note, and, fearing that the repossession company would snatch the vehicle, I instituted certain strategies. Instead of parking outside Joyce's house or KATZ, I would conceal the car two blocks from either location. The reappearance of the government in my life and my subsequent plummet in earnings only increased my drinking and sense of self-pity.

I discussed my financial situation with KATZ manager Marty Brown, who came up with a partial solution. His idea was what he described as customizing. Marty would pay me fifty dollars a week out of the station's petty cash box to make sure I wasn't humiliatingly penniless. He also arranged for me to eat my meals at restaurants that owed the station fees for advertisements as a type of trade-off.

In an effort to get the government off my back, I called the IRS to see if a payment formula could be established. This would also show Uncle Sam that I was willing to make a good-faith effort in the spirit of correcting a wrong. The sincere request for an arrangement of repayment ran into a stumbling block when the agent called back after checking my files. He was very belligerent and hostile and threatened to have me arrested for the unpaid taxes. It would take twenty-five years, he claimed, to repay the government with the salary deductions I suggested, and this was unacceptable. The government wanted all or nothing.

A DRINKING COMPANION at the Chatter Bar was a man who went by the name of Rags, a moniker that probably sprang from the fact that he was always as raggedy as a serving of sauerkraut. He was a derelict who was further distinguished by matted hair, bad breath, and yellowed teeth. His home was a shack behind the bar, and he was often perched on a stool imbibing his favorite beverage. One day on one of our whiskey-soaked adventures, I suddenly realized that I was pouring my heart out to Rags, revealing pain that I didn't share with many folks. After a drink was finished, he would coach me to take another shot, directing

Marie, the barmaid, to freshen my glass time after time. Before long, all reticence had been abandoned, and I told Rags the high points of the Rosedale killing, the abuse, stable life, the Smiths, marriages, and career choices.

Suddenly, in what seemed like a momentary loss of his senses, Rags knocked my glass of whiskey off the counter with a sweep of his grimy right hand.

"I'm gonna, I'm gonna kick . . . ," I stammered.

"You ain't gonna do a damn thing," said Rags. "You won't make it here in St. Louis. Go back home."

"Who the hell are you?" I asked.

Rags produced a book that he apparently had with him at the bar all along. Unbeknownst to me, the character who always hinted of a shipwrecked life was more keenly aware of my visits to the bar than I had realized.

"Look at this," he commanded, handing the book to me.

The book was actually a photo album. Flipping through its pages, I saw pictures of a conservatively dressed, well-groomed man in a tie with people whom I assumed were his wife and children. The photos captured images of a house and nice cars. Tucked away in back of the book were newspaper clippings and diplomas indicating that the person had received bachelor's and master of education degrees.

"What do you think of that?" Rags asked.

"Well, it's really nice, Rags," I said.

"Well, that's me," he said.

Even though I was trapped in the fog of a dozen shots of whiskey, I was still incredulous over what the homeless man was telling me. This pillar of society depicted in the album and Rags apparently shared the same identity. It became clear that my whole barroom confessional had been orchestrated by the derelict.

His message was clear: The path I was on was a dimly lit road of self-pity and self-destruction and I could discard the crutch of alcohol and beat the demons of depression and hopelessness on my own strength of character. It was remarkable that this insight did not come from a preacher, teacher, or psychologist or some member of the so-called upper gentry, but from a beaten-down homeless man. His lesson did much to help me escape the quicksand of alcohol and turn my sights toward self-preservation.

FEW KNEW THE DEPTHS OF MY SADNESS, although it was discernible that I was troubled. I hitched a ride with a woman friend one day and asked her to let me out at the bridge going over the Mississippi River. The woman went to the Illinois side of the bridge, turned around, and then drove back into St. Louis. After a few minutes I walked back into Missouri and went to a package store to buy liquor for a binge, despite Rags's warning. I missed two days of work, and the woman who dropped me off told the police that I may have jumped into the Mississippi River. Police had apparently begun dragging the river in an effort to retrieve my corpse. The chaos my disappearance caused was unknown to me until a hotel maid tipped me off.

"I think you are the man they're looking for," she said. The words startled me despite the haze that enveloped me after hours of uninterrupted drinking. I stayed in the hotel for several more hours before contacting authorities as to my whereabouts.

During that time in the hotel, my whole life flashed before my eyes, and I experienced a revelation. Mattie C.'s death floated back into the forefront of my consciousness along with the beatings from Slim and Aunt Emily. But I also experienced the realization that suffering with the burdens of alcohol and tax debt were punishment for disobedience to that inner voice. The decision to cut ties with Lucille was mine, but I had committed an unforgivable sin with this action. Lucille was an adult who could fend for herself, but my children were another story. God had entrusted them to my care, and I had planned to achieve so much more in regard to family stability than my father, Slim, had done. Then, in the face of ill winds, I had abandoned my responsibilities and consorted with self-pity and self-absorption.

When I looked into the mirror in the hotel room, I did not like the reflection staring back. The haggard, unshaven, rumpled man seemed to be the spitting image of Rags, the man sent to me by a divine hand. The tumultuous effect on my soul as a result of accepting the truth about my behavior was more painful than the electric shock treatment or abuse from relatives. I resolved in the hotel that I would not run away again from my family responsibilities and would take steps to rectify the situation with Lucille.

I finally notified city police and the radio station that I was still walking on the mortal side of eternity. However, I knew that I would have to be more earnest about accepting the import of Rags's lesson to me.

At KATZ the next day, I told Marty that I wanted to take steps to smooth out the tattered relationship with Lucille, and he allowed me to use the office phone. Lucille told me that I was washed up and that my professional career was sputtering to a close and she wanted nothing more to do with me. Her words were painful, but Marty tried to convince me that it was probably for the best that Lucille and I did not resume life together.

It wasn't long after my sojourn in the hotel that I decided to leave St. Louis after roughly six months in the city. Because of the inner truths uncovered during the hotel drinking binge, I knew I needed to move closer to Sherri and Shelley. Earl Neal was notified that I wanted to put on one last show at the Chatter Bar. Word about the swan song spread, and the night of the platter party people lined up for two or three blocks in an effort to get into the lounge.

"Here's the man y'all come to see," a cigar-smoking Neal said to the packed house.

I entered the room with a ghostly white sheet over my head in reference to the rumor that I had leaped into the Mississippi River and committed suicide. "Maybe I'm not Shelley or the ghost of Shelley, but I am gonna rock the house tonight," I said from beneath the bed linen that was now my disguise.

The performance was filled with energy and electricity as I introduced records and sang with unprecedented gusto and fervor. St. Louis would have something extra by which to remember Shelley the Playboy. Rags was observing the show from outside the lounge door. As was customary, Marie, the bartender, placed a glass of scotch on the counter for me to sip during the party. I ignored the glass and one that Neal had ordered for me also. Several customers had purchased drinks for me during the evening, and by night's end ten glasses of liquor lined the bar. As the evening wound down, I observed something about Rags that I found most peculiar. A smile spread across his face. Never had I seen Rags smile before in all the weeks we had drunk together. Now his facial expression radiated approval as he bowed his head and applauded the show. Neal, Marie, and Rags hugged me, and I was congratulated for the best performance ever witnessed at the Chatter Bar. Rags's mission in my life was now complete.

CHAPTER FIFTEEN

Dock of the Bay

IN MY CONTINUED FLIGHT from the tax man, I landed in Atlanta in 1965 at WAOK, a station owned by Zenas Sears and Stan Raymond. Atlanta was a large market and therefore represented a challenge: Conquer or be conquered. I became a success by most standards if that word can be measured in popularity and feedback from listeners. Aretha Franklin, Jackie Wilson, the Temptations, Wilson Pickett, and the O'Jays were some of the entertainers with whom I rubbed shoulders at the Royal Peacock Club on Auburn Avenue and at other trendy establishments. At a place on Hunter Street called Paschal's Hotel I would engage in conversations with Julian Bond and other political luminaries. But the government, in Sherlock Holmes fashion, soon caught up with me and placed a lien on my paychecks again.

The people with whom I interacted daily did not know the extent of my financial quagmire nor the depression I experienced over the situation. Now I could barely pay my rent in the rooming house on Fair Street, and the fact that I missed my two children, Sherri and Shelley, helped my despair to mushroom.

Sometimes I would run into the Reverend Dr. Martin Luther King Jr. and his wife, Coretta, at a place called the Birdcage Restaurant. King would invite me over to their table and end up paying for my meal. I am sure he had no idea that I could not return the favor with what jingled in my pockets.

Otis Redding was building a reputation from his home base in Macon, eighty miles south of Atlanta. At least two or three times a week Redding would drive to Atlanta on business and social excursions, and we would hang out together. As a token of friendship he gave me a diamond ring, which I always cherished. WAOK had been my workplace for a year when I accepted Otis's invitation to work with him in Macon.

His manager was Phil Walden, who co-owned RedWal Music with Redding. Phil and his brother Allen were familiar with my reputation and knew that I possessed skills beyond radio. They hired me as director of public relations for the company, a breakthrough job for a black man. Basically, I was to promote Redding and travel with him on some occasions.

We all had overlapping duties, but the common denominator for our energies was cultivating the success of Otis Redding, a task I approached with passion and enthusiasm. I helped book him into the Appollo Theater and the Cheetah Club, both of which were in New York City. Redding, in appreciation for the work I did for him and out of his decent heart, helped me wriggle out from under the government's paw. Through negotiations, I was able to reduce my IRS debt down to six thousand dollars, and Otis gave me a check for this amount, freeing me from at least one torment. The Clyde Smith family had brought kindness into my life with the shelter they provided in the 1940s. Now, two decades later, Redding was also making a generous gesture that would help ease a portion of my inner anxieties. In certain ways, the sympathetic actions of these people helped me to know that not everyone was as cruel as my father, stepmother, and aunt. Redding's gift helped to alleviate the sense of depression that had drained my spirit, and the success I achieved in my RedWal post also worked to chase away a portion of my blues.

Redding was a man bursting with big aspirations. We had gotten information that a disc jockey convention was scheduled for Macon. We viewed this as an opportunity to network with a group that could impact his career through airplay of songs and subsequently increase his name recognition. The decision was made to hold a barbecue at the singer's home and invite the radio personalities who hailed from across the South.

Redding, I noticed, had disappeared for a couple of weeks to prepare for the barbecue. Curious, I called his home, and his driver, a fellow named Speedo, answered the phone.

"Man, did you see that hole Otis has got at his house?" Speedo said. "He is building a swimming pool."

I could not believe what I was hearing. The barbecue party was just three or four weeks away, and apparently the singer had initiated a major construction project. I headed to the house to ascertain the exact nature of the project. In Redding's backyard, about five feet from the steps, was a circular hole about thirty feet in circumference and roughly fifteen feet deep. Apparently, Redding had hired a couple of guys to dig the pool who were not proficient at the exercise since the structure did not allow for drainage and appeared roughly executed.

"Otis, what in the hell . . . ?" I said.

"Shelley, this is the Big O pool. Other stars have pools, so why not me?" Otis said.

"You can't do this," I said.

"Just wait and see," he responded.

I got on the phone to Phil Walden, and we arranged for crews to work virtually night and day over a two-week period to finish the pool before the barbecue. All totaled, what

Redding said would be a six-thousand-dollar project ended up costing thirty thousand dollars. Meanwhile, I continued spearheading plans for the cookout and micromanaged every detail, from the amount of beef and pork needed to the alcohol. The cost was $1,064, and 225 people ate, drank, socialized, and networked.

Hits came at an accelerated pace for Redding during this period on the strength of his talent, and he compiled such successes with Stax Records as "I've Been Loving You too Long" (1965), "Satisfaction" (1966), and "Fa-Fa-Fa-Fa-Fa (Sad Song)" (1966).

After I worked a year with the Walden brothers and Redding in Macon, Birmingham radio's WJLD offered me a job as program director, and I returned to Alabama. I was still on Redding's payroll as a consultant and used industry contacts to promote his career. Redding was a man with a pleasant personality but who could almost be described as timid. He was proud of his racial heritage and always wanted the best for his wife, Zelma, and their children. However, he took chances and went against my recommendation against flying so often. As if to thumb his nose at fate, at one point he traded a Queen Air for a larger, more powerful Lear Jet. I had flown with Redding and his pilot once down to Columbus, Georgia, but for some perhaps not so obtuse reason, I felt a mild uneasiness about the purchase.

On December 10, 1967, Otis called me in Birmingham and asked me if I wanted to fly to Wisconsin for a show he was to perform. Inexplicably, I declined his invitation. Later that day I learned that the chartered plane had crashed into a lake near Madison, Wisconsin, killing Redding and members of the Barkays. Fate or perhaps Mattie C.'s guidance from a divine realm had spared me, but a great talent with a huge heart passed from our midst at the tender age of twenty-six. His song cowritten with Steve Cropper, "Sitting on the Dock of the Bay" (1968) became a number-one hit and revered rhythm and blues anthem.

BIRMINGHAM WAS A PLACE I could never stay away from no matter how many times I left. Sam "Double O" Moore and Dexter Alexander were among the talented personalities I recruited as WJLD program director to complement Erskine Faush and Paul "Tall Paul" White. We used our leverage to demand the hiring of a black secretary and had a simple formula of playing the best music mixed with helpful messages. Otis Dodge had moved off, and George Johnston Jr., son of Rose, had taken the helm. I continued my misbehaving ways in that I followed my own drumbeat in defiance of dictated rules.

Martin Luther King was assassinated on the balcony of the Lorraine Motel in Memphis on April 4, 1968. The action greatly saddened me and others who had known him from his days of brilliance in Birmingham. Personally, I felt that after King began expanding his focus beyond the rights of blacks and the poor and voiced vocal opposition to the Vietnam War, his life was in increased jeopardy. Many of the nation's urban centers erupted in flames. A wave of rage rippled across the country's fabric as people who had been dismissed as worthless exploded over the murder of a man who tried to show them the way toward worthwhile lives. King had written his "Letter from Birmingham Jail" and had done much to guide the civil rights movement toward constructive engagement of the white power structure in the United States. The seeds of peaceful change King had sowed in Birmingham had kept the city from erupting into riots like Detroit, Watts, Newark, and other municipalities. Flags at many public buildings across the nation were flown at half-mast in King's honor the day after his assassination.

On WJLD the next morning I began to receive phone calls from people saying that the flag at City Hall was not on the pole at all. I launched a monologue questioning why the Birmingham City Hall flag was not up and flying in a position to salute a man who had a role in so much of black America's quest for dignity under the law. Mayor George Seibels called in to respond to my query. The Republican Seibels had won high marks for his moderate views on race and for acting as a bridge away from the city's wrenching racial politics of the 1960s. Seibels stated that because it had been raining, the flag was not hoisted.

"You mean to tell me that you have people that raise the flag based on the weather?" I asked.

Seibels fumbled for words, stuttering and stammering, and offered what I considered another lame excuse for the perceived snub.

"If the flag does not fly, there will be hell to pay in this city," I said.

Before the day was over, the flag was up at City Hall, and King was saluted in a pivotal city in the nation's cultural evolution. But I had set in motion a series of events that would constitute a red-letter day for me in Birmingham. WJLD owner Johnston and others on the staff like Dave Davis, director of sales, were displeased with what they regarded as my disrespect for the mayor. Jim Lawson, a new announcer in Birmingham, was offered the job as program director on the condition that he fire me since apparently Johnston could not face me himself to conduct the hatchet job. Lawson found me at the Aqua Lounge and delivered the news that I had been terminated. The words were painful to hear, but I tried to accept the situation gracefully.

When the news spread about the dismissal, picketers showed up at the station, but I called them off after a few days.

A couple of nights after I had been fired from WJLD, I received a call from Shelby Singleton, head of Shelby Singleton International Productions in Nashville, Tennessee. Singleton and I had been in contact for years; he would keep me informed about news from his neck of the woods and vice versa. Singleton, while occupying an executive position with Plantation Records, had helped steer the career of a former record company secretary born Jeannie Carolyn Stephenson in Anson, Texas. As Jeannie C. Riley, her "Harper Valley PTA" sold ten million copies in 1968 and put Singleton on the country music industry map.

Singleton, who had worked with rock-and-roll pioneer Carl Perkins, was interested in creating a black label with musicians who were between contracts. WJLD's action made him joyful, he said, because he wanted me to come work with his company and help recruit performers. The experience I had accumulated with Phil Walden and Otis Redding, not to mention my contacts with scores of artists and promoters, were just right for his endeavor. He dangled a carrot, and I swallowed it, largely because pride would not allow me to be seen ambling around Birmingham without the airwaves underneath me.

Nashville represented a double-edged venture in that I would also work with Jimmy Keys, owner of New Keys Music. At Singleton's company I would be encased in artist relations, recruiting black performers for the record label; at Keys's shop I was to book black performers at various clubs and shows. Singleton provided a pool of cars for my convenience and an apartment in the Pinewood Park complex.

Booking performers was often as slow as a chunk of glacier drifting way from an Icelandic ice cap. It dawned on me that I could try my hand at arranging concerts and other appearances for the white country music artists. Keys was bemused at the assertion that I could handle the work and voiced reservations that a Negro would be accepted in such a position. To alleviate his doubts, I formulated an audition that I would conduct for him. The music executive went into the next room at my suggestion and picked up a telephone extension. On the other end of the line, I went into a routine to prove that I could carry out the job.

"Hey, Jim, how are things going?" I said in my most nasal, high-pitched Caucasian voice.

"Fine," he said.

"Listen," I said, still in character, "I have so and so available for some performances in your area. What do you think about us booking them?"

Keys was impressed with the charade and permitted me to start booking white acts immediately. I employed the "white voice" in that work.

The agency handled such performers as Bobby Beam, Jimmy Newman, and Jeannie C. Riley. Both Singleton and Keys seemed pleased with my competence in juggling the duties, but I noticed a certain condescension when they observed that a Negro could perform activities in what had been a "white" job. A piano requires the use of both black and white keys to play the Star Spangled Banner, I said, and it was essential that races learn to work together in harmony like a well-tuned piano.

About once a month I would drive down to Birmingham and then on to Columbus, Georgia, to see Sherri and Shelley. Contact with the black community remained on my agenda, and I visited radio stations in Georgia to keep up with the tempo of the industry. White radio personalities like Bill "Hoss" Allen and John Richbourg were icons at the fifty-thousand-watt WLAC, a station that played much black music. And there was

WVOL, where personalities like Gilley Baby had set up shop. Upon visiting WVOL on one occasion, I met a pleasant young part-time intern with an unusual name who would amaze me and others at how far she would go in her career: Oprah Winfrey.

My tenure in country music was groundbreaking and possibly paved the way for other blacks to be viewed as capable of competently handling nontypical jobs.

DESPITE SUCCESS ACHIEVED in the job and interacting with luminaries like Loretta Lynn and Tammy Wynette, I was still miserable without my children. Sherri was nine and Shelley was seven when I went to spend the Christmas of 1969 with them and their mother, Lucille. Lucille had been receiving money from me with which she was supposed to buy the children clothes for Christmas, but I discovered that, perhaps out of spite, nothing had been spent on them. Lucille attacked me verbally for some innocuous remark, and we both proceeded to vent hostilities that had been submerged in tolerance.

When my ex-wife mentioned to the children that Santa had brought them gifts, I angrily corrected her. "Santa did not bring you anything, I did," I said, aggravating Lucille further. Of course, to make matters worse, Sherri repeated her long-spoken desire to come live with me in Nashville.

BIRMINGHAM WAS A TOWN to which I kept returning like a divining rod seeking an underground stream. Nashville represented a breakthrough in the world of country music, but I was still crippled by scant money and tattered credit. The music industry was a family to me, and we shared each other's pains and concerns. When I determined that I would be cutting the tie with country music row and going to WENN again, I called many of my contacts to let them know that I was changing scenery in early 1970. These included Roebuck "Pops" Staples, patriarch of the Staples Singers, whom I had known for many years dating back to before the group was nationally known; promoter Roger Redding, Otis Redding's brother; Al Bell, a Stax Records vice president whom I had met when he worked at KOKY, a McClendon station in Little Rock, Arkansas; and Issac Hayes, a former Memphis butcher whose mellow songs turned into big hits for Stax.

Actually, it meant more to people in the industry for me to be on the air spinning records than to be working as a promoter. I related my financial predicament to them as a matter of sharing difficulties with kissing cousins.

I rented a truck for a return to Birmingham after spending a few months in Nashville. I moved into a modest domicile at 301-C Montevallo Gardens Apartments in Titusville. Harvey Menefee, the manager of the facility, cut me a deal on the fee and gave me a ride down to WENN so I could go on the air. Afterward, he said I could use the beaten-down maintenance truck as transportation. He was gleeful that I would be living there and said my "celebrity" status would help him attract more renters. WENN would pay me $125 a week for my services. However, I sensed resentment of my top-dog status from some of the guys that I had put on the air like Pat Williams, a former station janitor, and Paul "Tall Paul" White. Erskine Faush, who played gospel music as a successor to his brother William, welcomed me warmly, as did station office manager Jack Randall and traffic manager Daisy Giddings. The station had done little to publicize my return, but the masses of listeners let me know that they were aware of my presence.

After a few days back in Birmingham, I got a call from Al Bell. He told me that he, Isaac Hayes, and others had been discussing my situation and wanted me to book the Boutwell City Auditorium for a concert to raise funds that would help me reestablish myself. Hayes would be featured as well as Johnny Taylor, Pops Staples, the Dramatics, and the surviving members of the Barkays. I was grateful but told him that a poor-man's purse would not permit me to put down cash to reserve the facility, and my credit rating chased away any possibility of securing a loan.

"Damn," said Bell, "do you want us to do everything?"

"Yeah," I responded, somewhat bemused.

"How many handbills are you going to need?" Bell asked.

"Oh, about five hundred," I said.

"OK, we'll send two thousand handbills," he replied.

I reminded Bell that we had not discussed what I would owe artists out of the proceeds for the use of their talents. Before I could finish enunciating my reservations, the Stax executive hung up the phone. After I called back to the record company's headquarters, Bell hung up on me again. The third time had to be the charm, so I asked the switchboard operator to connect me to Issac Hayes, whom Bell had stated was visiting the building.

"How things going, Shelley . . . with your broke ass?" asked Hayes in his velvetlike baritone voice.

"Better," I said. "Listen, Ike, Al and I did not talk about how I was going to pay y'all—" Suddenly, the phone line went dead. Hayes had done an imitation of Al Bell.

After Bell wired me five hundred dollars, I was able to reserve the Boutwell for a March concert. Globe Posters, based in Maryland, printed up the handbills advertising the event. Although no other WENN on-air personalities would mention the upcoming show, the station did record a promotion tape that was played on the air. However, the quality of the entertainment ensured that the show as a sellout despite limited promotion. At show time, Pops Staples acted as a business manager for the group. Issac Hayes expanded his six-member backup band into an orchestra by adding an additional six musicians. Hayes, Staples, Johnny Taylor, the Dramatics, and the Barkays all performed to a thrilled and grateful Birmingham audience.

We gathered in an office in the Boutwell after the show to determine how much money had been raised so fees could be paid. A pile of greenbacks lay on a table. At twelve dollars per ticket and attendance of about five hundred people, the show possibly netted fifty thousand dollars. Pops Staples ascertained how much the artists would need for their bands' transportation and lodging and fees, and that amount was separated from the pile. Funds were extricated for other incidentals such as the sound system and security, leaving one mountain of money on the table.

Johnny Taylor, who called everybody Pete and who always kidded me about a mishap I suffered when he, Otis Redding, and I were horsing around in Georgia, started talking.

"Any poor dumb bastard who would run into a tree . . . Pete, you can just keep my part," he said.

The others had all agreed that I was to take the remaining mound of money on the table, which amounted to twenty-one thousand dollars, and they would forgo their performance fees as artists. As tears cascaded down my cheeks, Pops Staples's son Pervis asked the others if they wanted him to rough me up for crying.

"You wanted a house and a car, didn't you, Shelley?" said Hayes. "You have earned it. You are among the radio personalities that you can count on one hand that have earned it. Take it."

After most shows the performers customarily gather for a party somewhere. But this time Taylor asked us to bow our heads, and he led us in a word of prayer. Then it was my turn to voice appreciation for the generosity of folks whose talents I so greatly admired. With the money I was able to buy a car and a house at 1553 Sixteenth Way Southwest, in the city's West End area.

CHAPTER SIXTEEN

Family Turbulence

IN THE SUMMER OF 1970 I made another bid for the elusive sense of family that I craved deeply. I called my brother David who lived in Los Angeles and told him about my dream of all the siblings settling on the eighty acres of land that I had purchased in Shelby County in 1952.

"Man, are you crazy?" said David when he heard my suggestion. "Alabama has torn your ass up. . . . Birmingham is not for us. Looks like I'm going to have to come down there and show you how to live."

The last time I had seen David was in 1963 with his wife Betty and their three children. At the time, he was a chef at the International House of Pancakes in Los Angeles and was making an honest wage. David had to leave Birmingham in 1962 as the result of a fight with a man. He had sought revenge the day following the scuffle by firing a sawed-off shotgun at the man in a house on the west side of Birmingham. The case was handled in federal court, and U.S. District Judge Hobart H. Grooms ordered David to leave town within a month. The judge, I felt, was more lenient on David because I told the jurist the gist of our family history.

David was now making a living on the renegade side of the

law with a bookie or gambling joint and two or three after-hours lounges in Los Angeles and had no use for my Pollyannish nonsense. Now he was going to launch a campaign to straighten out my conventional mind-set. A month later he called to say that he and his associates would be visiting me like missionaries traveling to bring Christianity to a hermitic Amazon River–basin tribe.

Days later I looked out the window of my home in time to see David pull up in a beautiful black Buick Electra 225. Another vehicle in the two-car caravan was driven by a man I recognized as Ray Mallard, who also had Rosedale connections but apparently was living in California. David exited his car in an outfit that would draw attention anywhere. He was dressed completely in black with matching hat, lizard-skin shoes, and charcoal briefcase. Clusters of diamond rings embraced the fingers of the man now known as Black Jesus. I was later to discover that his house in Watts was painted black, for good measure. Although he had a diploma from Rosedale School because he could play football, he could read only at a third-grade level and could barely write. He now seemed to harbor resentment toward me and my celebrated belief in education and efforts to walk on the right side of the law.

"Man, who cooked this shit?" he said, turning up his nose at the mashed potatoes and roast beef I had sweated over in preparation for his visit.

He continued. "I thought you were doing something out here. You know books, but it looks like you are going backwards. I see it is up to me to step in and help you out. . . . I would not invest a dollar in this godforsaken state. This is the worst state in the world. Screw Alabama."

David said that he had a place for me in his organization as an office manager based on the book knowledge I had acquired.

He wanted me to ride with them "Over the Hump," which meant to drive up Red Mountain into Rosedale, but first he wanted to know if the house had a burglar alarm system, which it did not. He then placed the briefcase on the table and opened it to reveal stacks of fifty- and hundred-dollar bills.

"This is smart, bitch," he said, picking up a wad of bills and tapping me in the chest with it. He repeated the action and phrase sixty times. Sixty thousand dollars was in the case, but the money wore the unromantic stench of drug selling or some other illegal undertaking.

"Are you finished?" I asked. "David, you can take your money and go back to California because I am not going anywhere with you."

Before he and Roy left for their excursion, David warned me that he expected to see the stacks of dollars just the way he had left them. Several hours later they came back with two hustlers named Billy and Dog. Listening to their conversation from my bedroom, I understood that these guys had been in California also and were sought by authorities for such issues as gambling, drugs, and assault-and-battery violations.

The company David was keeping amounted to more evidence of his plummet into confusion and anger, which had escalated since I had visited him seven years earlier. I heard him tell his motley band of desperadoes that he would be leaving Birmingham but would return in a few weeks. After the parley, the group left again for the evening. The next day David headed back to California without me.

A month later David returned to Birmingham accompanied by a woman in her early twenties named Billie. Braless, she could have passed for a prostitute walking the steamy streets of any urban red-light district in the nation. They revealed that she was wanted on a fugitive warrant from California for some unspecified offense. David's treatment of the woman seemed to represent a perverted master/servant relationship. He ordered her to wash his face, give him a manicure, and basically cater to whatever selfish whim he displayed. When I objected to the treatment, David dismissed me as a man swimming in a sea of stupidity. Perhaps to demonstrate his power, he told Billie she could go to bed with me, an offer I respectfully declined.

The next day I returned from work to find another surprise. David had spread a bedsheet on the ground in the backyard and laid out from fifty to seventy-five pounds' worth of Colombian marijuana so that it could dry under the sun's gaze. Needless to say, I exploded in outrage.

"If you don't get that mess out of my yard now," I said, "I'm going to call the police. You are not ruining my life. I have suffered enough."

As I went toward the telephone, David pulled a knife from his pocket. Whenever any of the Stewart boys pulled a weapon, most likely it would be used; little margin was left for bluffing. Although I too had become skilled with knives during my days at Stringfellow Stables with Bubba, I decided to defend myself with another instrument. To tip the confrontation in my favor, I rushed into my bedroom and grabbed my .38 caliber revolver out of a drawer and pointed it at David. With a marksman ranking from my air force days, I couldn't miss a vital organ, and David knew this. The standoff quickly de-escalated.

"Damn," said David, "I forgot you'll kill a man."

The marijuana vanished.

David would hibernate in the day and stalk the town at night and usually end up at some lounge or club. Most times he would just camp at a table or barstool and engage in a ritual with others of similar stripe. These were con men, burglars, pimps, and small-time criminals lost in their pursuit of the big score, braggarts who boasted of how many women were in their stables or the volume of goods they had stolen or fenced. Most of the time they were networking, comparing notes and using that information to enhance their own dishonest trades like similar men had done at Ratkiller's Shoeshine Parlor and the Club Savoy in the '50s.

Billie had not been seen, at least by me, for a couple of days, so I asked David her whereabouts. Oddly, he asked me if I knew anyone at University Hospital. Before I could digest the question, he stated that Billie had fallen off the back steps and broken her arm. When I pressed him, he confessed that he had beaten her with a stick during a fracas. Images of Slim Stewart chasing my mother with the ax and the other beatings streaked across my mind as I rushed out of the house to the hospital. Billie was there, but she had not told hospital personnel what had actually happened. After her release, I told David they would have to leave.

A few weeks later David returned to Birmingham for a short visit with a new traveling companion named Carolyn. He said she had filled the position earlier offered to me as office manager in his organization. He still viewed my proposition for the three brothers to migrate to the Shelby County property as backward, idiotic thinking. The pair stayed a few days and then rushed back to the world of dim lounges and informal gambling.

"Mama, tell me what I should do. I cannot make it by myself. I know I will be in a strain if I go against you and make a wrong decision." Conversations with my mother's spirit were a mainstay of my life. The times when I talked with her were always in private, and her messages were key components in decisions I made. Her direction this time was for me to bring my children to live with me.

Sherri came to stay with me in Birmingham on Christmas of

1970, and I enrolled her at Jackson Elementary School. With great care I made sure her clothes were pressed and she was well fed. However, while cooking had never been a problem for me, one facet of her grooming and care made me feel as if each digit on my hand was a thumb: fixing her hair. To get around this, I bought her a wig.

I met Doris Richardson in the latter part of 1971. She had been dating a coworker at WENN, and I asked her out since the relationship did not appear to be consequential. Her boss at a day care run by the Jefferson County Committee for Economic Opportunity, an antipoverty agency, was married to a WENN station engineer, and we would double-date occasionally.

Doris lived with her two daughters, Lisa, nine, and Sharrone, two, and her parents, Abe and Anna Williams, in Pratt City, an old mining camp off the northwestern route U.S. 78 takes out of the city. Our relationship began to gel. Looking at the mechanics of the situation, I realized that my daughter, Sherri, needed the hand of a woman in her life. And I felt I could help enhance Doris's nuclear family with my income.

So, without either of us proposing marriage, we decided to live together. On July 3, 1972, Doris and her girls moved into my West End home. Her older girl had been from a teenage marriage, but the younger child was the product of a relationship with a man whose name she would not divulge. Her obstinance pained me because I felt if I was going to raise the girls, I should at least be privy to that information. So, Doris, Sherri, Lisa, and Sharrone were hopefully to be the framework of an ideal family, which I had failed to cultivate after two earlier marital misfires. A few months after we began cohabiting, Doris was pregnant.

Doris and I crossed swords since she did not seem to share my enthusiasm for education. Lisa would not study enough, and

Doris did not really push her as hard as I would have liked. Also, tension emanated from the fact that Doris's father, Abe, would buy toys for Lisa and ignore the other children. This made me flash back to the days when my stepmother, Marie, catered to her sister, Nettie, and ignored my brothers and me in Rosedale as if we were refugees from a leper colony.

Doris also accused me of being more overbearing on Lisa than I was on Sherri. Of course, I felt that I was evenhanded in my dealings with the children, and I even shied away from use of the word *step*. They were all my children equally, I felt, and I was determined to sculpt something grand out of our conglomeration. This was not going to be a case of yours, mine, and ours. All of the children would be *ours* without distinction. Since no father's name was on Sharrone's birth certificate, I went to the vital statistics office and had my name inserted as her father. To make the brood even more complete, on July 13, 1973, I was blessed with the joyous birth of another son, Corey.

———————

SAM, WHO HAD BEEN LIVING in California since 1963 and had become a poet, called me in August 1973 and told me that David had been shot and that he and I would now have to kill his wife, Betty. To make heads or tails of the situation, I jumped on a plane to Los Angeles and found Sam pacing in the International Airport terminal. He repeated the contention that Betty would have to die now. This was nonsense when I first heard the death sentence thousands of miles away in Birmingham, and the words remained gibberish and unfathomable with Sam standing three feet away from me in the airport terminal.

We went to Martin Luther King Hospital where I found David resembling a mummy because of bandages coiled methodically around his head. Chains fastened him to the bed since he was wanted on fugitive warrants, and hospital personnel said that a policeman down the hall was his guard. The fact that the man was unconscious and seemed near death made the chains seem even more inhumane. After my protests, a police supervisor came and took the restraints off while I offered a prayer for David's survival.

Sam said the shooting had taken place at the Watts home of a Mrs. Powell where David's wife, Betty, roomed. Betty had stormed out of their house after a confrontation with David over the fact that he had brought home the love child he had fathered with the woman I had met in 1970 named Carolyn, the so-called office manager. On his orders, David's henchmen had scoured the streets of Watts until they discovered Betty's refuge. David went to the boardinghouse to see Betty, but Mrs. Powell noticed a revolver in his pants and ordered him to leave it on a stand in the front hall before proceeding further.

Only seconds had past before Mrs. Powell heard a cacophony of screaming and hollering from Betty's room. Hurried footsteps in the hall preceded the crisp, unmistakable report from a handgun. The landlady jumped up figuring that David had somehow accomplished what he had actually come to do, but was startled to see my brother lying in a pool of blood on the hall floor.

Apparently, Betty had fled down the passageway to escape David, noticed the gun on the table, grabbed it, and fired backward over her shoulder. The shot may as well have been executed by a U.S. Army Ranger sharpshooter since the bullet tore through David's skull over his left eye. Fragments from the projectile could not be removed from his brain, but he survived and was to begin suffering seizures and blackouts attributed to the shooting. The marriage was irretrievably lost after that incident.

CHAPTER SEVENTEEN

Signing the Checks

DURING THE 1970s I began to grow weary of the Playboy routine. For years I had my sights set on sales, management, and station ownership. From working with Otis Redding, Phil Walden, and Shelby Singleton, I knew that the road to the front office would be through radio sales. Those who were in sales strived for management positions, and from there, the prize was station ownership. Often, I had observed the operation of the sales staff at radio stations during my career and absorbed any nuance of the craft that I could glean from periodicals and trade publications. But all of the salesmen at most black-oriented stations in the South were, of course, white, and I knew that the broadcast outlets were surviving off the talents of the black on-air personalities who were basically receiving crumbs in comparison. I had discussed the desire to be a salesman with the McClendon company but was always discouraged. Even Joe Lackey did not feel the town was ready for a black salesman at WENN. This time, in 1975, I put my request in writing that I wanted to be considered for a sales post if an opening resulted from an employee's death, transfer, or firing. The letter went unacknowledged.

In early 1976 WENN was placed on the market after the death of John McClendon. Joe Lackey, Erskine Faush, and I went to A. G. Gaston to secure a loan with which we could purchase the station. His executives turned the tables and persuaded the businessman to buy the station himself, which he did. Gaston, after having stated that all WENN employees would be rehired at the new operation, revealed that he had a problem with having a white man running one of his businesses. He told Lackey he was sweeping him out of the station. This stance led me to organize the staffers to walk off the job, and we picketed the station for seven weeks. Our protest actually went beyond Joe Lackey to the sense of justice that had been trampled by Gaston's action. During that time Gaston cut off my insurance coverage, which was critical since Doris and I were anticipating the birth of a second child.

Crescendo Broadcasting was operating a station, WATV, from the top of the Cabana Motel. An owner, Stu Hepburn, contacted Lackey and said that if he could deliver the whole staff of WENN, he would hire us and turn the station into a black-oriented format. In a relative instant, we all were employed again. The new station was called WATV 900 Gold AM, and we continued our policy of delivering great music and social messages with unquestioned professionalism.

During this period it became clear that the Playboy had seen his best, hippest days. Shelley Stewart never really liked the night life and the clubs and all the attendant flashiness and flamboyance. He did not consider himself a playboy and certainly was not a boy. It was time for Shelley Stewart to emerge from the shadows of the Playboy and tip his hat to the world. A lurking fear existed as to whether the quiet, introverted man could survive without the gregarious alter ego, but certain omens seemed to portend that my life was due to change course.

The platter-party circuit was still relatively lucrative when I was on my way to an engagement one evening at Willis and Ada

Reed's club in Columbiana, about thirty-five miles south of Birmingham in Shelby County. A fellow who assisted me had taken my sound equipment, records, and microphones to the club. I was barreling down U.S. 31 at about sixty miles per hour when suddenly, out of the dusk, two or three white horses, escapees from one of the rural farms, came rushing toward the car. As we closed in on each other, the creatures suddenly veered on either side of the vehicle. Shaken by my slow reaction and the closeness of the encounter, I proceeded on to the Reeds' club.

On my way to the same establishment about a week later, another incident happened. Sleepy and tired from a hectic schedule, I decided to pull over on the side of U.S. 31 to take a nap. Possibly an hour had passed when menacing Caucasian-sounding voices wafted into the car through an inch-wide opening in a rear window.

"There's a nigger in there asleep," someone said. "We've got us one. Let's get his ass."

Feigning sleep, I could see the forms of three white men outside the car. One was directed to find a brick to smash the windows and pull me out of the car, perhaps for the purpose of robbery or an old-fashioned lynching. Slowly I reached under the seat and grabbed the .357 Magnum I kept there for protection. Straightening myself up, I pointed the gun toward the men; I intended to shoot at them through the closed window if necessary. Instantly, the trio caught sight of the firearm and went scampering away into the night like frightened rabbits.

A week later the trilogy of omens was completed. On my way to the same club, I climbed into the car at my West End home and instantly was aware of a supernatural aura that permeated the car's compartment and my consciousness. Simultaneously, I heard my mother's voice as clearly as she had spoken and sang her favorite spirituals in our Rosedale home in 1939.

From her home in the enigmatic, hidden world of the eternal, she offered me fresh directions on the path my life should take.

"I don't want you in nightclubs anymore," she said. "You must retire Shelley the Playboy. Something is already planned for you."

Much of life, and its manifestations on earth and heaven, are unfathomable to mankind's limited mind. Perhaps we don't use all of our human capabilities, or maybe we have forgotten them in the swirling vortex of technology and materialism, but my mother's spirit reached through that barrier again that day. Her presence remained in the car communicating with me as I drove toward Columbiana, an hour's ride from Birmingham.

"The alcohol . . . ," she said. "That was not what I told you to do." The spirit told me that the decisions that caused me to go awry in my life were choices that she had not approved, and now it was time to quit the platter parties. The mother who was always with me in a subliminal way had made her presence starkly apparent again.

When I became aware of my location, I had been driving for two hours and was outside of Prattville, near the state capital of Montgomery. When I finally got to the club, William and Ada asked me why I was so late. I announced to them and the crowd that this would be my last appearance at the events. Everyone was shocked, but I knew that when I ignored the inner voice, whether it was God, Mother, or both, I always ended up spinning my wheels in the mud.

Doris wondered how we would survive on the $250-a-week radio salary, but I had my sights on the sales arena and knew Mike Bobyarcheck and Amory Johnson had raked in juicy commissions selling airtime on WENN and WATV. On Monday morning I went into the WATV office, cleaned out a vacant desk, and sat down and just stared at Joe Lackey.

"I'm here," I said, and began assisting with office calls. This was going to be my first step into sales and management, and Lackey knew not to try to hinder me now. He walked into his office and closed the door.

As part of the plan, I stopped calling myself Playboy. However, I was still playing records, and I resented it if anyone referred to me by the name that I was attempting to jettison. About a month later, Crescendo executive Hepburn showed up. I reminded him that he and I had had casual conversations on the matter of a position as a salesman, and I told him of the note to Lackey stating that I expected consideration for such a job when a vacancy was created. "That's a great idea," said Hepburn. "Why wait?"

Hepburn's position enabled me to begin immediately as a salesman. I went downtown to New Ideal department store and introduced myself to Gene Nunn and Mike Carroll, the manager and assistant manager, respectively. Using an amalgamation of persuasive techniques I had culled from selling shoes at Schiff's, booking acts for Jimmy Keys, and even my sack boy days at Yielding's, I walked out of the room with a huge twenty-five-thousand-dollar contract for the store to advertise on WATV. My income snowballed to between fifty-five and sixty-five thousand dollars annually, and sometimes more, from the 15 percent commissions I extracted from record-breaking sales. Amory Johnson, an old-guard type, retired within a year after I had started because apparently he felt working with me put us on equal footing. I became the top-selling salesman ever employed by Crescendo; at one point it was estimated that I was responsible for 80 percent of their radio revenue.

By 1979 I had stopped spinning records and concentrated on sales work and a new radio talk show I began hosting that year. Shelley the Playboy, for all intents and purposes, was officially retired.

———————

CY STEINER AND I HAD CONTINUED the relationship begun in 1958 when we met in Shreveport, Louisiana. Steiner had been hired at Shreveport's KOKA and WENN's predecessor, WBCO, on my recommendation and sold ads for that station for a few years. He had then gone on to do similar work at a television station and an ad agency. In an effort to flex his wings, he started his own agency in 1973 and had come to me to discuss the venture.

We both knew the heartbeat of the city's corporate power structure. In effect, he stated that I would be his partner, albeit a silent one, since we feared reaction from the business community if my role in the company's operations was known. As compensation for my advice and insights in handling marketing and public relations for clients like Bruno's pharmacy and grocery chain and Parisian's department stores, Steiner would give me payments. Sometimes I kept the money, but often I handed it back as an investment in the company.

Steiner was also teaching me aspects of the business such as constructing storyboards for ads and other workings of the production studio. The company picked up steam and developed an impressive list of clientele. The ledger showed that it had become an $18-million-a-year business.

We concluded that it would be better if I opened a sister company, Shelley Stewart and Associates, which I did in the mid-1970s. Business prospects that I felt Steiner could handle were referred to him, and he would steer projects to me in return. I continued to offer Steiner advice and learn more about the intricate workings of the business. Steiner teamed with

Harry Bressler of New York, but did not share the fact that our two companies were working in synergistic harmony.

My primary clients in Stewart and Associates included the city of Birmingham, City Councilman Richard Arrington, and other politicians and civic leaders. Years of gleaning information and knowledge were now being put into use on two horizons, as a salesman at WATV and as a marketing and public relations expert. Friends who were fond of the ostentatious Shelley the Playboy began to drift away, and I was accused of having an ambitious reach that fell short of skyrocketing aspirations. Businessman and salesman Shelley Stewart was markedly different from his alter ego. He had little stomach for nonsense and foolishness. Now the Playboy wouldn't be around to help conceal old wounds.

DORIS WAS HESITANT ABOUT having another baby in our common-law marriage, but I resolved that the child would be born and the marriage was going to survive despite multiple sources of friction. We got married in the Shelby County Courthouse in the county seat of Columbiana in March 1976, a few days before a daughter, Corlette, was born.

The idyllic life portrayed in teleplays has always been a Hollywood construct that I have pursued consciously and subconsciously, overtly and covertly. A family trip in the spirit of *The Brady Bunch* situation comedy was a brainstorm that occurred to me in the late 1970s. Our destinations were Monroeville, Pennsylvania, to see Doris's half sister Viola and Baltimore, Maryland, to visit my father's brother Doug. Doris, Sherri, Lisa, Sharrone, Corey, Corlette, and I piled into our Caprice Estates station wagon for the journey that I hoped would help us to bond and become more like the real family I had been chasing since I walked away from Slim and Marie's house in 1940 at age six.

The trip was a moderate success, but we did not have a united front in handling the children, and I was portrayed as a villain. Doris sided with Corey when his granddaddy wanted to buy him a gun. "It's all right with me, but you know how your daddy is," Doris said.

The uneasiness between Lisa and me boiled over after about five years under the same roof. One day I heard Sharrone admonish Lisa about some matter.

"Daddy is gonna get you if you do that," Sharrone said.

"He's not our daddy," said Lisa, as she had done several times over the years. On this occasion, I did not bite my tongue and quickly interrupted them in their conversation.

"If I am not your daddy, then who is?" I asked Lisa.

It was not long before she moved out of the house and began staying with her grandparents Abe and Anna in Pratt City.

Richard Arrington

Birmingham was in a state of transition in the mid '70s as it struggled to grasp symbols of maturity almost as a teenage boy attempts to grow side whiskers as a sign of manhood. The convergence of history and human dynamics positioned the Magic City to peek in the mirror of time to see just how far it had evolved from the stark bigotry that had operated helter-skelter in the 1960s.

The Jefferson County Citizens' Coalition, the brainchild of City Councilman Richard Arrington, a zoology professor at Miles College, was establishing itself as a force with which to be reckoned in the game of power brokering. Arrington had followed Arthur Shores as the second black person on the Birmingham City Council in the early 1970s, and talk arose in various quarters that he would be a candidate for mayor. Some blacks, including influential ministers, did not feel that it was time for such a step. But the question was proffered, If not now, when?

Even businessman A. G. Gaston hedged at supporting Arrington over incumbent mayor David Vann in the Democratic primary election. He donated only a hundred dollars to Arrington's coffers as opposed to a thousand dollars for Vann. But Arrington, to the consternation of many, beat Vann, a progressive Democrat and veteran lawyer who had been among the few rational white leaders in the city during the hysteria of the 1960s.

Vann could trace his loss to the shooting death of Bonita Carter, an unarmed black woman killed accidentally by a city police officer. The precipitating incident was an altercation between a male customer and a convenience-store clerk in an eastside neighborhood called Kingston. Ms. Carter was apparently attempting to move the customer's car when the officer came upon the scene and fired into the vehicle. The policeman was vilified as a lawman who had used his gun without assessing the situation correctly. Many in the black community felt Vann had given the officer a slap on the wrist when he was reassigned to administrative duties and the mayor stated that no other so-called punishment for the man was warranted.

Frank Parsons, a local attorney, captured the Republican nomination for the job. He had predictably pledged fairness for all city residents if elected mayor.

Often I would take walks downtown from radio station WATV. One particular day my route found me walking past the Parsons headquarters, which was located at Twenty-first Street between Third and Fourth Avenues North. Since I knew Parsons well, I decided to stop in and chat for a minute.

"Hey, Shelley," Parsons greeted me. "You know I will have a spot for you at City Hall after I win."

"Okay, Frank," I said, with all insincerity.

As I scanned the crowd, I noticed insurance man Joe Reid in the room. He had been one of Bull Connor's right-hand advisers. Former mayor George Seibels and Vann had cleaned out most of Connor's cronies from the city's rough-and-tumble days, but now Parsons, a potential mayor, seemed to be gravitating toward them again. I excused myself and ran at a gallop to Arrington's nearby headquarters.

Joy overwhelmed my soul as I rushed into the building where Arrington advisers Tony Carter and Willie Davis were milling about on campaign activities.

"We've won the election!" I shouted, then went on to explain. Parsons had talked a good game in his campaign with vows to cast off the old baggage of racial division. Now we would use Joe Reid to expose the lawyer's true colors, I told them. I hatched a plan to lure Parsons onto my radio program. A candidate's forum that had already been scheduled at Lawson State Community College would also figure into the scheme.

On the radio program I talked with Parsons about his goals for the city. At some point I mentioned Reid's name without noting his connection to Bull Connor, and Parsons praised the man and confirmed that he would be part of his team. A few days later at the Lawson State forum, Parsons and Arrington appeared together and fielded questions from the audience. A campaign operative stood up in the audience and asked Parsons about Reid, and he again affirmed that the man would be on his team. The questioner then revealed Reid's relationship to the segregationist Connor, and Parsons was asked if that was the type of person he had in mind to lead the city. Parsons responded lamely, but television and newspaper representatives were monitoring the program. The next day's *Birmingham News* featured an article with a headline that said the ghost of Bull Connor had resurfaced.

This incident gave momentum to blacks and fired them up to vote against Parsons. In view of the heavy black turnout at the polls, the Reid exposé probably helped galvanize black voters and ensured the strong showing that put Arrington into office as mayor. Reid later served time in jail for a scandal that would engulf him on the city water board in the late 1980s.

George Wallace

George Wallace wanted to cleanse his soul of old, grievous sins. On his road to redemption he tried to mend fences every way that he could. In his final term as governor of Alabama in the late 1980s, he had become a shadow of the fiery Alabama chief executive who had stood in the door of Foster Auditorium at the University of Alabama and attempted to block the admission of Vivian Malone Jones and James Hood in June 1963. He was now only an echo of the man who had proclaimed "Segregation now, segregation tomorrow, segregation forever," in his inaugural address in 1963. He had traveled a long road from the time I was introduced to him in businessman A. G. Gaston's office in the late 1950s, when he was a moderate candidate for governor. He lost to state attorney general John Patterson, who played hardball racial politics. Wallace had vowed, by some accounts, never to be "out-segged" again, and he never was. His anti-integration rhetoric, many observers have concluded, did much to contribute to the tone of violence and the bombings that peppered the state during the civil rights movement and claimed several lives.

A back problem had put me in the hospital for disc fusion surgery in 1988. Delois Pickett, a former actress who found work as Wallace's liaison, came to Baptist Medical Center Princeton with flowers from the governor and said he wished me a speedy recovery. Not long afterward, Ms. Pickett brought me a proclamation of appreciation from Wallace and stated he wanted to meet with me. Assuming that neither one of us had anything worthwhile to say to the other, I shirked off the invitation and told Ms. Pickett that I wasn't ready to meet with Wallace yet. Ms. Pickett, a black woman, had come under criticism in some quarters for working for a man with Wallace's overt antiblack track record. She told me that she wasn't trying to glorify Wallace and was bothered because she felt he had not fully atoned for his past, but she believed she could make an impact within the system through her job.

Four years later, in 1992, Wallace's son George Jr. came by WATV and said his father wanted to meet with me. An earnest, likable man, he was to become the state treasurer, but apparently did not possess his father's political savvy. The elder Wallace was not in the best of health, he said, principally because of the bullets Arthur Bremer had fired into him on May 15, 1972, in Laurel, Maryland, which left him paralyzed from the waist down. The shooting interrupted Wallace's third run for the presidency, although he did remain in the race after some recuperation. George Jr. had heard his father speak well of me, and he asked me if I would meet with the governor if he arranged the event. I agreed to do so.

When I met with the Wallaces at the ex-governor's residence, George Jr. told me that his father was practically deaf and that I would have to scribble my remarks down on a pad for him to read. After exchanging amenities, the elderly Wallace began to say what was on his mind.

"We fought each other back then, but I thought I was doing the right thing," Wallace said. "There were strong black preachers telling me that I was right about segregation and civil rights, and of course there were whites that I was listening to who were telling me the same thing. Now, maybe I would've done things differently." Wallace said that he respected me for standing up on the integration issue and asked me to forgive him if he had harmed me with his policies.

"Governor," I said, "I can forgive, but I can't forget the harm you brought to many of the state's Negroes with your actions. Anything else is between you and God."

Wallace accepted my comments graciously, and we chatted about other matters, including a trip he had taken to China. He stated that his aide, a black man, had traveled with him, and the Chinese acted as if they had never seen a black person before. We all laughed when he said that the Chinese had rubbed the man's skin to see if the color would come off.

The bottom line between us was that we each had respect for the other. At least you knew where Wallace stood, whether you supported him or not, and he said he admired the degree of fortitude I had displayed in the 1960s.

CHAPTER EIGHTEEN

Driving the Bus

IN THE MID-1980s Cy Steiner and I talked more about making our business partnership public, but hesitated for the old, obvious reasons. Another life change saw Cy, in his fifties and a widower, marrying a woman in her early twenties whom he had met during some of his travels around the country. Although I was skeptical of the union working based on their age difference, this apparently meant nothing to Steiner.

On the radio front, as a reward for breaking company sales records, I became a stockholder in Crescendo Broadcasting. Then in 1988, Erskine Faush and I purchased WATV under the umbrella of Birmingham-Ebony Broadcasting. Also, I ventured into other civic and professional endeavors including presidency of the Birmingham Park Board. I was also a promoter and manager of a local singing group, the Dynamic Soul Machine, which cut a record for Stax called *Your Love Is Like a Boomerang.*

By 1992 Cy was depressed for cloistered reasons at which I could only guess, and he used a gun to end his life. At Elmwood Cemetery, friends and acquaintances were filled with inextinguishable grief at the demise of an astute businessman and loyal friend. An almost mystical ambiance permeated the burial ground as Cy returned to the bosom of mother earth. John Zimmerman, the company's creative director, and I looked at each other in a silence that communicated volumes. Somehow we understood that we were dancing about the precipice of a special drama. Simultaneously, we walked toward each other and embraced as brothers. Our action caught the attention of the other mourners—a long-haired young white man and a middle-aged black man ignoring the usual awkward impediments that often spring up in the dynamics of racial interaction. Observers had to wonder why the "creative guy" and "the radio man" were bonding in a personal moment that no one in the cemetery could fathom, except perhaps for Cy Steiner himself.

"Whatever it is, John, I've got you," I said.

"We've got each other," he responded. "What are we going to do?"

"Are you going to try to save the company?" I asked.

Zimmerman agreed that it was imperative to keep the firm afloat, and we pledged to work in a symbiotic relationship toward that end. Later I got a call from him during which I revealed my relationship to Steiner-Bressler. The fact that I was functioning as a hidden arm of the firm struck him as a situation that needed correcting.

Steiner had talked with me about Zimmerman, a fellow who was in his early thirties when he came aboard the company in 1988 and was toasted as a creative wizard. Steiner had also discussed me with John without sharing the true nature of our relationship.

Zimmerman and I began buying out Bressler, and in 1993 the company's name was changed to Steiner-Bressler-Zimmerman. By 1994 Bressler's share had been completely purchased. Legal papers were executed listing both John and me as owners. Since I had often forgone payments for so-called consultation work during my years associated with Steiner, my investment amounted to fees owed and liquid assets that I presented. I became executive vice president of the company and had an office in the building that I never used; John was chairman and chief creative officer.

Zimmerman and I both shed tears when our partnership was made legal. A long, arduous road had been traveled since I met Cy Steiner in 1958. The road was even longer when Rosedale and the horse stable were used as measuring points. In my heart I knew my mother, Mattie C., had to be smiling down on my achievement.

"You have paid your dues. I am proud of you as my partner and as my 'dad,'" Zimmerman said. "You don't have to worry about anything; your back is covered."

Zimmerman was an individual with roots in provincial Baton Rouge, Louisiana, but he earnestly shepherded the idea of making us a legal and *public* partnership. He had been the odd man out, a motorcycle-riding rebel among his siblings, some of whom were high-achieving career military officers and lawyers. Later he had settled down to thoughtful work in the office among his abstract artwork and contributed much ingenuity to the company's lifeblood before Steiner's death. Now his rebellious instincts were raging against the hush-hush nature of my role with the company in the fading light of the twentieth century.

"The world should accept us as we are, black and white, older and younger," he said. "I am good, and you are good."

We understood that we were situated in a city that had owed much of its post–World War II reputation to incidents of racial intolerance, but Birmingham's albatross did not have to be ours. Nevertheless, we did not openly broadcast the fact that I was co-owner, principally at my request. The voice of circumspection and restraint, I still feared revealing this information in a race-conscious society that I felt had not matured far enough from the attitudes I experienced in the air force in 1952.

Although he was a talented individual, John had to cultivate his management skills. He did not believe in a hierarchy and ran the company in an almost egalitarian manner without the totem pole stratification that prevails in most businesses. After finishing his work, he would assist someone else on a project and even share office space. For my role, I continued to offer input into the company, much as I had done before Steiner's death. With all of us working valiantly and professionally, the company's revenue escalated from twenty million, to thirty million, and on up to about forty million dollars per year.

The staff expressed ebullience when we broke the news that I was a co-owner of the company. They were told that we would not be pigeonholed as a black and white entity but would project ourselves as a corporation inclusive of different races and ages and genders and present service of the highest quality. Zimmerman, in particular, made it a point to bring more blacks into the company as a symbol of our commitment to equal opportunity in the marketplace.

Eventually, we decided to gradually spread the word that I was a co-owner. We chose a meeting with Parisian department store executive Donald Hess to make the revelation. An approving Hess congratulated us enthusiastically at the news. The same scenario played out with Ronnie Bruno, chairman of the huge, homegrown Bruno's grocery and drug store chain, who expressed endorsement of the relationship and hailed it as a business breakthrough. From those contacts we anticipated that word would spread into the corporate community.

John and I set our sights on changing the name of the company in 1997. Zimmerman-Stewart seemed too ridiculously close to a name you might find on a highfalutin New York law office. Besides, we knew we wanted the company's reach to extend globally and not be constrained by the borders of Alabama. Whether our clients were situated in southern Africa or Central Europe, we knew the name should have a universal appeal to which all customers could relate. Literally hundreds of names were considered for the firm, but we settled on O2 Ideas. The name was derived from oxygen, the element that serves as the basis of life and creativity.

Jesse Lewis, head of an advertising agency, sought a meeting with O2 Ideas executives to talk about the lack of black representation in advertising and communications companies. At the arranged meeting, the Tuscaloosa native, who was also publisher of a black-oriented weekly, the *Birmingham Times,* began his presentation as Zimmerman and I listened patiently. Lewis mainly seemed to direct his message to Zimmerman and apparently viewed me as a "Negro in the window," which refers to the old practice of strategically placing a token black person in a conspicuous position in a business to allay suspicions about fair hiring practices; the technique was quite common in the early days of affirmative action.

Finally, during a pause in Lewis's speech, Zimmerman and I looked at each other in an attempt to decide who should break the news.

"Jesse," Zimmerman said, "you ought to know that this company is owned by that man over there, Shelley, and myself."

Lewis seemed flabbergasted and mildly incredulous at the contention, but I never heard him publicly make any reference to my position at O2 Ideas. Perhaps to have done so might have erased some of his own revenue if potential clients gravitated toward our company because of our interracial partnership.

O2 Ideas persisted in its success and developed more and more global accounts. Certainly many clients greeted us with open arms, but an undercurrent of racial bias may have steered some work away from us. Nevertheless, while discriminatory attitudes may be entrenched in some quarters of business as a reflection of the general society, this obviously has not been an impediment to the success of O2 Ideas since we grew from twenty-seven employees and twenty million-plus dollars in accounts in 1992 to about eight-five employees and ninety million dollars in accounts in 2000 with interests in interactive communication and Barking Dogs Productions.

Zimmerman and I respect each other's cultures without sublimating our respective heritages; we have blended our own business skills and personal insights to work toward the good of a dynamic, thriving firm. Not a month passes that we don't ride into the back alleys in the black sections of town and talk with the so-called street people. Some days we may lunch together at an upscale area restaurant; on other days we may eat at a modest soul-food establishment. Secondarily, these ventures help us to learn each other's cultures. They also keep us in touch with the masses who have slim access to corporate boardrooms and the so-called business elite.

Some of our contacts with prostitutes and winos have allowed us to refer some of them for work, which has helped them climb out of their valleys of confusion and self-destruction. The hypothesis is that none of us in the human family is successful unless we are all successful; there are no "Big I's" and "Little Yous." What impacts one individual has a ripple effect through the collective soul of us all. John and I know this, and we have earnestly used our leverage to help anyone who wants to break his or her cycle of despair. Any one of the downtrodden who listens to our message of "cleaning yourself up and going back to school" is halfway out of the rut if the desire for change is within their heart.

EPILOGUE

If THE HOURS OF A DAY can be analogous to the breadth of an individual's life, then I would say that I am in the late afternoon of the journey. The sun has not yet set on boundless opportunities, and for this I am most grateful. Positive energy still flows from the kindnesses of God and the mercies of fate. The tears I cried daily for fifty-seven years of life have dissipated through the catharsis of candid revelations to attentive audiences.

In 2001 John Zimmerman and I reorganized the structure of O2 Ideas. I relinquished the title of president, which I had worn since 1999, and was designated vice chairman and chief consulting officer while John continued as chairman and chief creative officer. But professional achievement and recognition, while satisfying, take a backseat to the importance of a loving, caring, and nurturing family. This, for sure, is a major cog in a fully satisfying and constructive life. My brothers Sam and David were not able to channel their emotional pain into avenues that would have brought them or society the most benefit. Jerome met an early death, but showed signs of volatility as he too tried to fit into a culture that was not particularly sympathetic about his own bumpy life.

Even Jerome's demise makes me wonder about the "what ifs" in the context of American society. The sniper who killed him in Korea placed him in the company of 686 other Alabamians who lost their life fighting for freedom in that war. But he and I both knew that many in America would look at his blackness first before categorizing him as a man.

My brothers never really had much of a chance with the cards destiny had dealt to them, but I, as their companion on the chinch bug–infested mattress, could fathom the pain they endured until death. Whereas we were products of the same crucible of life, I was able to harness my old demons for better use, thanks to a divine hand who wanted me to tell our story. But in a greater sense, my achievements are theirs. And from that I can receive a measure of comfort. Everyone has portions of good, and they were no exception, but the forces of fate were less kind to them.

SAM STEWART ALWAYS SWEATED OVER modest jobs in Birmingham and Los Angeles, where he had been since 1963. At some point in California he began receiving work disability payments, for some reason that always remained obscure. He became a personality of sorts by writing poems and selling them on the streets. In some way, this literature may have been his own purgative to help him discard ancient agonies. His poem "Hello, Black Woman" seemed to me (as a psychologist without portfolio) a method of paying homage to a mother who had been abruptly extricated from our lives. Sam also wanted to write of his own experiences about walking to California. But he had little to say about Scooba, Mississippi. That I understood, because of my own horror stories that I had secreted away for so long and from so many people.

Sam's final days in 1994 represented a crisis. Lung cancer had spread, and chemotherapy had left his body weakened. A Birmingham oncologist told me that if I could get Sam to the city, he would take him as a patient. Moving a dying man who needed oxygen tanks more than three thousand miles was a formidable task when expenses and logistics were considered. I had to take the chance, even though I knew that I would have only about a twenty-four-hour window of opportunity. A Delta Airlines representative gave me the name and phone number of a man he said could possibly help for a fee. The contact said he needed Sam's medical records, and his crew would be at Martin Luther King Hospital in Los Angeles to pick up my brother at around 5 P.M. on the agreed-upon day.

Meanwhile, childhood friend Jimmy Bonner's wife, Alma, and I drove a van bearing oxygen tanks to their daughter's home in Atlanta. An airplane ride took me to Los Angeles for the hospital rendezvous. On discharge day, as promised, men helped Sam leave the hospital, placed him in an ambulance, and took him to Los Angeles International Airport. Passengers and onlookers looked baffled as the attendants wheeled the stretcher with Sam on it through the terminal and up near the loading ramp where a wheelchair was waiting. They transferred him into the chair and rolled him into the plane and to his seat where they connected him to oxygen tanks. Sam was still unconscious when I placed sunglasses on his face; a baseball cap from the airport souvenir shop made him look like any dozing, healthy plane passenger.

In Atlanta, Alma was waiting with the van, which also contained oxygen tanks. We climbed in and sped toward Birmingham, where Sam was placed in hospice care at my home.

A few days after we brought him home, Sam smelled food Doris and I were preparing, and a deathly ill man seemed to ignore his pain. "What are y'all cooking?" he said, sitting up in bed.

Later that day Sam was to walk around in the backyard,

which convinced me of the soundness of my idea of bringing my brother back to Alabama. If elephants can travel miles for a special dying place, then at least my brother could spend his final hours in the company of people who loved him despite the misfortune life had heaped upon him. I am comforted to know that this would have been what our mother, Mattie C., would have wanted. I was expressing my love for one of the sons she had abruptly left in the secular world when she entered her spiritual journey upon her physical death in 1939. Sam died a few months after I brought him home to Birmingham.

DAVID STEWART PERSISTED IN his slide into oblivion, partially, I believe, because of the gunshot wound to the head he suffered at his wife Betty's hand in 1973. He suffered from seizures and blackouts and could not hold a job, legitimate or otherwise; he ended up homeless. The medications he relied on were Dilaudid, an addictive narcotic painkiller, and phenobarbital, a sedative that also arrests muscle spasms.

Sam spotted him on a CBS broadcast in the mid-1980s sleeping in a box on a street in Los Angeles. Soon David had taken his most consequential step on the slippery slope of a mountain called misfortune. On August 28, 1989, the anniversary of our mother's birth, David was handling security at a shelter, Outreach Missionary Church at 5875 South Main Street in Los Angeles, when a belligerent man named Clement Guitry came onto the premises. David attempted to remove the man from the scene, and a minor scuffle ensued. The pair, according to California court transcripts, disengaged. Guitry left the scene and returned a few minutes later, and another fracas erupted between the two. Witness Lester Pink said David kicked and stomped the man, who then began to run from the area. David followed Guitry to

124 West Fifty-eighth Place where he stabbed him in the chest and in the abdomen below the rib cage. Guitry died on the scene.

When I learned of the situation, David had already been dealt a sentence of twenty years to life in Corcoran State Prison, where his fellow inmates included Charles Manson and Robert Kennedy's assassin, Sirhan Bishara Sirhan. I petitioned the California Parole Board to review his case with the hope that he would be freed due to extenuating circumstances. These included the fact that he was a functional illiterate and unaware that he was waiving the right to a jury trial, inadequate counsel, and blackouts and memory lapses that I attributed to the gunshot wound. Also, an attorney I hired, Estelle Schleicher, determined in her investigation that Guitry had himself displayed a knife at some point during the confrontation. Nevertheless, the board refused to issue a parole for David.

David went on to become a Muslim and studied the Koran with the help of an imam, a spiritual leader. I greatly appreciate any relief that this faith could provide a man so sorely twisted by life. The imam would even read correspondence for David and helped him compile his thoughts in presentable literary fashion.

When David discovered he was wasting away with lung cancer, he asked me to get a message to his former wife, Betty, incapacitated by a stroke. He was sorry for the tough times he had thrown her way and sought her forgiveness. Betty, in response, sent word to David that she was praying for him and had indeed wiped away any hard feelings over their wrecked marriage.

The last time I saw David alive was when I visited him with his sons Huell and David Jr. They collapsed in tears at the sight of a once aggressive man weakened and attached to a menagerie of tubes. He instructed them to listen to whatever advice I would offer. A corrections officer said that a picture of David, his sons, and me was out of the question. A female guard, overwhelmed at the scene and my revelations about David's past, came to my aid.

"You'll get your picture," she said before returning with an instamatic camera. She snapped a cherished photo that I always carry around in the glove compartment of my car.

David died March 8, 1996, in Corcoran Prison, three days shy of his fifty-seventh birthday.

———————

A PERSISTENT HUNGER FOR meaningful family bonds has become obvious in my life. The fact that my original nuclear family was dissected so soon in my life's journey pushes me to seek cohesion within my immediate and extended families. But, to my distress, I have not been able to construct a solid, caring structure of love and trust among people who are my kin by marriage or through bloodlines. Even today most of my children are not close, and we have never all sat down for a family dinner because of distrust, jealousy, and mutual antagonisms. My desire for a loving family has also prompted me to gauge possibilities and potentials among the outer circles of relatives. While I have made overtures of friendship to various segments of my extended family, the reactions from these individuals have been less than rewarding. For instance, I have contacted the Buttses, the branch of my maternal grandmother, but several felt that my ulterior motive was to gain something from them. On the Stewart side, many disliked my assertion that laid my mother's death at Slim Stewart's feet. Despite my successes in business, the void generated by absent love is my greatest torment.

Doris and I have had emotional tangles like other couples, which distracted us from the true goal of marriage. Again, a portion of the friction stemmed from the fact I have been very much in the public eye. The fact that I have had a high profile as a radio station owner and successful communications executive makes me fair game for busybodies. Any harmless luncheon with a female coworker, acquaintance, or business partner has been fodder for friends who might call her to say, "Guess who Shelley was seen with?" These and other tensions helped contribute to a chasm to the extent that I have sometimes dreaded being sick at home because I doubted that I would even receive proper care. But it seemed my mother's spirit directed me to hold the family together to at least ensure that her youngest grandchild, Corlette, would receive an education.

Overall, despite my love for my children, my relationship with many of them is distant, and their lives have been less spectacular than I had hoped. For the most part, there is little bonding among them, a situation that has disturbed me deeply. Although I know the cities in which they live, I have little contact with most of them. Corey went to Arrington Middle School but struggled to pass course work there and at West End High School because of a mixture of poor study habits and a possible learning disorder. He was shot in the leg in Birmingham during an incident that likely stemmed from gang warfare, and fathered two illegitimate children during his carefree, irresponsible years. A friend of Corey's hung around the house and ended up impregnating sixteen-year-old Corlette, an honor student at West End High who was afflicted with ulcerative colitis and was often sickly. To her credit, and in salutation to my devotion to education, she went on to Talladega College and then Auburn University where she received a degree in engineering. After that she waded into graduate school at Georgia State University and pursued an MBA degree in marketing.

Lisa, because she did not adhere to my emphasis on education, did not score well enough on a college entrance examination to be accepted, to my consternation. The distant nature of the relationship between Lisa and me was clear when people started telling me about her then-pending six-thousand-dollar wedding to Frederick Brown at Metropolitan A.M.E. Church in the early 1980s, an event that I knew nothing about. The day before I was scheduled to go to Atlanta on business, Lisa came by WATV with a request. "Granddaddy is going to give me away," she said. "Would you walk my mama down the aisle in the church?" Of course, I was not going to break my appointment at that late date.

Sherri displayed some anger at me for various reasons, but she did not defect like the others did. She eventually worked for my radio station and went on to pursue a degree at Birmingham Southern College in her adult life.

Sharrone made decent grades at West End High School and went on to Jacksonville State University. I never saw her grades for the first semester, but she did say she needed $1,800 for tuition and room and board. Soon I learned that she had been on academic probation, and by the end of the second term she had flunked out. Shelley, or Kip, was offered an education, but he did not accept. He lives in Arizona.

One of the few bright spots among relationships with my children has been Sheldon, my son with Gwen. He came back into my life in recent years after a lengthy absence following the deaths of his mother and grandmother. He admitted that he had harbored resentment toward me, but we did have a reconciliation. We both discovered that Doris had made misleading comments to make him believe that I did not want to build a relationship with him.

WHILE I LONG FOR STURDIER family bonds, ironically, other relationships have stepped in to fill the gap to a certain extent.

After Papa Clyde and Mama Bessie broke up several years after my tenure at the rock house, he remarried. His new wife, Mama Smith, bore three sons, Clyde Jr., Ricky, and Dwight. I lost track of Mama Smith and Papa Clyde and their brood when they moved to Mobile for a few years. Mama Smith, the rest of the family, and I found each other years after Papa Clyde had died in the early 1960s. A childhood friend, Jimmy Bonner, heard me say that white people had helped raise me and knew that some people assumed I was telling a yarn. Coincidentally, Bonner knew of Clyde during his travels through Vestavia Hills as a public works official in that Birmingham suburb. Smith had moved there after living in Mobile and had set up a restaurant. Bonner helped him to sell equipment from the eatery after it was closed down. Jimmy called Mama Bessie and asked her about me, and she confirmed that I was her "son," to his surprise.

The Smith boys had been told about my existence, and they thought of me as their brother. In the 1980s, at a family gathering, I was introduced as their sibling. Their wives call me their brother-in-law, and their children call me their uncle.

A humorous incident happened in the 1990s when I received an honorary doctor of humane letters award from Miles College in Birmingham. As I sat on the podium, I noticed an elderly white woman and a young white man enter the room. The woman seemed to be waving at me frantically, and I did not gather who she was at first. A few minutes later someone told me that a white woman in the room had inquired about me and said that she was my mother, and the man had stated that he was my brother. The messenger looked incredulous as he related the conversation, but I knew it was Mama Smith and Clyde Jr.

John Zimmerman and I have also become close friends and developed a relationship that extends beyond mere business partners. The Zimmerman family's holiday stationery even includes my name. When I visited John's father, I was warmly greeted by the retired Louisiana engineer as his son's "other dad." It was ironic that in the 1940s Papa Clyde and his family had adopted me, so to speak, and now, fifty years later, I was adopting a young white man, not as a ward but more in the manner of offering consultation and advice within the confines of mutual love and respect. John and I began to pray together daily, and we knew that the venture in which we were involved could trace its source to a divine scheme. In a sense, the friendship with Zimmerman is reminiscent of the one I enjoyed with Otis Redding. It seems that the people who should have been just simple business partners were fulfilling extradimensional roles as kinfolks.

———

THE HOUSE THAT ISAAC HAYES, Pops Staples, Johnny Taylor, and others had helped me purchase with the concert in 1970 was a blessing from heaven. But I had several ideas kicking around in my head about building another type of home. This would be a haven for family, including my brothers, and a monument to my mother. Sam died while it was in the planning stages, and David was incarcerated. But it seems my mother's spirit was directing me to renovate the old house Aunt Emily had lived in until her death in the early 1990s.

"I'll never live in those woods," Doris said. "You will have to go there by yourself."

I moved into the house and began remodeling it, expanding it from 1,100 square feet to 1,400 square feet in a project that took me six months. But the remodeling work was not quite what my mother had in mind, I don't believe.

In 1994 I approached an architect named Melvin Smith and told him I wanted to build a new house that would encompass

Aunt Emily's abode on the land off Bear Creek Road near the small town of Sterrett in Shelby County.

"The best thing you could do," said Smith, "would be to tear the house down and start fresh." Smith, a graduate of Southern University in New Orleans, felt that the logistics of the construction made such an undertaking absurd aside from the fact that I would be driving thirty miles to work daily.

"Just keep drawing, Melvin," I told him every time he called me with an impediment he encountered with the plan.

Finally, Smith apparently saw the same vision that had been planted in my soul and announced that the project was within the realm of possibility. His sketches and designs were beginning to take on a credible shape and form; the monument was indeed possible and workable, he said. But contractors estimated that costs would range from $300,000 to $800,000. Finally, a home builder figured that it could be done on the low end of the estimate. With eighty acres of land as collateral, I was able to secure a commercial loan from businessman Elton B. Stephens, the same man who, I discovered, was a co-owner of WBCO, the station I had worked at in high school.

Work began on the house with Sam dead and David in prison. But the monument was built regardless. As a further tribute to my mother, I had a blue stained-glass window featuring a cross installed high above the living room.

A VACUUM WAS CARVED INTO MY LIFE with Mattie C.'s death, and I have been trying to fill it ever since. For years I never heard the words "I love you," and I had been hugged only twice by the time I reached adulthood. That is why I often greet O2 Ideas family members with hugs rather than handshakes. One lesson I learned from the pain was that there can never be enough positive influences. Money and position are inconsequential when measured against the permanence in this world—and the next— of loving familial bonds. From my story people can discern a pattern of triumph over adversity especially when a generous and considerate gesture is offered. The world has boundless room for more love, faith, trust, understanding, and kindness. Conversely, any modicum of hate, distrust, and indifference should be categorized as excessive; it represents the heavy albatross that threatens to keep humanity "a little lower than the angels."

ACKNOWLEDGMENTS

In February 1999 I received an honor of which I am most proud from the Sixteenth Street Baptist Church in Birmingham called the Footsteps for Freedom Award in a ceremony held at the Scrushy Center. Co-honorees were Time Inc.'s Don Logan and Alabama Power President Elmer Harris. The church, site of the 1963 bombing that killed four black girls, encased our footprints in cement. My friend and business partner John Zimmerman recounted my past to the crowd, tearfully summarizing my life on a back porch, abuse at the hands of relatives, habitation in a horse stable, and the rescue of my brothers from 1950s' slavery on a Scooba, Mississippi, plantation.

After the ceremony, Logan suggested that I write a book. Actually, my coauthor, Nathan Hale Turner Jr., was already working on my life story. Nate had appeared at my WATV office unannounced in August 1996 in search of a freelance writing project. While I was impressed with the credentials listed on his résumé, I had hoped that my cousin Sharon Childs-Long or goddaughter Candace Bonner would chronicle the story. The inner voice told me, however, that Nate should write the book, and in 1997 we began work on the project. I appreciate the work he has done and know also that his appearance out of the blue that summer day, and Don Logan's sincere interest and support, were manifestations of a divine scheme.

11/22
$ 13.82

2/03

DATE DUE

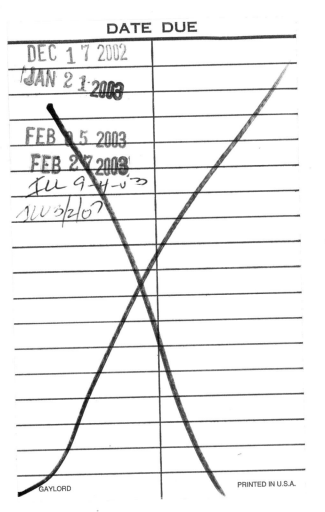

DEC 17 2002

JAN 21 2003

FEB 15 2003

FEB 27 2003

ILL 9-4-03

ILL 5/2/07

GAYLORD   PRINTED IN U.S.A.